W9-BQS-153

Microsoft©
Office 365

Connect and Collaborate
Virtually Anywhere, Anytime

KATHERINE MURRAY

PUBLISHED BY
Microsoft Press
A Division of Microsoft Corporation
One Microsoft Way
Redmond, Washington 98052-6399

Library of Congress Control Number: 2011932154
ISBN: 978-0-7356-5694-9

Printed and bound in the United States of America.

First Printing

Microsoft Press books are available through booksellers and distributors worldwide. If you need support related to this book, email Microsoft Press Book Support at mspinput@microsoft.com. Please tell us what you think of this book at http://www.microsoft.com/learning/booksurvey.

Acquisitions and Developmental Editor: Rosemary Caperton
Editorial Production: Waypoint Press
Technical Reviewer: Mitch Tulloch; Technical Review services provided by Content Master, a member of CM Group, Ltd.
Copyeditor: Roger LeBlanc
Indexer: Christina Yeager
Cover: Twist Creative·Seattle

*To all users of technology who are willing to take a chance,
make a choice, and try a new way of doing things so that
we can nurture and enjoy a happy, healthy planet.*

—*K.M.*

Contents

What do you think of this book? We want to hear from you!

Microsoft is interested in hearing your feedback so we can continually improve our books and learning resources for you. To participate in a brief online survey, please visit:

microsoft.com/learning/booksurvey

What do you think of this book? We want to hear from you!

Microsoft is interested in hearing your feedback so we can continually improve our books and learning resources for you. To participate in a brief online survey, please visit:

microsoft.com/learning/booksurvey

About the Author

Katherine Murray has been writing about technology since the mid-1980s, which means that over the years she's seen lots of changes in the way technology is used. She loves the potential cloud computing offers and often writes about software that enables us to connect and collaborate in a variety of ways. The author of *Microsoft Office Plain and Simple* (Microsoft Press, 2010), *Microsoft Word Plain and Simple* (Microsoft Press, 2010), *Microsoft Word Inside Out* (Microsoft Press, 2010), and co-author of *Green Home Computing for Dummies* (Wiley, 2009), Katherine is a member of the Society of Environmental Journalists and writes frequently about earth care topics. She also writes regularly about Microsoft Office and other software for CNET's TechRepublic and Windows Secrets.

Introduction

LET'S HEAR IT for freedom. Freedom from your desk. Freedom from those boring managers' meetings. Freedom to work anywhere, with anyone, anytime, on almost any device. Sounds good, right?

Office 365 is Microsoft's smart and simple answer to cloud computing. Using the various programs in Office 365, you can do all the tasks you're used to doing in your favorite Office applications—write documents, create presentations, check email, manage your calendar, crunch numbers, and more—and then share what you create in real time on a team site, design and publish a website, and even create and host live online meetings while you're traveling on the train, sitting in a coffee shop, or dialing in on your phone.

This book shows you how you can use cloud computing—and specifically, Office 365—to get more done, collaborate more easily, and work more flexibly than you ever have before. From the necessary how-tos about creating and administering your Office 365 account and working with the various Office 365 programs to sharing files with your team, creating a team site, using Office Web Apps, and holding online meetings, you'll discover how easy it is to work online and off, accessing and sharing your files whenever you need to. After you learn about each of the core programs, you can try strategies for building successful teams, and get some good ideas on practical ways you can put all this cloud power to work.

Who This Book Is For

Microsoft Office 365: Connect and Collaborate Virtually Anywhere, Anytime is all about cloud solutions for small businesses, focusing on the core software services (Microsoft Exchange Online, Microsoft SharePoint Online, Office Web Apps, and Microsoft Lync), and demonstrating ways you can create, manage, and lead teams effectively using the communications and collaborative online tools.

You'll find helpful ideas and solutions in *Office 365* if you

- Own or work in a small business and want to be flexible where and when you work.

- Need to collaborate with others near or far.

- Want to store and work with files online from any point you have web access.

- Lead a team online or face to face.

What Is Cloud Computing?

The phrase *cloud computing* brings to mind for me the feeling of stretching out on a hillside on a summer day while my sons pointed out the animals and shapes they saw in the clouds above. Cloud computing is a little like that—the ability of your technology to take on the shape you need for the type of project you need to accomplish. Want to put together a project team? You can do that in the cloud so that team members all over the globe can collaborate and communicate easily. Need to create a meeting space for your regional sales reps? You can create a team site for everyone in the cloud, using web servers and software, and you can enable every person to log in from any point they have access to the web.

So where is this *cloud*? The real definition of the phrase *cloud computing* simply means the ability to access files and applications online through multiple devices—your computer, browser, or phone. Microsoft has already been offering cloud services through the web in various ways:

- Windows Live SkyDrive is one of the Windows Live Services, a free web-based application that enables you to save, store, organize, and share files easily.

- Microsoft Office Web Apps are available for Word 2010, PowerPoint 2010, Excel 2010, and OneNote 2010, making it possible for you to save and work with your Office files online and collaborate with other authors. Office 2010 Web Apps are free to registered Office 2010 users.

- Microsoft Office Live Small Business is a web-based suite of services that enable you to create and market a website, communicate with others by email and instant messaging, and store and share files online. The basic services are free, and you can add specialty features for a monthly fee.

- Microsoft Business Productivity Online Suite (BPOS) is a suite of messaging and communications programs designed to provide the kind of collaboration support companies need. BPOS includes Microsoft Exchange Online, Microsoft SharePoint Online, Microsoft Office Communications Online, and Office Live Meeting, all for a monthly, per-user fee.

The best news about cloud computing for you as an end user is the added flexibility the services offer you, without additional investment in either hardware or software. You can simply use your web browser—which is open anyway, right?—to get to the files you need to work with, make any changes, and save and share the files as you see fit.

The great thing about cloud computing for companies is that it enables them to expand the services they offer both staff and customers without adding to their own hardware infrastructure. Web services enable companies to connect workers and make collaboration possible on a global scale without adding servers, setting up datacenters, and more. The environment is secure, flexible, and expandable to accommodate as many users as businesses need to support.

Introducing Office 365

Microsoft Office 365 is Microsoft's latest venture into cloud computing, bringing together tried-and-true programs that make communicating and collaboration natural online. Office 365 includes Microsoft Exchange Online for email and scheduling, Microsoft SharePoint Online for sharing files and creating team sites, and Microsoft Lync Online for instant messaging and online meeting. Office 365 mixes the capabilities of those programs with cloud versions of Office Professional Plus programs.

What Cloud Computing Means for You

Office 365 makes using Office in the cloud a simple, natural, and affordable way to make the most of services you are already familiar with, in ways that easily extend the technology you are probably already using. Sound too good to be true? It's not. Office 365 enables you to easily and naturally

- Collaborate globally in real time.

- Use programs you already know.

- Create a virtual office where you can work with information securely while you're on the go.

- Use your PC, browser, or phone interchangeably.

- Keep your information secure.

- Keep your hardware costs down.

- Use multiple devices to access and work with files.

- Create a shared team site.

- Boost productivity by making it easy for people to work together.

- Give users instant access to each other with presence technology and instant messaging.

- Incorporate social networking in your team communication.

Office 365 Versions

Because different types of organizations and businesses have different needs, three different versions of Office 365 are available for end users. These three versions are

- **Office 365 for small businesses** Small businesses and professionals who don't have large IT requirements will find just the set of tools they need in Office 365 for small businesses. This version is easy to try (free for 30 days) and then low-cost ($6 per user per month at the time of this book's publication), and it offers businesses Office Web Apps, Microsoft SharePoint Online, Microsoft Exchange Online, and Microsoft Lync for instant messaging and online meetings.

- **Office 365 for enterprises** Enterprises have larger-scale IT needs than small businesses or individuals, requiring software that can handle a large number of email accounts, messages, and attachments; provide guaranteed uptime; offer reporting and support options; and deliver Active Directory features that enable a single sign-in for end users. Office 365 for enterprises offers all these features and adds on to standard BPOS services to extend the collaboration and online meeting capabilities. Office 365 for enterprises also offers flexible plans so that businesses of different sizes can tailor the features to get just the kind of cloud support they need.

- **Office 365 for education** Educational users face a unique set of challenges—they need to provide students with access to the latest software possible, but they have to do it on a shoestring (and perhaps diminishing) budget. Cloud-based services can help users in education save money and give students the tools they need to create projects, collaborate in real time, and learn how to use software in the cloud.

WHAT DOES OFFICE 365 ADD TO BPOS?

Microsoft Business Productivity Online Standard Suite, also known as BPOS, has 40 million users all over the world. This highly successful online software suite offers communication and collaboration features that make it easy to connect in real time and work together on projects large and small.

Office 365 for enterprises extends the features of BPOS by adding Microsoft Lync for instant messaging and online meetings, Outlook Web App for management of email and scheduling, Office Web Apps, and the ability to create reports and administer the account through a web-based dashboard. The educational version of Office 365 also includes the latest version of Microsoft Live@Edu, which offers cloud solutions to thousands of schools and millions of students around the globe.

A Quick Roadmap

Microsoft Office 365: Connect and Collaborate Virtually Anywhere, Anytime is organized in three parts to help you learn about different aspects of setting up and working with Office 365.

Part I, "Finding Your Place in the Cloud," takes a look at the way people are working in the cloud today and introduces you to Office 365. Chapter 1 looks closely at teams, both inside and outside the office environment, and it takes a look at the way Office 365 offers a greener choice for small businesses. Chapter 2 shows you how to create an Office 365 account and set up a profile, and it gives you a big-picture tour of Office 365 so that you can begin planning just what you want to do with the tools. Chapter 3 is for the team manager or person who will be managing the Office 365 site; you'll learn how to customize the site, add mobile devices, and set up and manage Microsoft Exchange, Microsoft SharePoint, and Microsoft Lync online.

Part II, "Teamwork in the Cloud," is your guide to setting up, organizing, managing, and helping your team be successful using Office 365. Chapter 4 spotlights all the team features you can use to get everybody on the same page, calendar-wise; you'll also find out how to share files, hold online meetings, instant message each other, and broadcast presentations. Chapter 5 walks you through creating, editing, and sharing a team site. Chapter 6 shows you how to create document libraries, share files with team members, and manage the files in SharePoint Online. You'll also find out about working with file versions, tracking file changes, and comparing and merging files. Chapter 7 shows you how to create and use workflows to keep your team moving in the right direction, and Chapter 8 introduces all things Web App by shining a light on the capabilities of the various tools and showing you how to work with files online, coauthor documents, edit worksheets, broadcast presentations, and share notebooks. Chapter 9 rounds out this part of *Office 365* by focusing on mobile technologies: find out how to use the various Office Mobile applications to review, edit, and share the files you develop with your team.

Part III, "Connecting in Real Time," shows you how to use the communication and instant-messaging options in Office 365 to stay in touch with your team in real time. In Chapter 10, "Email and Organize with Office 365," you learn how to use Outlook Web App to import and manage contacts, set email preferences, organize mail folders, work with your calendars and tasks, and more. Chapter 11, "Talking it Over with Microsoft Lync," shows you how to connect in real time to other online users through instant messaging, voice calls, and online chats. You'll learn how to manage transcripts, invite others to the conversation, and host web meetings. Chapter 12, "Designing Your Public Website," shows you how to use the web tools in Office 365 to create a website to showcase your products and services and give your customers a sense of who you are and what you offer. Chapter 13, "Integrating Office 365," presents a set of examples that show how you and your team can use the various tools in Office 365 together to create and share business projects.

Let's Get Started

Now that you have a general sense of the road ahead, let's get started using Office 365. In Chapter 1, you learn how small businesses are using cloud computing to accomplish business-critical tasks in a flexible way. You'll then get to dream a little about the cloud shapes you want *your* Office 365 to take as you begin using this powerful suite of cloud-powered tools.

Acknowledgments

One of the best things about writing books is working with the talented team that makes it all come to life. Big thanks go out to the team that made it possible for you to be holding this book in your hands today:

Thanks to my editor, Rosemary Caperton, who managed this project with expert care, championing it from the very start and helping to improve and further the idea, while dissolving obstacles, finding a path to the resources we needed, and troubleshooting problems as they arose. (I'd add "She's able to leap tall buildings in a single bound," Rosemary, but I think someone has already used that.) This book *truly* would not be here without her.

To Steve Sagman at Waypoint Press, Roger LeBlanc, and Mitch Tulloch for their many talents, expressed though their wonderful design and layout (Steve), always excellent editing (Roger), and a careful, conscientious, and constructive technical edit (Mitch).

To Michael Stroh, author of *Microsoft Windows Phone 7 Plain & Simple*, who generously contributed some of the illustrations in Chapter 9, and to Kenyon Brown, Senior Editor at O'Reilly Media (Microsoft Press Division) for his help in getting us needed resources at a critical hour.

And to Brent Watanabe, Windows Phone 7 Developer, for his suggestions and friendly help as we figured out how to capture live Office 365 mobile images to share in the book.

Thanks to one and all! Your efforts and care are very much a part of this book!

Errata and Book Support

The following sections provide information on errata, book support, feedback, and contact information.

Errata

We've made every effort to ensure the accuracy of this book and its companion content. Any errors that have been reported since this book was published are listed on our Microsoft Press site at oreilly.com:

> *http://go.microsoft.com/FWLink/?LinkID= 221811*

If you find an error that is not already listed, you can report it to us through the same page.

If you need additional support, please email Microsoft Press Book Support at mspinput@microsoft.com.

Please note that product support for Microsoft software is not offered through the addresses above.

We Want to Hear from You

At Microsoft Press, your satisfaction is our top priority, and your feedback is our most valuable asset. Please tell us what you think of this book at:

http://www.microsoft.com/learning/booksurvey

The survey is short, and we read every one of your comments and ideas. Thanks in advance for your input!

Stay in Touch

Let us keep the conversation going! We are on Twitter:

http://twitter.com/MicrosoftPress

1

Finding Your Place in the Cloud

WHETHER YOU'RE just learning about cloud computing for the first time or you've been saving and sharing files online for a long time, it's plain to see that having an online component is a smart way to make sure your files are always available where and when you need them. This part of the book starts out by giving you a glimpse at how the work world is changing—setting the stage for cloud computing—and then you discover how to create an Office 365 account and set up the roles and permissions you need to get started.

CHAPTER 1

What's Happening with the World of Work?

IT'S NO SECRET that computers, the web, and social media have all dramatically changed the way we work. What we used to compose on typewriters (remember those?) or file away in clangy, metal filing cabinets, we now take care of completely electronically with just a few keystrokes and a click of the mouse button.

What you used to do by writing, printing, folding, putting in an envelope, stamping and mailing, you can now do by simply composing and clicking Send—and the message reaches the other person almost instantly.

Although you used to spend hours camped around a big board-room table, doodling on your legal pad while someone presented a workshop that wasn't entirely relevant to your job, today you can log in to a webcast to catch the bits of a presentation that directly impact what you need to do today. And you can form teams on the fly to accomplish specific project goals and then disband the team to go back to your regular tasks.

Technology now enables us to work faster, more productively, and with more flexibly than ever. You can easily pull together the resources you need for as long as you need them and then let them go when you're done. This is a smarter use of resources—and greener, too—and it results in less overhead for your business. You don't need to add computer systems or people to work on specific project tasks that require some extra help. You can simply go to the cloud.

Teams, Teams Everywhere—In the Office and Outside of It

We seem to be in a perfect storm of technology and workforce development, where several important aspects of the way we work are coming together. Since the early '60s, the use of work teams has been on the rise. Fortune 500 companies are full of them. Most mid-sized businesses have realized that work teams can boost productivity, help managers manage, and give groups more ownership of the work they perform.

Teams enable individual workers to get together in the name of a common goal— producing the annual report, for example—and bring their own respective talents to the mix. Your work team for the annual report might include a writer, an editor, a graphic designer, a production and layout person, a corporate communications person, and someone who can provide the financial detail. And here's the good news—data is showing that working in cohesive teams boosts creativity and productivity, and people seem to be happier at work when they're part of a successful team. That's all good.

But add another new development to the mix. Now workers are often on the road, traveling from region to region, stationed overseas, or perhaps remotely accessing a corporate network from another continent. The development of new hardware options— more powerful and affordable laptops, netbooks, and smartphones, as well as improved video conferencing tools—make this easier than ever to do. In this global and mobile workforce, how will your team meet its goals? Will the editor know when the writer has finished the draft? What happens to the deadlines?

The simultaneous development of the pervasive and always-on web and the explosion in social media technologies has made it easier to stay in touch with all members of your team wherever they travel and whenever they appear. From any point of web access on the globe, your teammates can communicate with you. Nice. Working virtually has even bigger benefits as well—when a team works successfully from remote locations, there's a reduced need for centralized office space, which means lease costs for your company go down. And that daily one-hour commute into the office? Gone, if you're working from home. That saves fuel and reduces the carbon your car is pumping into the atmosphere. Those are just a couple of the large-scale benefits that, multiplied exponentially across the planet, make the world a whole lot greener.

But this brings us back to a critical question. In this flexible time of go-anywhere, do-anything work styles, how do you stay focused on your team objectives and complete your original assignment? How do you organize the work, build libraries of files you all need, meet together in the same space and time, and keep track of all the pieces of the project? Facebook isn't going to help you with that. And your email client—even if it's Microsoft Outlook 2010—is limited as far as group space goes.

That's where Microsoft Office 365 comes in. Now you have a shared team space, always available online, where you can build document libraries, share assets, assign tasks, and collaborate on all kinds of Office projects. Office 365 builds on four key technologies— Microsoft Exchange, Microsoft Lync, Microsoft SharePoint, and Office Web Apps—to give you all the tools and abilities you need as a team to be successful, no matter when or where you work.

Worldwide Collaboration Is Here

Teams form for all sorts of reasons and have all sorts of goals. Some teams are developed to meet a specific project objective—for example, putting together an annual report. There are also leadership teams, program teams, departmental teams, and formal and informal teams. Pretty much anything you want to create—short-term or long-term, with a few other people—can be done better in a team. (OK, that's an editorial opinion—but experience proves it.)

If your team involves one or more people who seem to be always on the go, you need

- A way to make files accessible to the remote worker

- A means of assigning and sharing tasks, appointments, notes, and more

- An online meeting space groups can call in to or use to gather together

- A shared site that can be accessed by multiple technologies—laptops, smart-phones, et al.

- Translation tools, if your team member's primary language is different from your own or you are working on multilingual documents

If you can create a team space that provides all these types of tools, your global team can log in, share their information, get feedback, and contribute to the project in a way that makes global access a moot point. They could just as well be logging in from the coffee shop on the corner!

THE SOFTER SIDE OF GLOBAL TEAMS

Throughout this book, you'll get many ideas about ways to create and manage teams successfully. But here's something to consider if you're working with global teams: different cultures have different expectations about relationships and communication, so if your new team member is from an Asian country, trust might build more slowly—and you might need to lay more groundwork—than when you begin to work with a new teammate from Canada.

In "Tips for Working in Global Teams" (which you can find at *www.ieee.org*), author Melanie Doulton describes "high-context" and "low-context" countries. In high-context cultures—Indian, Arab, Asian, or Latin—relationships with family and colleagues is paramount, the entire relationship provides the context for communication, protocol is valued and followed, and decisions are made slowly and are often based on relationships.

In low-context cultures such as North American, Germanic, and Scandinavian cultures, communication is based less on relationships and more on facts. In other words, the message carries the meaning, whereas in higher context cultures, the relationship sets the stage for the way the message is received.

For this reason, be aware that when you're working with team members from different cultures, they might hear what you're saying differently than you think. Take time to build trust and establish relationships with your global team members and, when in doubt, check it out.

Going for the Green—With Groups of All Sizes

One of the best aspects of cloud computing is the way it uses—and conserves—resources. Instead of using millions of computers on desktops that are tied into hundreds of thousands of servers that are purchased, maintained, and repaired by thousands of individual companies, cloud computing offers a scalable alternative.

Because applications used in cloud computing are web-based, the number of servers used increases as more are needed to support the demand. The additional servers then return to rest when they're no longer needed. This share-the-load approach, on a large scale, saves electricity, reduces the need for hardware components, and increases the efficient use of the resources used to provide the services.

As part of a green strategy, companies can choose to use cloud computing to

- Downsize or offset their office space

- Expand their ability to work globally

- Support a mobile workforce

- Reduce use of consumable office supplies (paper, ink, file storage)

- Reduce computer hardware (desktop computers and server systems)

Heads in the Cloud (Computing)

So what are companies doing in the cloud today? IBM commissioned a survey in July 2009 ("Dispelling the vapor around cloud computing," which you can find at *www.ibm.com*) to check the pulse of cloud adoption, and they found that many groups are considering cloud computing in various forms. The survey included respondents who work in communications, financial services, the industrial sector, and public services. The following table shows the distribution of respondents by country.

TABLE 1-1 IBM Survey Participants by Country

Country	Percentage
Canada	5
China	10
France	10
Germany	10
India	15
Japan	11
UK	9
USA	30

Many companies are already using or are open to using private cloud computing for the following functions:

- Business continuity and disaster recovery

- Data mining

- Data warehouses

- Long-term data archiving
- Security
- Testing environment infrastructure

A smaller percentage of companies have adopted a public cloud approach, which includes the following capabilities:

- Audio/video/web conferencing
- Data center network capacity
- Desktop
- File storage
- Server
- Service help desk
- Test environment infrastructure
- Training and demonstration
- Voice over Internet (VoIP) infrastructure
- Wide area network (WAN) capacity

Office 365 enables you to create a cloud computing approach that offers just what your business needs require. The four main technologies—Exchange, SharePoint, Office Web Apps, and Lync—enable you to stay in touch by email and scheduling, create a shared team site (for both intranets and the Internet), collaborate on all sorts of projects using familiar Office applications, and stay in touch with instant messaging and video conferencing. The next section gives you a bird's-eye view of the features in Office 365.

A Closer Look at Office 365

Office 365 makes it easy for you to work with the applications and programs you're familiar with in the easy-access, always-on world of the web. You can use Office 365 to

- Create a shared team site where you create data libraries, assign tasks, schedule calendars, and more

- Check everyone's availability, and schedule online meetings

- Connect instantly by instant messaging, email, or video calls

- Keep your files and user accounts secure and keep email safe from spam and scams

- Create documents, worksheets, presentations, and notebooks, and share them seamlessly

- Always work with current updates of Office 365 software

- Create blogs and wikis for your team and for public view

You Can Use What You've Got

One of the big features of Office 365 is the software's ability to work with whatever device you're using at the moment—your desktop PC or Mac, laptop or netbook, Android phone, iPhone, Windows Phone, Nokia, or BlackBerry.

You can log in to your Office 365 account, work on files, share documents, update tasks, post to your discussion forum, join a meeting, send instant messages, and more—from wherever you are at the moment, with whatever device you've got. Sweet!

Big-Time Security

Office 365 invests in state-of-the-art security, reliability, and recovery technology to ensure that your files and messages are secure, your data is safe, and you are always able to access and work with your information. Office 365 offers

- A guaranteed 99.9% uptime Service Level Agreement

- Data centers with SAS 70 and ISO 27001 certification

- Geo-redundant, enterprise-grade reliability and disaster recovery

- Multiple data centers and automatic failovers to ensure your data is safeguarded

- Up-to-date antivirus and anti-spam protection

THE IMPORTANCE OF UPTIME

One of Office 365's big promises—and something its users depend on—is the guaranteed 99.9 percent uptime promise. This means that your team site, your files, your public website, and all the tools you need will be accessible online 99.9 percent of the time. This might sound like marketing lingo, but it's an important promise for teams and companies that run the majority of their business processes in the cloud.

Nowhere was this need more evident than in a recent cloud outage suffered by Amazon's cloud services. In April 2011, a simple error in one availability zone started a domino-like effect that affected other areas, which resulted in a "re-mirroring storm" that overwhelmed cloud capacity temporarily. This affected a number of sites—for example, FourSquare, HootSuite, Quora, and Reddit—and caused a temporary outage.

Microsoft is providing a financially backed service level agreement (SLA) for Office 365 users and has designed Office 365 as a comprehensive geo-redundant service so that data is replicated between geographically distant sites. This means if one site experiences a failure, other sites around the world can continue the processing so that Office 365 users won't experience any loss of services.

Keep It Simple with the Office 365 Home Page

When you first log in to Office 365, you see a simple and clear home page that shows you how to get started with the tools you want to use. The various tools you'll use in Office 365 are all available on that first page, making it easy for you to find your way around and get to the tools you need. This clean screen design also makes it easy for you to navigate, regardless of whether you're viewing the site on your PC, in your browser, or on your smartphone.

As you can see in Figure 1-1, the navigation bar at the top of the window gives you easy access to the primary views in Office 365. You can get back to your Home page from any of the other pages; you can click Outlook to work with mail, schedules, and tasks; or you can click Team Site to display your SharePoint team site. If you are the administrator of the Office 365 account, you can also click Admin on the Home page to access another screen where you can set up the various programs the way you want them, add and manage users, and set up the domains you want to use.

Note	What's an administrator? A person with administrator privileges in Office 365 is able to create new accounts, set up users, configure the services they'll use (for example, Microsoft Exchange, Microsoft Lync, or Microsoft SharePoint), set permissions, and get updates to the software. If you have administrator privileges, check out Chapter 3, "Administering an Office 365 Account."

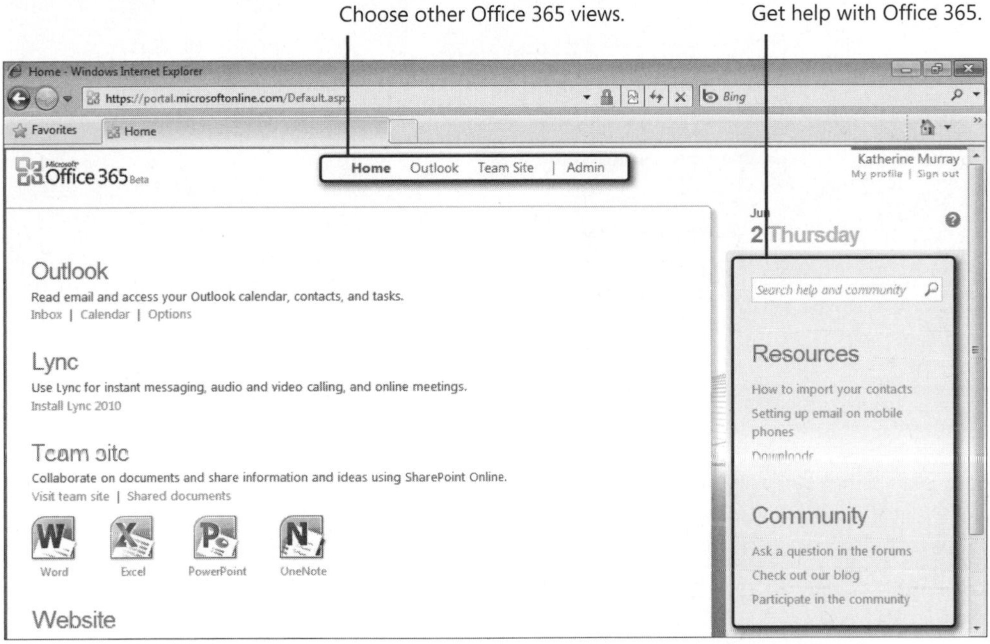

Choose other Office 365 views.   Get help with Office 365.

FIGURE 1-1 The Office 365 Home page makes it easy to begin setting up your space in the clouds.

Stay in Touch with Outlook

When you click Outlook at the top of the Office 365 window, you are taken to the Outlook view, where you can check email, compose new messages, organize your mail, add appointments to your calendar, create notes, and add tasks. (See Figure 1-2.) If you've used Outlook Web App in the past, Outlook in Office 365 will look very familiar to you.

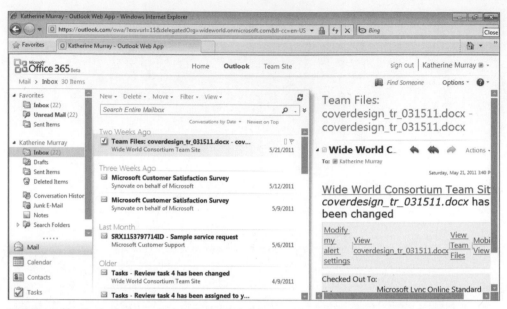

FIGURE 1-2 The Outlook view, which includes tools for organizing email and contacting colleagues and friends.

The folder view on the left side of the screen is where you manage and file away all the mail you receive. You can create new folders and subfolders as needed, just like you do in your desktop version of Outlook. Click Mail, Calendar, Contacts, or Tasks in the lower left corner of the screen to choose the view you want to use to add, modify, review, or delete those different types of information. The center column of the Outlook window shows you the contents of the folder you've selected (in this case, the Inbox folder). In the far right panel, you see the contents of the currently selected message. This type of display enables you to scan your email quickly without opening and paging through each message, saving you time and trouble as you move quickly through your mail.

Also in the Outlook view, you can use the presence icon of a contact (located to the left of that person's name) to see his or her online availability. If the icon is green, your contact is available online. When you click the icon, a list of contact options appears, giving you a range of choices for contacting the person. You can send an email message, schedule a meeting, invite the person to chat, and more. (See Figure 1-3.)

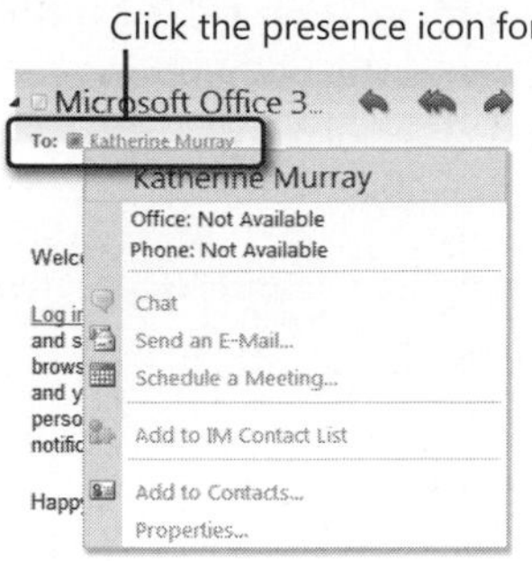

Click the presence icon for direct contact options.

FIGURE 1-3 You can click the presence icon to display options for contacting someone online.

Sync Your Team with Microsoft SharePoint

If you're organizing and managing a team effort, chances are you'll spend lots of time in SharePoint. SharePoint makes it easy for you to create both a team site—where you can communicate with team members, create document libraries, and more—and a public website, for the information you want to show the world.

When you click Team Site at the top of the Office 365 window, your SharePoint site appears, looking similar to the one shown in Figure 1-4. Here you can design your team site, adding content and images and choosing a theme.

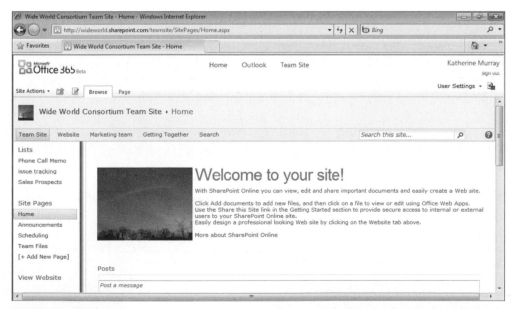

FIGURE 1-4 Clicking Team Site displays the SharePoint site your group can use as a common workspace.

You can click the Edit tool to the left of the Browse tab to display the editing tools for the SharePoint site. The Ribbon changes to display the Editing Tools tab, which enables you to format the text on your page and insert new page elements such as pictures, videos, tables, and more. (See Figure 1-5.)

FIGURE 1-5 To edit and format your SharePoint pages, you'll find what you need on the Editing Tools Format tab.

You can click Site Actions on the left side of the Ribbon to display a list of ways you can modify and interact with your SharePoint site. You'll learn all about customizing, formatting, and sharing your site in Chapter 5, "Creating Your Team Site with SharePoint Online."

Real-Time Connection with Microsoft Lync

So we've talked about using Outlook to handle your email and scheduling needs and using the SharePoint team site to keep everybody on the same page—what about those times you need to communicate in real time, using instant messaging or online meetings? Enter Microsoft Lync 2010. Microsoft Lync is an exciting addition to this suite of online services, enabling you to keep in touch with all your contacts and make calls, set up meetings, and send ideas and messages on the fly.

> **Note**   When you first log in to Office 365, you might need to download Microsoft Lync by clicking the Install Microsoft Lync link on the control panel page. The process is pretty painless. You'll find the steps in Chapter 2, "Getting Started with Microsoft Lync."

The Microsoft Lync window resembles Windows Live Messenger, but you'll find that it includes a different set of tools. (See Figure 1-6.) Adding new contacts is something done by the administrator so that everyone on the team is using the same address book. (As an administrator, however, you can change that setting so that individuals can add the contacts they'd like to include.) You can call a contact by clicking the Call button to the right of the contact name and choosing the command you want from the displayed list.

FIGURE 1-6 Microsoft Lync includes the tools you need to make instant calls and set up online meetings.

With Microsoft Lync, you can make instant contact with others, make Internet calls, share audio and video, and host online meetings. You'll find out how to use the various features in Microsoft Lync in Chapter 11, "Talking It Over with Microsoft Lync."

Work with Office Web Apps

Office Web Apps make it super simple for you to save your Office 2010 files online, where you can easily access them from your PC, browser, or phone. If you plan to download, deploy, and license Office 2010 Professional Plus with the pay-as-you-go option, you can use the Install Your Office 2010 Professional Plus subscription link on the Home page to download the software and sync it with Office 365.

This subscription solution is a great way to ensure that you have the latest updates on the Office 2010 software you use. Additionally, you don't need to have a big IT team to handle the deployment for you, and you can get help 24 hours a day, 7 days a week and even make tech support calls as part of the deal. What's more, you can use the Office 2010 applications on your desktop, in your browser, or via your smartphone; save them to your SharePoint libraries; or share them with others on your team through email, by instant message, or in a meeting.

What's Next

This chapter explored the ways our work world is changing and showed that the time is ripe for cloud computing. Whether you plan to use the cloud yourself—to trade files and access documents from home, from work, and on the road—or you need to create, manage, and lead a team, this chapter gave you a sense of the big picture in Office 365. The next chapter shows you how to create an Office 365 account and set up a profile, and it shows you how easy it is to accomplish specific business tasks in Office 365 so that you can begin planning just what you want to do with the tools.

Getting Started with Office 365

BY NOW, YOU'RE an old pro at creating a new account and setting up an online profile, right? You create accounts all the time and are very familiar with the process of posting your information—just what you want others to see—in the public profile portions of your accounts. In this way, Office 365 is similar to other sites that want to get you up and running as smoothly as possible. You'll set up some of the basics of your account—user name, password, type of account, and so forth—and then begin building on those basics to create the kind of online cloud experience you want to have and share with others.

Businesses of all sizes—with teams of all configurations, working from all locations—will find that Office 365 makes connecting, sharing information, and collaborating on projects easy and intuitive. Because you already know the programs—all the Office 2010 favorites—you won't have a big learning curve. And with its 99.9 percent uptime guarantee, Microsoft promises the site will be working round the clock—whether or not you have the IT staff to support it.

So, whether you find this exciting or not, it all begins here. Fortunately for you, Microsoft makes the whole process pretty painless. This chapter shows you how to create your account, set up your profile, and envision the services you want to make available for your team in Office 365.

Creating Your Office 365 Account

The first step in accessing the wonders behind the Office 365 curtain involves creating your own account. Begin by going to *www.office365.com* to sign up. The first question Office 365 will ask you is to decide whether you want to use the Small Business version or the Enterprise version of Office 365. This book focuses on the features you'll find in the Small Business version, which gives you everything you need for creating a team site, sharing documents, working with email and instant messaging, hosting online meetings, and more. The Enterprise version is designed for larger organizations that have sophisticated data needs and require advanced archiving and Active Directory capabilities.

After you choose Small Business, Office 365 presents you with a simple form to fill out. You provide your name and Windows Live ID (and you can sign up for one during this process if you don't already have one), and then you pass muster by typing the validation key and clicking OK. When you click Continue, Office 365 lets you know that it will send your new user name and password to the email address you specified. The Office 365 home page then appears, and one by one the various services that are part of Office 365 begin to load. (See Figure 2-1.)

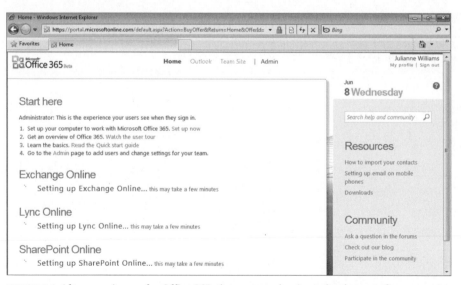

FIGURE 2-1 After you sign up for Office 365, the program begins to load your software services.

Tip	You'll see the note, "This may take a few minutes…" only the first time you access Office 365. After the services are added to your account, you won't have this kind of wait time again.

WHAT'S A MICROSOFT ONLINE SERVICES ID, ANYWAY?

When you first visit *www.Office365.com*, you might think the site is asking for your Windows Live ID. However, if you try to sign in using that tried-and-true user name and password, you'll get a rather unfriendly message: *You are now required to sign in at Live.com* or *You are now required to sign in at MSN*. What does that mean, and how does it get you into Office 365?

The answer to the mystery is that your Microsoft Online Services ID and your Windows Live ID are two different things. To keep Office 365 secure (and paid for), site security is enforced by admitting only licensed users into the site. This means that the administrator of your Office 365 site needs to generate your Microsoft Online Services ID and password, and that's done through the Microsoft Online Office Subscription website. If you don't have a Microsoft Online Services ID, contact your administrator to get your ID and password so that you can get into your group's Office 365 site.

You'll notice also that whatever name you select, Microsoft adds "onmicrosoft.com" to the name you've chosen for your Office 365 account. You'll also find that the URL for the public-facing website that is part of your account has "sharepoint.com" appended to it. These name additions won't cause you any problem, but make a note of them so that you remember how to get into your team site and find your website easily later.

A Look Around the Office 365 Home Page

After you enter the necessary Microsoft Online Services ID (or create a new account), you are presented with the Office 365 Home page. The Office 365 Home page has a minimalist design, offering you primary site choices across the top (Home, Outlook, and Team Site—plus Administrator if you're, well, the administrator). As Figure 2-2 shows, on the left side of the screen, you see categories that introduce you to the overall process and then to each of the primary Office 365 services:

- **Start here** walks new users through the simple tasks involved in setting up Office 365 for everyday use. New users learn how to set up their computers, and learn about the basics of Office 365. Users who will serve as administrators for the site can go to the Admin page and add new users to the account.

- **Outlook** is short for Outlook Web App, the familiar web version of Office 2010. You can use Outlook to check and send email, schedule appointments and tasks, and set up email and calendar options.

- **Lync** contains the settings you configure to send instant messages, set up online meetings, and share audio and video clips with others on your team using Microsoft Lync.

- **Team site** contains all the options you need to create a team site with Microsoft SharePoint. You can access your team site, view documents you're sharing with others, or create a new Word document, Excel worksheet, PowerPoint presentation, or OneNote notebook.

> **Note** Clicking each one of the Office 365 icons launches a different Office Web App—Word, Excel, PowerPoint, or OneNote—and opens a new document. (You'll learn more about working with Office 365 Web Apps in Chapter 8, "Working with Office 2010 Web Apps.")

- **Website** lists the link to your public website, which you can easily modify with the content, pages, and pictures you want the public to see.

FIGURE 2-2 The Office 365 Home page gives you the links you need to access your mail and manage your calendar, connect with your team in real time, and work on your Office documents.

CHECKING OUT YOUR RESOURCES

On the right side of the Office 365 home page, you'll see the Resources column, which includes links to more information that can help you get started using Office 365. At the top of the column, you see a search box, which you can use to locate help content on any topic related to Office 365. Just click in the box, type a word or phrase that describes the type of information you'd like to find, and click Search. A pop-up window gives you a list of search results with links to the information you're looking for. You can return to Office 365 by simply clicking the close box.

Back on the Office 365 Home page, the top article in the Resources area shows you how to import your contacts to your Outlook Web App address book. You can also find out how to set up your smartphone to receive your Office 365 mail (which you'll learn more about later in this chapter), and you can click the Downloads link to install additional Office 365 services.

At the bottom of the Resources column, you'll see a set of Community links that display ways you can interact with other Office 365 users. You can ask a question in one of the Office 365 forums, read the Office 365 blog, or add your own thoughts and content to the forum, wiki, or other community efforts.

Setting Up a Profile

Your first task, after you create your Office 365 account, is to tell the program a little about your preferences and interests. Your profile—similar to ones you've probably created on social media sites—lists the basics about who you are, where you live, and what language you use. There's nothing fancy or too involved here, as you can see from Figure 2-3. Note, however, that the basic info about you—your name and address, for example—aren't editable in the profile screen. That's because the Administrator of your account is the one responsible for making changes to user accounts. You learn how to set up and edit user account info in Chapter 3, "Administering an Office 365 Account."

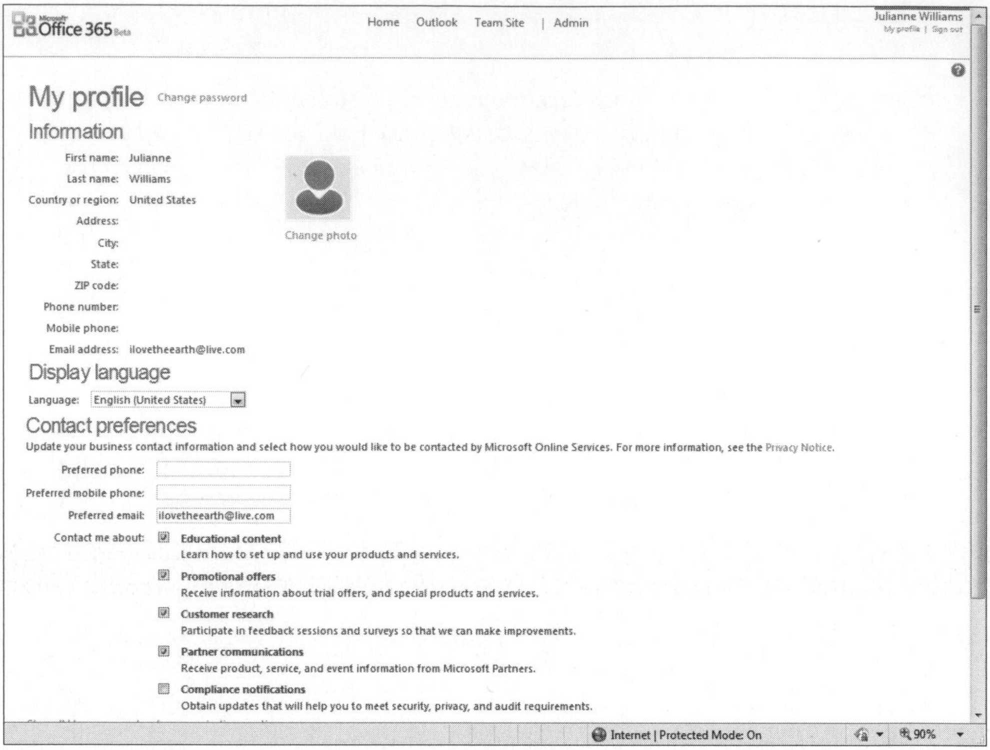

FIGURE 2-3 Configuring your profile.

Changing Your Password

If your Office 365 account was created for you—which means that instead of you signing up for the service and entering the password you want to use to access your account, an administrator did this for you—you will have received an autogenerated password that you'll most likely want to change when you log in to Office 365. Here's how to do that:

1. Click My Profile.

2. Click Change Password.

3. If prompted, sign in again using your user name and password; then click Close.

4. In the Change Password window, type your old password. (See Figure 2-4.)

5. Click in the Create New Password box, and type a new password for your account.

6. Type the new password a second time.

7. Click Submit.

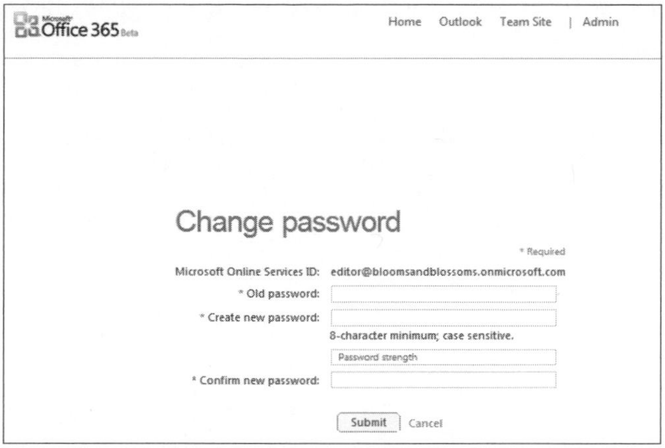

FIGURE 2-4 You can change your password in your profile page.

WHAT MAKES A GOOD PASSWORD?

Your password for Office 365 needs to be at least eight characters in length. To increase the strength of the password—which decreases the risk that your password will be deciphered by someone else—use a variety of uppercase and lowercase letters, numbers, and special characters.

The Password Strength bar shows you how strong the password you're suggesting will be; you can revise the password as needed to make it as strong as possible.

Changing Your Profile Picture

Office 365 also gives you the option of adding your own photo to your profile so that others will be able to see your image—or your favorite character, animal, or place—in various places on Office 365. To change the profile picture, follow these steps:

1. On your profile page, click Change Photo. (See Figure 2-5.)

2. Click Browse, and navigate to the folder containing the picture you'd like to use.

3. Click the picture, and click Open.

4. Click Upload. (See Figure 2-6.)

FIGURE 2-5 Click Change Photo to begin the process of changing your profile picture.

> **Add a profile photo**
>
> Upload an image to appear in services where profile photos are displayed.
>
> C:\fakepath\woman01.jpg   Browse...
>
> Upload   Cancel

FIGURE 2-6 Click Browse, and navigate to the folder containing the picture you want to use.

The new photo appears in your profile photo. You can change the photo at any point by repeating steps 1 through 4 and choosing a new photo.

Setting Office 365 Preferences

You can also change some of your preferences by scrolling to the bottom portion of the screen, where the items you can change are located. (See Figure 2-7.) You can change the language in which Office 365 is displayed, enter your phone numbers, update your email address, and sign up to receive more information on various topics related to Office 365.

If you want to change the display language, click the Language arrow and choose the language you want to use. In Contact Preferences, enter your Preferred Phone and Preferred Mobile Phone numbers if you like. You can also change your Preferred Email by clicking in the box and typing a new email address.

In the Contact Me About area, you can indicate which (if any) of the topics interest you enough that you'd like to receive more information about the products and services listed. To remove yourself from any of the topics, click to clear the checkmarks or click the Clear All link at the bottom of the list.

To save all the changes on your profile, click the Save button at the bottom of the page. You can then return to the office 365 Home page by clicking Home at the top of the Office 365 window.

FIGURE 2-7 Save your profile changes by clicking Save at the bottom of the profile page.

Tip

How Do I Change Everything Else?   Because Office 365 is set up so that the Administrator of your site sets up and manages user accounts, some of the profile information is beyond your ability to change. If you're also an Admin of the site, you can log in as an Administrator, click Users, choose the account you want to change, and click Settings. There you'll be able to change some of the basic user information, such as location, address, and more.

How Does All This Work?

Getting your mind around all this cloud possibility—especially when a number of configurations are available—might feel like a lot to try to imagine all at once. *Cloud services* are called that because the software and data centers appear when you need them and vaporize when you don't, like clouds—in other words, the resources you need to use applications, store data, and enable teams to connect are there when you need them and used elsewhere when you don't.

This enables businesses of all sizes to get access to the programs and services they need through a web-based service model. And it means that small businesses—who have the need for reliable technology but might not have a robust IT staff to support it—can benefit by having guaranteed access to technology that is hosted, supported, and deployed from the service provider (in this case, Microsoft Online Services). And the icing on the cake is that the cloud approach is better for the environment because data centers share resources and services, which also reduces the systems and servers your own company needs to have to support the work you do.

When you think of all the different services required to keep your business or team running efficiently and effectively and put them in a cloud, the whole configuration might look something like this simplified diagram:

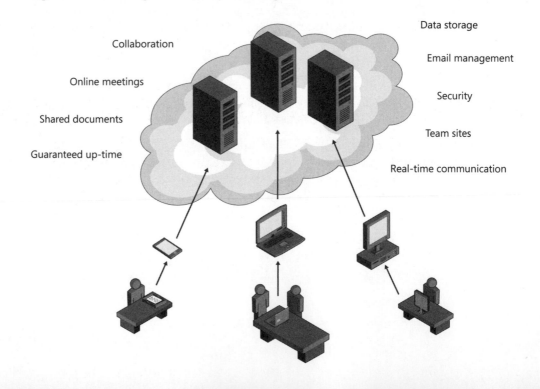

Collaboration

Online meetings

Shared documents

Guaranteed up-time

Data storage

Email management

Security

Team sites

Real-time communication

What's Your Service? Different Setups, Different Services

Office 365 is available in three different versions that are designed to give you just what you need—no more, and no less. Here's the quick rundown:

- **Office 365 for Small Business** (which is the focus of this book) includes access to Office Web Apps, up to 50 user accounts, a 25-GB mailbox for each user, mobile support, the ability to stay in touch with instant messaging, presence technology, audio and video, and team sites with SharePoint Online. The subscription cost for Office 365 for Small Business is $6 per user.

- **Office 365 Enterprise** includes all the features of Small Business as well as the full Office Professional Desktop software and pay-as-you-go pricing options. Enterprise users can also add kiosk plans that offer access to email, documents, and team sites in Office 365. Enterprise users can choose from two different subscriptions: existing Business Productivity Online Suite (BPOS) customers pay $10 per month; enterprise users who want to purchase the pay-as-you-go Microsoft Office Professional Plus 2010 service pay $24 per month.

- **Office 365 for Education** provides students with access to the Office 365 services—Office Web Apps, instant messaging, audio and video, and team sites—plus the latest version of Microsoft Live@edu, an online community of thousands of schools. Pricing for Office 365 for Education is $10 for educators and staff; the service is free for students.

IS OFFICE 365 THE NEW OFFICE LIVE SMALL BUSINESS?

In a word, yes. If you previously used Office Live Small Business (OLSB) for web creation and hosting, email, marketing, and more, you might be wondering how that service might overlap with Office 365. Office 365 includes all the greatest features of Office Live Small Business, and in late 2011 or early 2012, Microsoft plans to offer existing OLSB users a free transition to Office 365 for three months. After the initial free period, you can continue with your Office 365 for Small Business account for only $6 a month.

Getting Ready to Use Office 365

After you set up and log in to your Office 365 account, you need to do a few more things to get all the services ready to use. Specifically, you need to

- Download and install Microsoft Lync so that you can use instant messaging to contact others on your team, share audio and video, and hold online meetings.

- Get ready to use your existing Office programs.

- Set up your mobile phone to work with Office 365.

This section walks you through those tasks so that you can begin to arrange your cloud experience just the way you want it.

Installing Microsoft Lync

Microsoft Lync 2010 is the service that enables you to send instant messages to any member of your team who is available for contact. You can see the online presence of team members, share audio and video files, and schedule online meetings, phone calls, and more. Lync Online is the utility that connects your team in real time, whether you have something important to discuss or just want to ask somebody a quick question.

Begin the process of downloading and installing Microsoft Lync by clicking Install Lync 2010 in the Lync category of the Office 365 Home page. On the Downloads page (shown in Figure 2-8), choose your version (32-bit or 64-bit) and click Install.

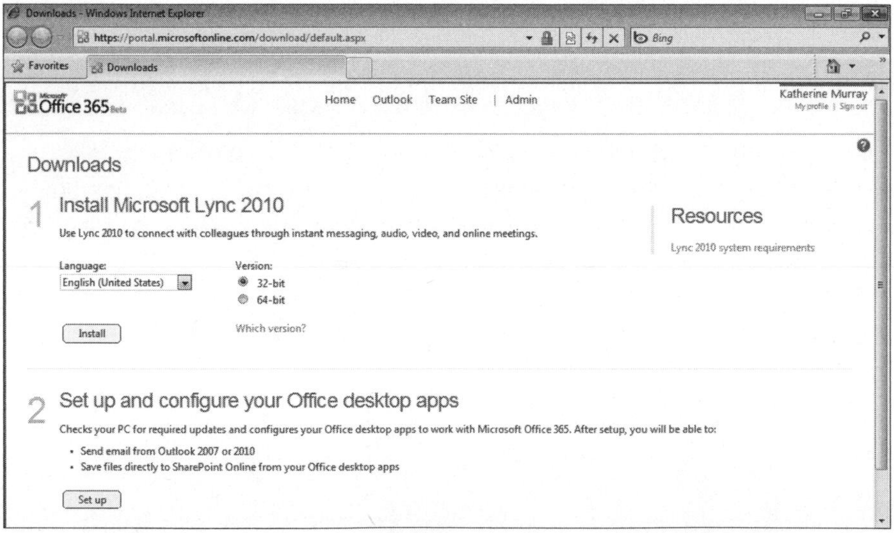

FIGURE 2-8 Install Microsoft Lync 2010 to add instant messaging, presence, audio, and video to your Office 365 capabilities.

Tip ✓ Not sure whether you have a 32-bit or 64-bit system? Here's how to find out: Click the Windows Start button and, on the right side of the Start menu, right-click Computer. Click Properties. In the System settings on the right side of the screen, you'll see whether you have a 32-bit or 64-bit system by looking at the System Type value. Note that if you have a 64-bit version of Windows, you can install either the 32-bit or 64-bit version of Lync. Microsoft recommends that you use the 32-bit version

After you click Install, the File Download – Security Warning dialog box appears so that you can choose whether you want to run or save the Lync install file. It's OK to go ahead and run the installation utility directly from Office 365 (unless your business has a policy to the contrary—in which case, you can click Save and save the file to your desktop, where you can launch it after downloading by double-clicking it).

It will take a few minutes for Lync to download; then you might be prompted to restart your computer. (Not all computer installations require this, however.) If prompted, restart your system normally, and Microsoft Lync 2010 should start automatically. If it doesn't, follow these steps to launch Lync 2010:

1. Click Start.
2. Click All Programs.
3. Click the Microsoft Lync folder.
4. Choose Microsoft Lync 2010 to start the program.

After Lync launches, it displays the window shown in Figure 2-9. As you can see, it resembles an instant messaging client such as Windows Live Messenger. There's one big difference, though—where are your contacts? Because Office 365 is built to be secure and enable your work with your team, only team members who are part of your Office 365 group appear in your Lync window, unless you use Lync for logging on to other domains as well. Within Office 365, your administrator is the one who adds user roles and permissions so that others will appear in your Lync window, ready for contact. You'll find out more about setting up user accounts in Chapter 3.

FIGURE 2-9 Microsoft Lync enables you to reach your colleagues instantly and set up online meetings.

> **See Also** You'll find all kinds of step-by-step procedures for using Microsoft Lync 2010 in Chapter 11, "Talking It Over with Microsoft Lync."

HARDWARE REQUIREMENTS FOR HAPPY LYNCING

One thing you'll notice throughout Office 365 is that the services are designed to be flexible. Almost nothing about this program is a one-size-fits-all answer. And that springs directly from the idea of the cloud—use what you need, and leave the rest for somebody else to use. Toward that end, the hardware requirements you need to run Lync 2010 depend on what you plan to do with the software. Understandably, sharing video or hosting online meetings in real time requires more bandwidth and processing power than simply sharing data or making a phone call now and then. The following list shows you the recommended hardware requirements so that you can see whether your system has what it takes to Lync successfully:

- **Display** Super VGA 800x600 [recommended: Super VGA 1024x768 or higher]

- **Operating system** Windows 7 or Windows Vista 32-bit, (64-bit for the 64-bit version of Lync); Windows XP SP2, or Windows 2000 Professional SP4

- **Microprocessing power** For just data and voice: Intel Pentium 500 MHz or higher; For video: 1 GHz or higher; For online meetings 1.8 GHz or higher

- **Memory** 512 MB RAM

- **Hard-disk space** 1.5 MB

- **Video card memory** 64 MB RAM

- **Audio** Microphone and speakers, or headset with microphone

- **Video** Video camera or webcam

- **Bandwidth** For data only: 56 kbps (kilobyte per second); For data, voice, video, and online meetings: 350 kbps

Tip ✓ If you work with team members all over the world—no problem. The early version of the Office 365 Beta was available for users in Canada, France, Germany, Hong Kong, Ireland, Italy, Japan, Mexico, Puerto Rico, Singapore, Spain, United Kingdom, and the United States, but as the program goes to wider release, support for additional countries will be added.

Getting Ready to Use Office 2010

Office 365 offers you different ways to work with the Microsoft Office 2010 applications, depending on what you need to do with the various programs. As part of Microsoft Office 2010, you can access and work with Office Web Apps:

- Word Web App

- Excel Web App

- PowerPoint Web App

- OneNote Web App

Additionally, Outlook Web App enables you to receive and send email, set up meetings, assign tasks, and perform the most common tasks you use in your desktop version of Outlook 2010.

Office Web Apps are available to you as part of Office 365 no matter which version you are using. These Web Apps are great for creating, editing, sharing, and reviewing content. What's more, you can work collaboratively on documents with Word Web App, partner on presentations with PowerPoint Web App, and co-edit in the same worksheet with Excel Web App. You'll find out more about the capabilities of the Web apps—and get the play-by-play on how to accomplish different tasks—in Chapter 8.

> **Tip** ✓ Office 365 Enterprise users also receive access to the latest version of Microsoft Office 2010 Professional Plus, which they can use on a pay-as-you-go basis. When Enterprise users click to use an Office application, Office 365 checks to ensure the user has been assigned a license for the software. The administrator of the Office 365 account handles this task and ensures that users have the necessary licenses. The cost for the license is included in the Office 365 package the organization selects.

Running Office 365 Desktop Setup

You can set up your desktop Office 2010 applications to work seamlessly with Office 365 by clicking Downloads in the Resources area on the right side of the Office 365 Home page, which takes you to the Downloads page. Click the Set Up button in the Set Up And Configure Your Office Desktop Apps area. Click Run (shown in Figure 2-10) to install and run the utility.

FIGURE 2-10 The Office 365 Desktop Setup utility connects Office Web Apps to your Office 2010 desktop applications.

After you run the Office 365 Desktop Setup utility, you'll be able to open and work with files from Office 365 in your Office 2010 applications. You'll also be able to sign in to your Office 365 account by using your Microsoft Online Services ID directly in your Office 2010 programs. So it's a convenience issue, but it also enables you to smooth out any wrinkles your desktop applications might encounter when you go to save or access files you've saved in Office 365.

In the Microsoft Office 365 Desktop Setup dialog box, click Continue to set up your applications and download any necessary program updates. (See Figure 2-11.) Click Continue. You will be asked to review and access the Office 365 user agreement, and then the utility begins searching for and downloading any available updates.

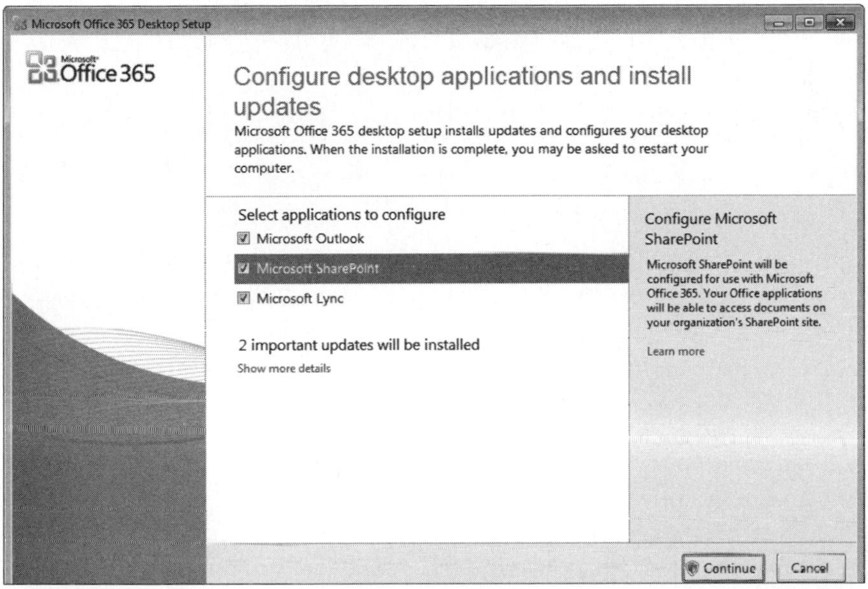

FIGURE 2-11 The Office 365 Desktop Setup utility configures the applications and downloads any available updates for your programs.

You can get more information about what's being downloaded by clicking the Show More Details link toward the right end of the status bar. The program items being updated are listed in the center column of the dialog box, and the link wording changes to Hide Details. (See Figure 2-12.) When the process is finished, click the Restart Now button to close all applications and reboot your computer so that the changes can take effect.

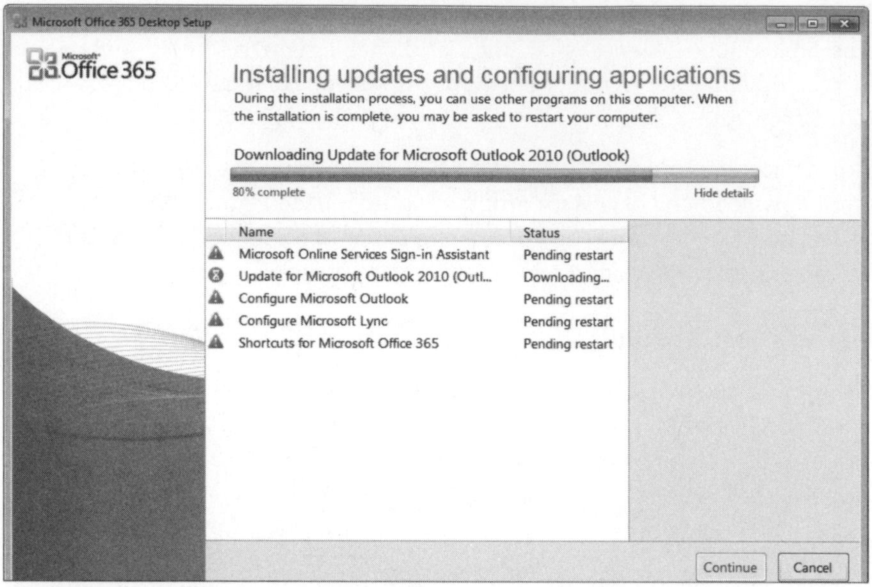

FIGURE 2-12 You can view the changes being made by clicking Show More Details and reviewing the list of updates in the center of the dialog box.

Setting Up Outlook 2010

When all is said and done, your computer restarts and pops back up with one more configuration screen, most likely telling you that a little manual work is required on your part. You need to create an email account in your desktop version of Outlook so that the Office 2010 Outlook Web App can interact seamlessly with your desktop version of the program. The process is simple:

1. Open Outlook 2010.

2. Click on the File tab, and click Add Account.

3. Outlook might add your information automatically in the Auto Account Setup page. Change the entries if necessary, and click Next.

> **Tip** ✓ Check with your administrator if you are unsure about the settings you need to enter here.

4. Outlook searches for your Exchange Online settings and prompts you to enter your email address and your use name.

5. Click Finish to complete the process.

> **Note** If you have trouble setting up your Office 365 email in Outlook 2010, return to your Office 365 account and type the phrase Connect Outlook to this account to find more help on this topic.

Now your desktop versions of Office 2010 applications are ready to work with your Office 365 account. You'll find out more about this—and all the related how-to tasks—in Chapter 6, "Posting, Sharing, and Managing Files."

Setting Up Your Mobile Phone

Ah, now we get to the fun part. Who wants to be stuck at a desk all day working on some ho-hum report or trying to get some worksheet numbers to balance? Why not do it at the coffee shop, on the train, or while you're waiting for the movie to begin? You can set up your mobile device to access and work with Office 365 data in a number of ways. After you connect your phone, you can check and send email, check your calendar, schedule appointments, and update your contacts information. You can also use Office 2010 Mobile Apps—for Word, Excel, PowerPoint, and OneNote—to carry on the work you started in Office 365.

To set up your mobile phone to work with Office 365, follow these steps:

1. On your Office 365 Home page, click Setting Up Email on Mobile Phones in the Resources column on the right side of the window.

2. In the window that appears, click Mobile Phone Setup Wizard.

3. Begin by clicking the arrow and choosing your mobile phone operating system. (See Figure 2-13.)

4. Finally, choose what you want to be able to do with your phone.

> **Note** The options displayed in the What Would You Like To Do? list depend on the capabilities of the phone you selected and also on the account type you have with Office 365. For example, if you chose Windows Phone as your mobile operating system, your choices are Set Up Microsoft Exchange Email On Your Windows Phone and Set Up POP Or IMAP Email On Your Windows Phone. However, if you choose a BlackBerry device, your only choice is Set Up POP Or IMAP Email On A G1.

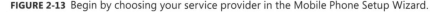

Mobile Phone Setup Wizard

You can use this wizard to get personalized instructions for setting up your mobile phone to access your account. Answer the questions below to receive instructions for your mobile phone. Choose your mobile phone operating system, model, or mobile phone company, and then choose the type of help you need.

Choose your mobile phone operating system.

Please make a selection

Windows Phone

iOS

Symbian OS

Android

BlackBerry

I don't know.

FIGURE 2-13 Begin by choosing your service provider in the Mobile Phone Setup Wizard.

Setting Up POP and IMAP Email

If you want to check your Office 365 email by using a POP or IMAP email account (which is the default if you don't use Microsoft Exchange), you can easily set up the account on your phone by following these steps (note that these instructions were written for the Windows 7 HTC HD 7 and might change slightly for different phones):

1. On your phone, tap Settings.

2. Tap Email & Accounts.

3. Tap Add An Account, and tap Other Account.

4. Enter your Office 365 email address and password.

5. Click Sign In.

The new account opens, and Windows 7 Mobile checks all your settings. After a moment, the email is synchronized and you will be able to check and send email from your mobile phone.

How Office 365 Meets Small Business Needs

In the chapters that follow, you'll see all sorts of ways you can use the various Office 365 services to collaborate with team members, accomplish tasks, create projects, look up data, and share what you know. The key to all this is flexibility, creativity, and using just what you need. As you log in—from *wherever* you log in—and work with files, messages, sites, and more, you'll discover that you really can get in and out quickly and complete the tasks you want to complete. And you can do all this without the huge overhead of servers, desk space, office rent, and transportation costs. And it's support-able even without a highly trained IT department (because the Office 365 IT group has you covered).

In essence, Office 365 does what many of us have been waiting for a long time. It offers us the worry-free, easy-to-afford, and easy-to-support option of using our software to do what we need to do without having to struggle through all the technical details required to install and maintain it. This section takes a look at how Office 365 might fulfill some of your critical business needs. The idea here is to provide some common ex-amples to spark ideas in your mind and inspire you to try things that work in your unique situation.

The Big Picture: Online and Off

Remember the days when you felt like you had to rush from home to office because you were afraid you were going to miss an important email message? Because email has become a common feature on most phones, that particular anxiety has dissolved for many of us. But often, reading and even responding to email on the phone can be limited. What if you need to look something up in a document you just created? What if another team member has the answer to the question the sender asked? You still need to wait until you get to the office to pull together the information for a satisfactory answer.

Office 365 makes it simple and seamless to stay in touch with your team and your files no matter where you are. You can easily move from your desktop computer to your laptop to your phone or even to a kiosk in the hotel lobby—looking up report information, checking your notes, or sending along a file that a teammate needs to review. You can easily move online and off, knowing that your files are stored in a place you can access them easily on any device that has web access.

Email, Calendars, Meetings, and More

Being able to access and send email is nothing new; chances are that you've been doing it by phone for a while now. But having your email easily connected to your schedule, group calendars, appointments, tasks, and more is a plus that helps you stay organized and synchronized with your team.

In Office 365, you can easily get to your inbox and calendar right from the Home page by clicking the appropriate links under the Outlook category. Outlook Web App enables you to check and compose email, manage contacts, set up meetings, arrange appointments, and create and track tasks, all in a single webpage. (See Figure 2-14.)

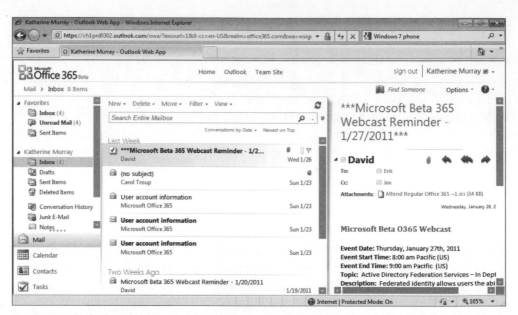

FIGURE 2-14 Outlook Web App makes it easy to access and work with your email, schedule, and contacts, and complete tasks all from a single interface.

> **Tip** ✓
> Office 365 Enterprise users have access to Exchange Online, which functions as a back end to manage communications while Outlook Web App is the front end. Exchange Online synchronizes received and sent messages, completed tasks, and more between all the different email access points you might use—desktop, Web, and phone. In functionality, Exchange Online is based on Active Directory services, which enable Enterprise users to access the global directory with all the contacts available in the organization.

Creating a Team Workspace

One of the challenges of working with a remote team is that there's no common space to share files, gather for meetings, or brainstorm about new ideas. Now Office 365 enables you to create a shared site where you can keep in touch with your team members, create workflows to track your projects, add project resources, schedule meetings, and much more.

The team workspace capability is built on SharePoint Online. As you can see from Figure 2-15, you can customize your team site by adding all sorts of tools, web parts, media, and more. You can also create document libraries so that your team members all have access to the files they need, and you can add pages and content related to the projects you are creating.

FIGURE 2-15 Your team site in SharePoint Online enables your team to stay in touch, share documents, schedule events, and much more.

Sharing Documents with Your Team

You can easily open, edit, and share the documents you save in your team site in SharePoint Online. When you choose to work with a file—a Word document, for example—it opens in Word Web App. You can choose to edit the document if you like, which opens the file in your version of Word while still keeping the file on the SharePoint server. You can also choose to edit the file in the Web App if you like.

You can then share the document window with another person on your team if you want to collaborate on the project in real time. When your other colleagues are working with the same file, the Office Web App you are using lets you know. (See Figure 2-16). The program locks areas where others are editing and then syncs all the changes so that the most recent changes to the document are preserved. In this way, you can collaborate on important files without fear of overwriting another team member's changes or losing an important change.

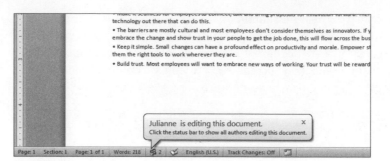

FIGURE 2-16 You can easily work collaboratively in Office 365.

Instant Messaging, Calls, and Web Meetings with Microsoft Lync

If you use instant messaging to get anything done—for business or for fun—you know the benefit of being able to communicate in real time, either one-to-one or one-to-many. Microsoft Lync Online, available as part of Office 365, provides all the real-time connection you need by offering an instant communications client with instant messaging, social media tracking, easy-to-use phone and video calls, and even features for setting up and hosting meetings. Figure 2-17 shows a Lync Online window in which two contacts are having a one-to-one conversation.

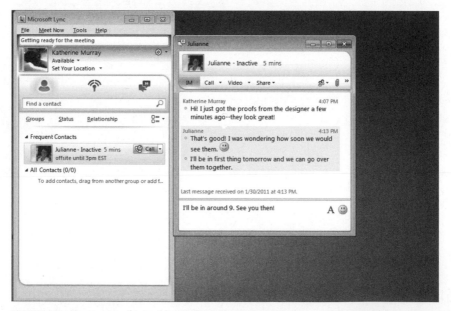

FIGURE 2-17 You can easily send instant messages to your team members, initiate audio or video calls, or host meetings with colleagues.

By default, Lync Online is set to offer as contacts only those included in your Office 365 team, but your administrator can set up your group so that you can communicate with others inside or outside your organization. What's more, others outside your group can be invited in for the meetings you host, so access and permissions don't pose a problem (while at the same time giving you the security you need to protect your information).

Behind-the-Scenes Support: Security and Reliability

Office 365 meets all kinds of needs for small businesses, but perhaps none is more important than this: you are working in a completely secure cloud, designed to provide multiple layers of protection so that your files, conversations, and collaborative efforts are safe. Office 365 services use 128-bit SSL/TSL encryption, which means that if communication is intercepted by an outside party, the file will be unreadable. Additionally, Microsoft Trustworthy Computing initiatives are in full force; antivirus signatures are continually updated, and Forefront Online Protection for Exchange protects and filters messages.

Tip ✓	You can take a closer look at the security measures Microsoft uses for its Online Services by reading the "Security Features in Microsoft Online Services" paper available at the Microsoft Download center (*www.microsoft.com/downloads*).

Reliability is another promise Office 365 keeps well for small businesses. Because all services are in the cloud, you need to have guaranteed access to Web services to work reliably and productively. To help ensure that your work is always accessible to your team, many data centers all over the world host redundant network configurations. So if one data center is unavailable, another one takes its place so that your work can continue uninterrupted.

◼ What's Next

In this chapter, you got the roadmap for creating your account, setting up your profile, and downloading the software you need to get started. You also had a chance to think through some of the tasks you want your teammates to be able to accomplish using the various Office 365 tools. If you will be administering the site—that is, managing user accounts and permissions—the next chapter offers the how-tos for managing Office 365 from the administrator side of things.

CHAPTER 3

Administering an Office 365 Account

IT CAN BE LONELY at the top. If you're the person responsible for setting up or at least managing the Office 365 account, you have a whole set of tasks and decisions to make that will affect the way your team interacts in the space. But don't worry—the choices are pretty simple, and they're easy to change later if necessary. And what's more, there's a community of administrators (and Microsoft MVPs) who are waiting in the wings to answer your questions if you get stuck along the way. Nice!

As you think through the way you want your team to interact in the cloud, you'll need to make decisions about who will have access (and what kind of access they will have), which services you want to use, how you want to manage your email, and how the various services will be set up to work for your team. This chapter walks you through all those choices and more so that when it's time to get everybody moving, you can hit the cloud running.

Are You an Administrator?

Administrator is an important-sounding word, and what it really means is this: you get to make decisions about your Office 365 account and get things set up the way you want them. With that glory comes responsibility, and this chapter will help you determine which items are important for your group and which are not. Specifically, you are an administrator if

- You are creating and managing the account.

- It is up to you to add and manage users in the site.

- You assign and administer the different licenses your teammates use in Office 365. (I'll say more about that in a minute.)

- You are charged with setting up the various services the way you want them.

- You have been charged with a specific goal you'll be helping your group to achieve.

- You are the visionary behind the whole virtual team plan, and you want to see it work.

- You'll be designing, updating, and managing the SharePoint team site in your account.

You might be taking on one or more of those tasks—or perhaps your role is bigger or smaller. No matter—in Office 365, you can have more than one administrator, so if you want to share the wealth of features all the better. Just to keep things simple, though, it's generally a good idea to have one person in charge of things such as user accounts, permissions, and licenses. And if you have more than one administrator in the site, be sure you communicate about big-picture decisions such as whether you want to migrate email accounts so that other accounts combine with Office 365 mail or whether you want to allow members to include external contacts in Lync Online. Orchestrating those types of management choices helps you not duplicate—or undo—each other's efforts.

Tip   This is a philosophical consideration, but one great benefit of being an administrator is that you can think through the kind of team experience you want your members to have. How collaborative will it be? What types of projects will you be working on? What, ultimately, will a successful group look like? Thinking through those questions will help you make choices consistent with that vision when you set up the services in Office 365.

An Overview of Your Administrative Tasks

So you already know you're a special person because you've got the keys to the kingdom. When you log in to your Office 365 account, if you're an administrator you'll see the Admin link at the top right side of the choices at the top of the screen. When you click Admin, the Admin Overview page appears, as you see in Figure 3-1.

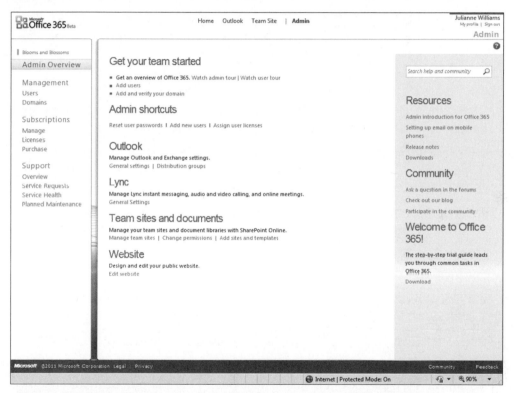

FIGURE 3-1 The Admin Overview page gives you access to the various ways you can administer the Office 365 account.

When you first click Admin after creating your Office 365 account, the Admin page shows the Get Your Team Started area at the top. This special group of links gives you what you need to know to begin setting up your site for your team. Specifically, you can

- Watch a video clip about the administrative tasks in Office 365.

- See a video of user tasks and learn about Office 365 services.

- Add new users to your account.

- Add and verify the web domain you want to use with the account.

The Admin Overview page is divided into three main areas. On the left side are links you use to manage the users and domains that are part of your Office 365 account. Here you add and remove users, set permissions, enter and change passwords, and update user properties and licenses. You can also view information about the various domains you set up to use with Office 365, manage your service subscriptions, and check the status of the system, get help, and review any existing technical support requests you created.

Tip What's a domain? The *domain* of your website is the name of the space online where your Office 365 account is stored. For example, in the examples in this book, the domain is wideworld.onmicrosoft.com.

The area in the center of the page lists the various services available to you in Office 365. Clicking the various links under each of the service names, you will be able to

- Use the Admin Shortcuts to accomplish common tasks you will likely need to do regularly—such as reset user passwords, add users, and assign licenses for working with Office 365 services.

- Set up Outlook to work as you'd like for your computer, complete with email defaults and group usage.

- Prepare Lync for your team, and choose whether users can use Lync to communicate with groups external to your team.

- Work with your team sites, set user permissions for the site, and create new sites and pages.

- Create, design, and edit the public-facing website that is part of your Office 365 account.

The column on the right side of the Admin page offers links that provide more information about administering your Office 365 site, connecting a mobile device, accessing release notes, and downloading the utility you need to connect Lync Online and the Office Web Apps with your desktop applications.

First Things First: Key Tasks to Complete

As you can see, that's a lot to do! The good news is that you don't have to tackle it all at once—you can grow into the features as you get familiar with the services. The most important thing when you're starting out if you're a small business is to accomplish the following tasks:

- Make sure team members have the permissions and licenses they need to log on and access Office 365 services.

- Make sure email is working the way you want it to for all your team members.

- Get started on the team site to provide access to the information your team needs.

- Set up Lync Online to allow file transfer and audio and video transmission if you want your group to have access to those features.

- Know how to get help, create service requests, and check system status.

In the sections that follow, you'll find out how to do each of these core tasks and prepare Office 365 for the happy arrival of your colleagues.

Adding and Managing Office 365 Users

Your first and perhaps most important task as the administrator of the Office 365 account is to make sure that your team can access the site. Click Users in the Management area to open the Users page. (See Figure 3-2.) In the Users screen of the Admin view, you can add and delete new users, edit permissions, and reset user passwords.

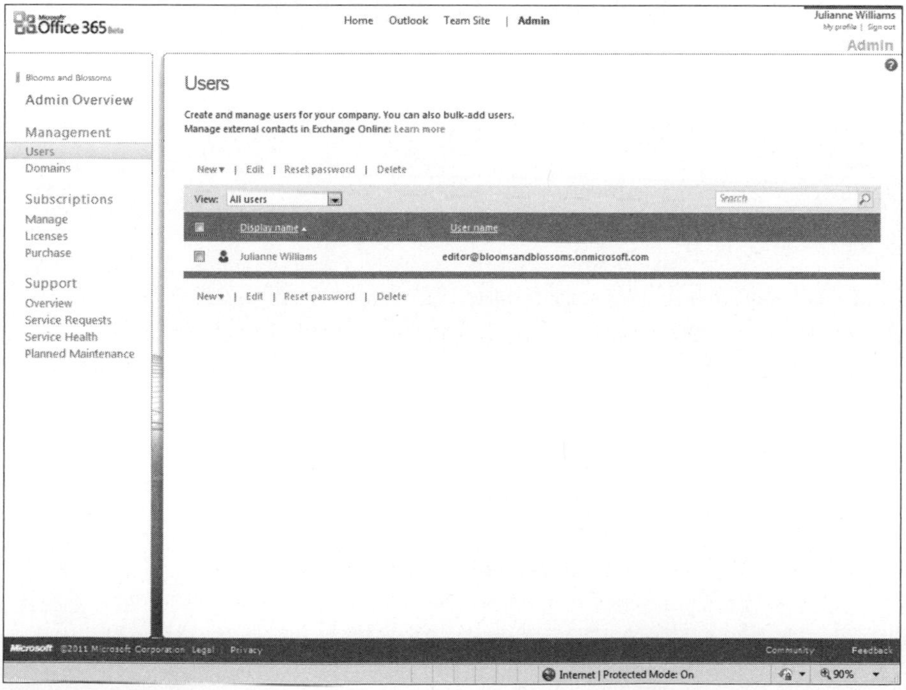

FIGURE 3-2 Click Users to add, edit, and update user information in Office 365.

Adding Users

After you click Users, the listing of team members already added to the site appears in the work area. If you're the only one who has accessed the site so far, yours might be the only email listed. You can add users one by one, if you're working with a small list, or you can add many users using a slightly different process. Here are the steps for each—choose the one you need.

Adding Users One at a Time

If you'll be working with a small team, or you've already created a team and just want to add a new user or two, the task is as simple as clicking the mouse and typing in a few pieces of information. Here are the steps:

1. Click New in the Users screen and click User.

2. In the New User Properties screen, add the name, display name, and email address you want to create for the new user

3. Click Additional Properties if you'd like to add additional information about this user in the site. (See Figure 3-3.)

4. Click Next.

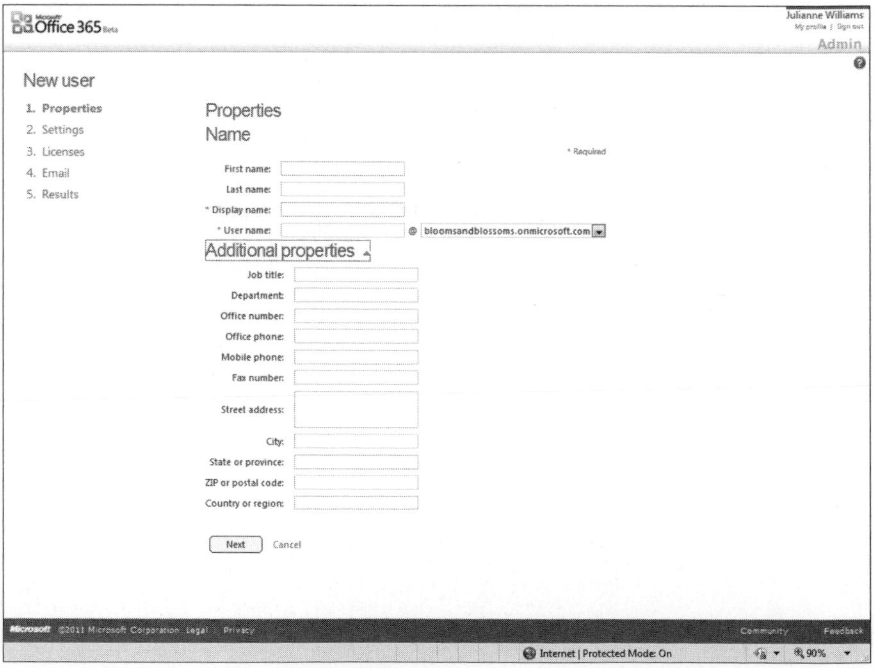

FIGURE 3-3 Adding a user is as simple as entering a display name and an email address.

> **Note** You don't have to enter the person's first and last name, but you *do* need to enter a display name that will be visible to others in the site. Also, note that at this point you cannot add an existing email address outside of your site domain. Later if you'd like to connect an existing email address to this account, you can do so. See the section, "Migrate Your Email," to find out more.

> **Tip** Other users will be able to view this information in the user's profile, so if you're working with a large team, fill in as much information as you have. This helps team members feel they know each other and begins the process of creating a more connected group experience.

After you've specified the basic properties for the new user account, you still need configure additional settings and permissions that control the way the new user will interact with Office 365 services. For more about how to do this, see the section, "Setting Permissions, User Location, and Sign-In Status," later in this chapter.

Adding Multiple Users at Once

If you have a number of users to add all at once—perhaps a department manager at work sent along a file of all the contact information for your team—you can simply upload the data file directly into Office 365 and create users that way.

To add multiple users all at once, follow these steps:

1. Click New, and choose Bulk Add Users.

2. In the Bulk Add Users page (shown in Figure 3-4), click the Browse button to open the Choose File To Upload dialog box.

3. Navigate to the folder containing the CSV file you want to use, click it, and click Open.

> **Tip** What's a CSV file? CSV stands for *comma-separated values*, and this common file format is used to store data from tables, worksheets, or databases. So a CSV file that includes information for your team might include information that looks like this: *User name, First name, Last name, Display name.*

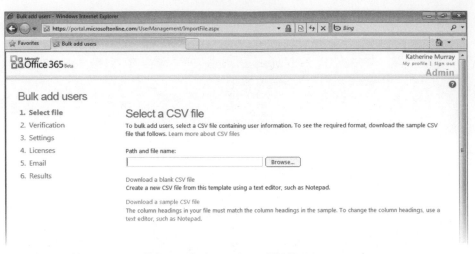

FIGURE 3-4 Add many users all at once by importing a CSV file.

After Office 365 uploads the file, the user names are verified to ensure that all information is ready to use. The verification screen shows you which information passed muster and which produced errors.

You can view any errors produced by clicking the View link in the Log File category. If you need to make a change to the data file, click the Back button at the bottom of the screen and then return to the data file, make any corrections, and upload the CSV file once again.

CREATE AND UPLOAD A CSV FILE

If you have user information you'd like to enter for everybody at once, you can download the sample CSV file Office 365 makes available for you, fill in your own data, and upload the file as described in the previous section. Alternatively, you can download a blank CSV file, add your own contact information, and upload the file to Office 365. Here's the process for creating your own CSV file for your team:

1. In Admin Overview, click Users.

2. Click New, and choose Bulk Add Users.

3. Click Download A Blank CSV File.

4. Click Open. This opens an Excel worksheet so that you can copy and paste or type your team information into the file. (See Figure 3-5.) Be sure to include the user's full email address in the User Name field.

5. Save the file to your Documents library (or another folder where you store team-related files).

6. Return to the Bulk Add Users screen, click Browse, navigate to the CSV file you just created, and add the file normally.

7. Click Next. Office 365 verifies the addition of the new users to make sure the information has been entered correctly.

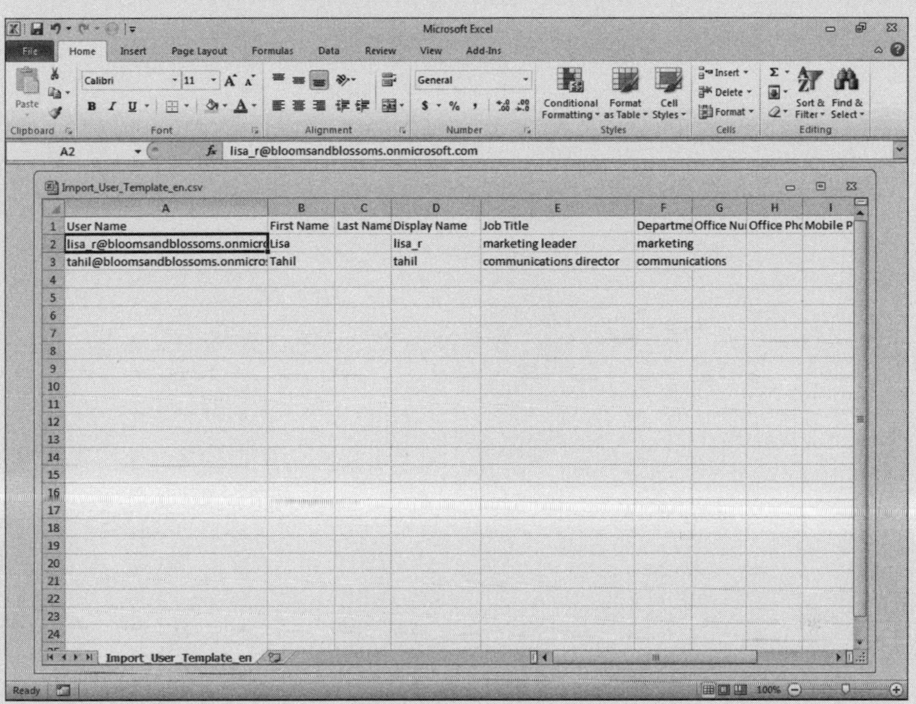

FIGURE 3-5 When you click Open, Office 365 displays an Excel file with fields already set up to record user information.

Setting Permissions, User Location, and Sign-In Status

The next step in the process depends on whether you are adding a single new user or are bulk adding new users. If you are adding only a single new user, the Settings screen is where you assign permissions and a location to the user. For the Permissions option, you can choose whether the user is to be an Office 365 administrator or not. To set the user location for an individual user, click the Select A Location arrow and choose the user's country from the displayed list. Office 365 is available in a number of countries around the world, but not all countries have access to the same services. Select the user's country for the displayed list, and click Next.

If you are bulk-adding new users, however, the Permissions option is replaced with a Set Sign-in Status option, where you choose to allow or block access to Office 365 services by the user. If you bulk-add new user accounts before employees are ready to use these accounts, you can choose Deny to keep the accounts inactive. Then when an employee is ready to use an account, you can change the sign-in status from Blocked to Allowed. In addition to configuring sign-in status, you must also specify a location when bulk-adding users.

Assigning Licenses

The next step involved in getting your users set up to use Office 365 involves assigning them the licenses they need to use the services in the site. Depending on the version of Office 365 you are using, you might have two different sets of licenses available, as Figure 3-6 shows.

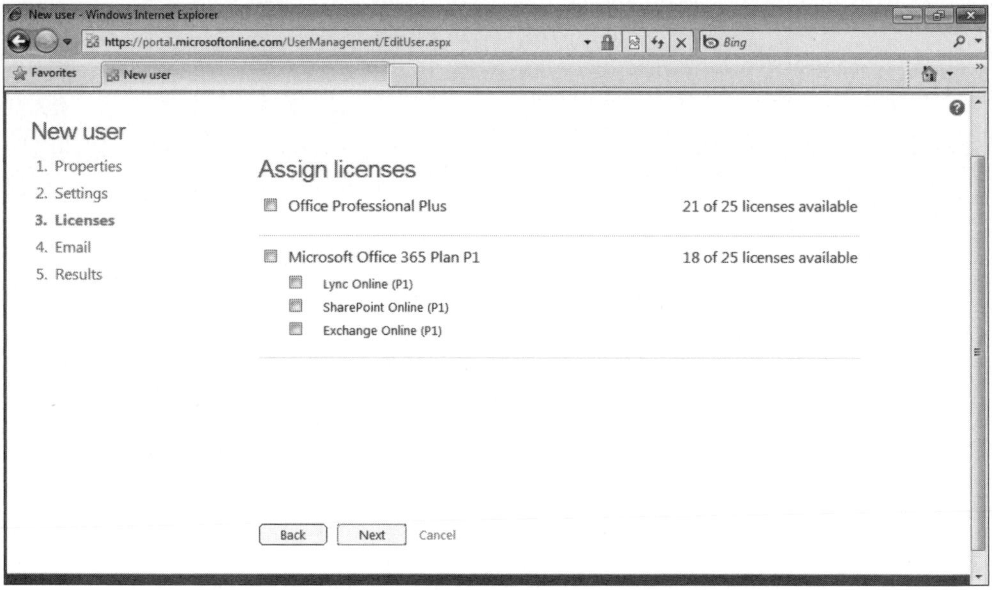

FIGURE 3-6 Click the license you want to assign to the new users you are adding.

Select the check box of the services you want the new user to be able to access. Office 365 shows on the right side of the screen the number of licenses you can assign to your various team members. When you are satisfied with your selections, click Next.

> **Tip**
> ✓
>
> If you find that as your group grows you're worrying about the number of licenses you have available, you can remove user accounts that are no longer needed to reclaim their licenses so that they can be assigned to other new users.

Sending an Invitation Email

Next Office 365 will walk you through the process of sending an email message to the new team member that includes an autogenerated password. By default, Office 365 enters the email address of the administrator who is creating the account. For security purposes, this email should generally be sent to an administrator and not to the new user account that is being created. The admin should then communicate the temporary password to the new user. This is especially true when creating bulk users because you don't want each new user to know the temporary password of every other new user being created.

Click Create. Office 365 generates and sends the message, and then displays a report so that you can see that the message is on its way to the new user. (See Figure 3-7.) Click Finish to close the Results window and return to the Users window.

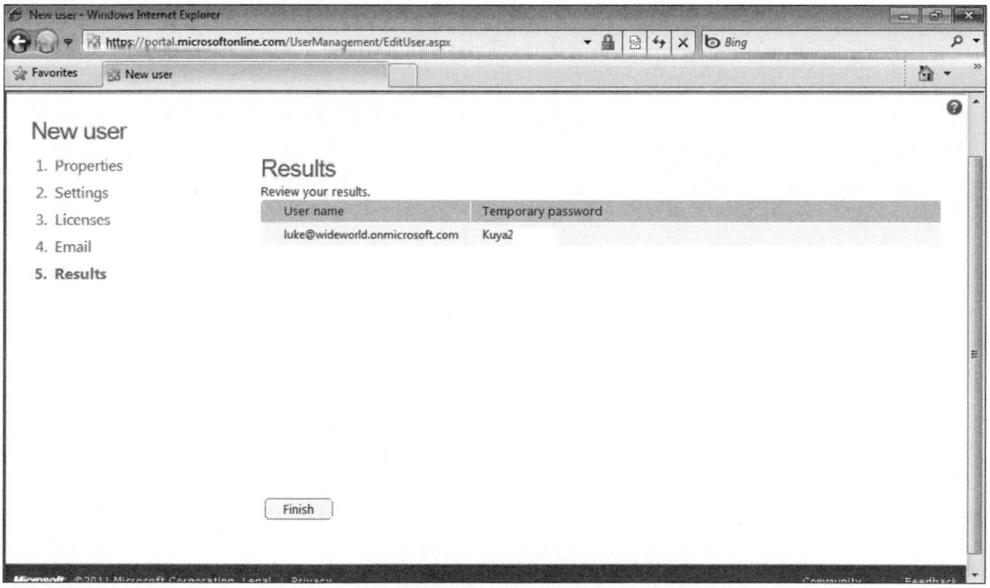

FIGURE 3-7 Office 365 lets you know that the email has been sent successfully.

That's the whole process for adding users to Office 365. At any time, you can add users individually, add another set of bulk users, or update properties for individual users as needed. You need to keep an eye on the number of licenses you have available, of course, but the process itself is a simple one.

Changing Passwords

The users you added will be able to access your Office 365 site and log in using the temporary password that was generated for them when their account was created. Depending on the security systems in place in your particular business, however, users might not receive the email or might have trouble logging in. And, of course, some users—including yours truly—just lose stuff from time to time (which is another reason to have the temporary password emailed directly to you as the admin).

Office 365 knows that as an admin, managing passwords might be one of your biggest headaches. Luckily, it's one that can be healed easily. When you get a request to change a user's password and help that user access the site, you can do it in five simple steps. Here's how:

1. Log in to Office 365, and click Admin.

2. In Admin Shortcuts, click Reset User Passwords.

3. Select the check box of the user whose password you want to change.

4. Click Reset Password. (See Figure 3-8.)

5. Again, your email address as the administrator will appear in the text box. Click the Reset Password button to email yourself a copy of the new password, which you can then pass along to the user.

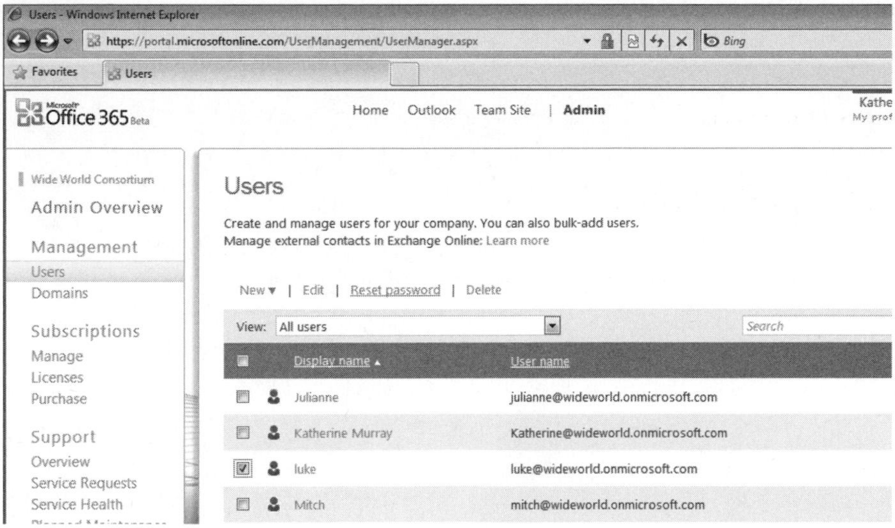

FIGURE 3-8 You can easily reset the password in the Users screen of Admin view.

Viewing Domain Properties

Another part of your responsibilities as administrator involves keeping an eye on the domains that are part of your account. Depending on how complex your needs are, this might be super simple: you might have only one domain registered with Office 365. This enables you to track your team, create a team site, access the services you've sign up for, and so on.

But if your scenario isn't quite so simple and you are managing multiple domains and many different sites, being able to display the domain information will be helpful. You can view the domains in use with your account by clicking Admin and then clicking Domains in the links on the left side of the Admin Overview screen. (See Figure 3-9.) The Status column on the right shows you whether the site is currently active or inactive. You can display the properties of a selected domain by clicking the domain's radio button to the left of the domain name and clicking View Properties.

FIGURE 3-9 View the domains included on your account by clicking Domains in the Management area of Admin view.

Adding a Domain to Office 365

When you sign up for your Office 365 account, you are assigned a default domain name of the form *yourcompany*.onmicrosoft.com, where *yourcompany* is a name you specify during the signup process. This domain name is then used to set up your services, set up email, and more. You can also add a domain name you already have to your Office 365 account if you'd like. If your domain name is registered, you can add it to Office 365 by using the Add A Domain link in the top left column of the domain listing.

> **Note** You must own the domain name you choose to add to the Office 365 domains. At any point in the process, you can purchase a domain name from a domain registration site, such as Network Solutions, and click Add A Domain to assign it to Office 365.

On the Specify Domain screen, click in the text box at the bottom of the page, type the domain name you want to add (for example, wideworld.com), and click Check Domain. Office 365 displays the information found about that domain in the Domain Confirmation screen. (See Figure 3-10.)

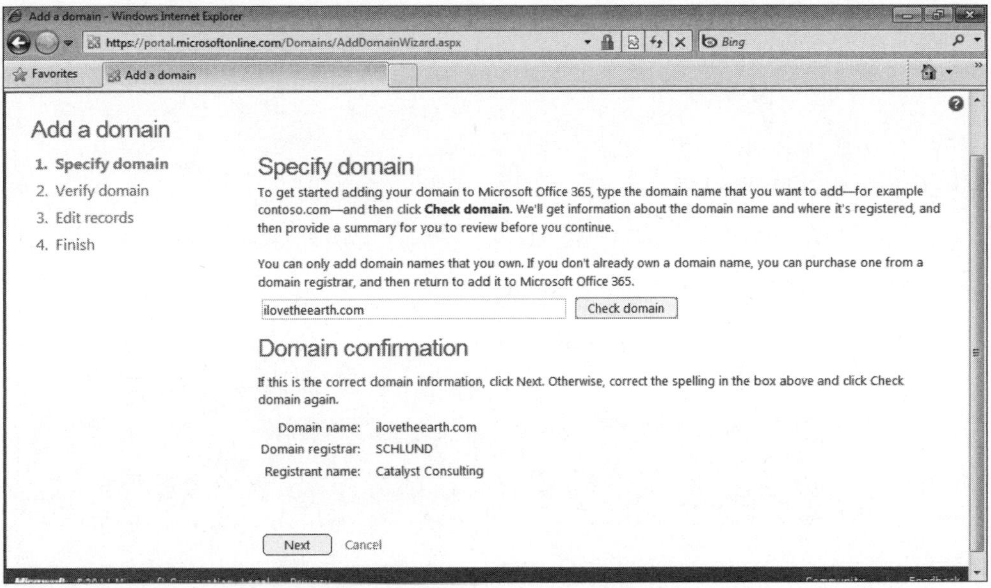

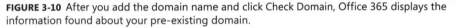

FIGURE 3-10 After you add the domain name and click Check Domain, Office 365 displays the information found about your pre-existing domain.

Click Next to continue the process. In the Verify Domain window, if you're ready to transfer the domain to your Office 365 account, follow the instructions provided to create a subdomain, edit the DNS settings, and complete the necessary permissions. You might need to involve your domain registrar in this process.

Finally, click Verify to finalize the process and make the domain available to Office 365. The entire operation might take up to 72 hours to complete. In the meantime, your added domain will appear as Pending Verification in the domain table in the Domains window.

Setting Up and Managing Outlook and Exchange

Now that you've got your users set up in the site, you're ready to begin setting up your services. Let's start with Outlook and Exchange, which you can use to create new mailboxes, create groups, set up calendars, and more.

Begin the process by clicking Admin and, in the Admin Overview window, click General Settings in the Outlook area. The Exchange Online screen appears (shown in Figure 3-11), where you can set up defaults for a number of features, including the following:

- Add mailboxes

- Create distribution lists

- Set up external contacts

- Add other email accounts to Exchange Online

Tip ✓ The Exchange Online settings you enter control the settings available in other aspects of Office 365 as well, including the way email works for your user accounts and the types of lists and contacts that are available in the Outlook Web App and in Lync Online.

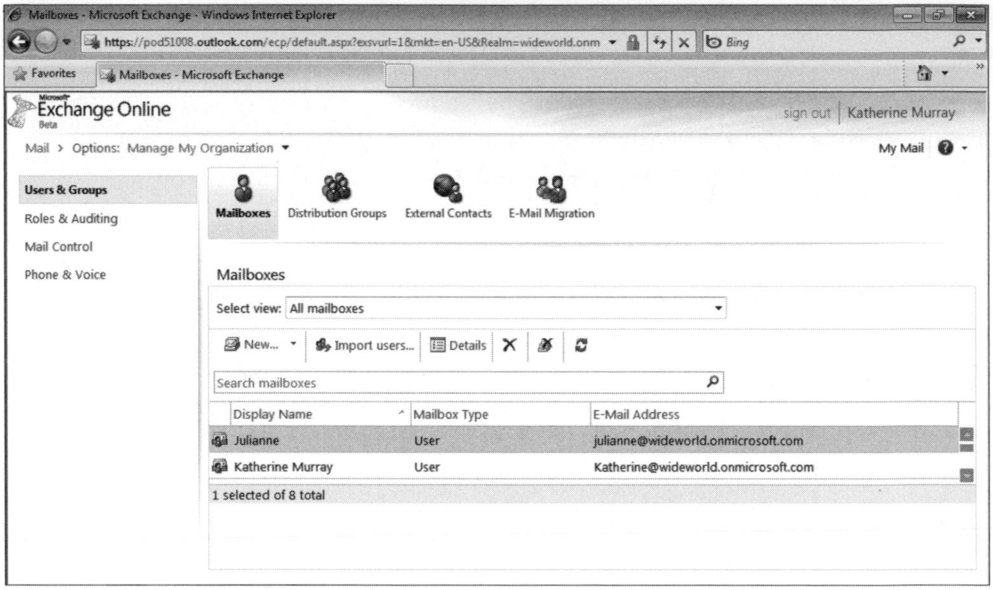

FIGURE 3-11 Exchange Online enables you to set up the way you want email to work in Office 365.

The Mailboxes features in Exchange Online follow steps similar to the ones you've already taken to set up your users in Office 365. You can click New in the Mailboxes screen to add a new user or click Import Users to upload a CSV file. The list of current users in your Office 365 account are displayed in the table at the bottom of the screen.

> **Tip** ✓ One neat feature in the Mailboxes area is the ability to create a Room Mailbox. This feature is intended for times when you need to schedule a real, physical location, like a conference room, training room, or lunch room. You can set up a Room Mailbox and then, when you send out meeting requests to the team, simply include the room mailbox on the To list. The room is then scheduled automatically, and others in the organization know it is no longer available during that time. This, of course, isn't a resource you would use if your team members are all working in the cloud from remote locations, but it's a cool feature if you occasionally get together for face-to-face meetings.

Create a Distribution List

You can create a distribution list in Exchange Online to control the flow of outgoing communications. If you regularly send out status updates from the site, for example, or you publish a list of site changes on a weekly basis, you can create a distribution list to make sure that all the users who need to receive that information get the message. To create a distribution list for your users in Exchange, follow these steps:

1. In the Outlook area of the Admin Overview page, click Distribution Groups.

2. Click New on the Distribution Groups tab.

3. Enter a name, alias, and description for the distribution list.

4. If you want the group to be secure so that people can join the group only by requesting to be added to the secure list, select the Make This Group A Security Group check box. (See Figure 3-12.)

5. Click the Membership area, and click Add; then click the user or users you want to add to the list. Click Add at the bottom of the dialog box and click OK.

6. Choose any additional options—or add other users as owners of the list—and click Save.

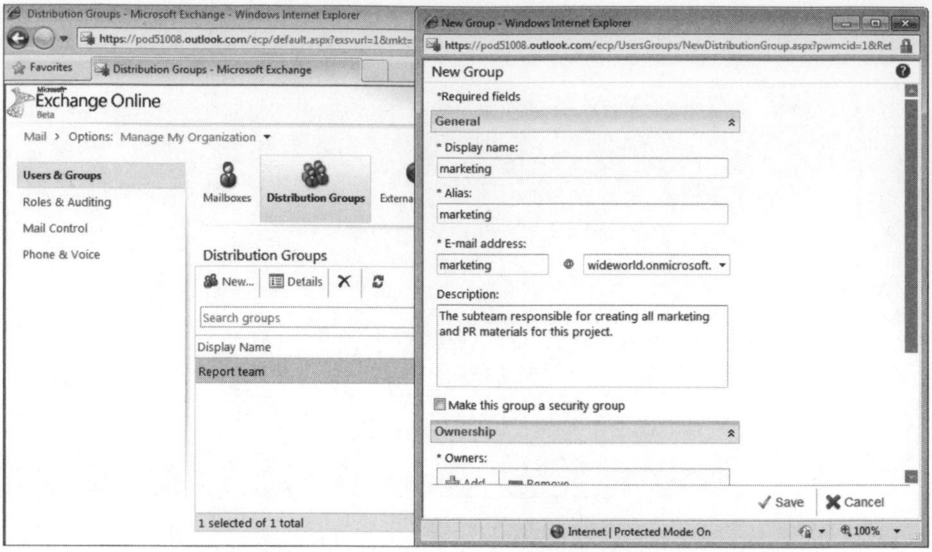

FIGURE 3-12 You can create a distribution list to send specific communication to selected users.

Add External Contacts

One of the great things about your Office 365 account is that you can create a completely secure space in the cloud where your team can collaborate and focus on specific tasks at hand. But part of your work is sure to require correspondence with contacts outside your happy little group, whether they are customers, contractors, or other colleagues who aren't part of your Office 365 team.

You can set up external contacts to allow users outside your organization to receive email from and send email to your team. The users you add will actually appear in your team's address book, but they won't be able to access your site. To add an external contact to your list, follow these steps:

1. In the Admin Overview page, click General Settings in the Outlook area.

2. In the Exchange Online screen, click External Contacts.

3. Click New.

4. Enter the name, alias, and email address of the external contact.

5. Click Save. The external contact is added to the list at the bottom of the External Contacts screen. (See Figure 3-13.)

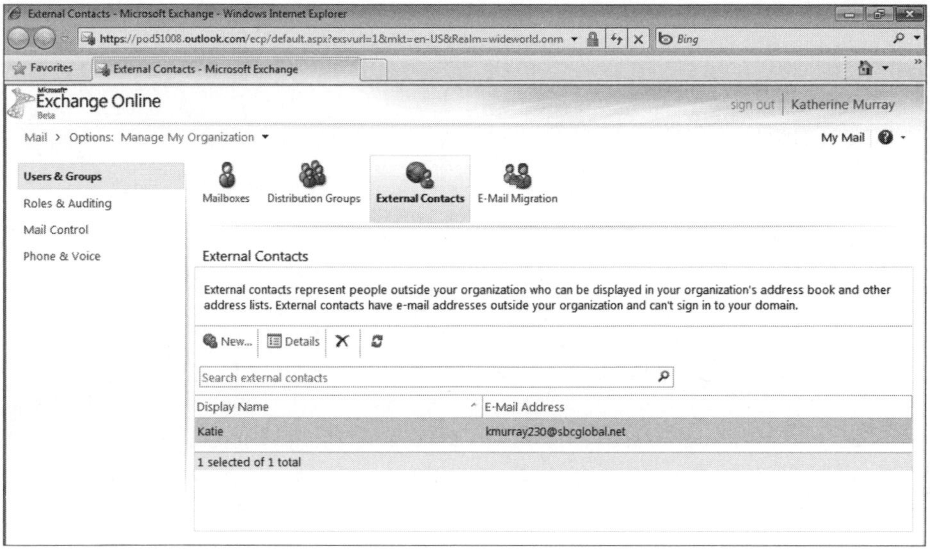

FIGURE 3-13 You can create a list of external contacts who will be able to communicate with your Office 365 team.

The external contact will show up in your address book so that you can send messages to and receive messages from the person you've added to the list.

Migrate Your Email

As you lead your team into the cloud, you might be considering migrating your email from your traditional server-bound configuration to a new cloud address at Office 365. This enables you to keep all your messaging—address books, rules and alerts, messages, and more—available online from any point of access, anytime. You can easily move your existing mailboxes to Office 365, or you can keep the mailboxes on the server and use your Office 365 mail alongside the server-based setup.

Office 365 enables you to coordinate your various email accounts in a couple of different ways. If you're using POP accounts, you can use Connected Accounts in Outlook Web App to add access to those accounts to your Office 365 account. (You'll learn more about this in Chapter 10, "Email and Organize in Office 365.")

For other types of email accounts such as IMAP accounts , you can use the Email Migration tool to move your email accounts to the mailboxes in Office 365. Here are the steps:

1. In the Admin Overview screen, click General Settings in the Outlook category.

2. Click EMail Migration.

3. Click New.

4. Select the type of email account you'll be migrating, and click Next.

5. Specify the account information as requested.

6. In the Start Migration page, click Run.

After the migration is complete, Office 365 sends you a status email giving you information about the migration—how many mailboxes and distribution groups migrated successfully, whether any errors were produced, as well as a report providing login keys for the migrated mailboxes. Your users will need these keys to log in to their mail in Office 365 after the account has migrated, so be sure to save this information. Users will change the password after their first login to the migrated account.

Setting Up SharePoint Online

You will use your SharePoint site to stay in touch with your team, share documents, assign tasks, post questions, provide updates, and more. You can also use SharePoint to create your own public website, giving your customers or clients a professional-looking site where they can find up-to-date information about your products or services.

As an administrator, your first task is to make sure all your team members can get into the SharePoint site and that the basics are in place so that people can begin creating the team experience you want them to create. This section focuses on setting up users and permissions, and the rest of the customizing experience (as well as all the how-tos for basic SharePoint Online tasks) is covered in Chapter 5, "Creating Your Team Site with SharePoint Online."

Adding Users for SharePoint Online

Your first task involves adding users to your SharePoint team site. Even though you have already set up user accounts in Office 365, those users aren't automatically added to

SharePoint—you need to do that yourself. To add your team members to the SharePoint site, follow these steps:

1. In the Admin Overview page, click Manage Team Sites in the Team Sites And Documents area.

2. In the Team Site Settings screen (shown in Figure 3-14), click People And Groups in the Users And Permissions area.

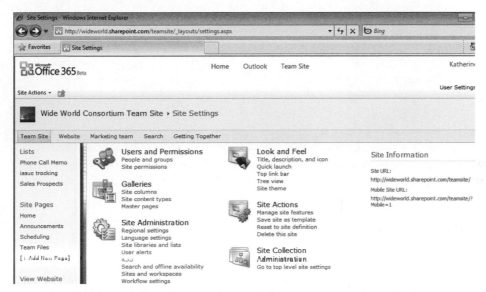

FIGURE 3-14 SharePoint Online offers a whole world of settings you can use to tailor the way your site looks and acts.

3. Under Groups in the navigation area on the left side of the screen, click Members and click New.

4. Click Add Users. The Grant Permissions dialog box appears. (See Figure 3-15.)

5. Enter the email addresses of your team members, separating them with semi-colons.

6. In the Personal Message box, type a message you want your team members to receive.

7. Click OK. The new users are added to the Members list.

FIGURE 3-15 Add your team members to the Users/Groups field by typing their email addresses, separated by semi-colons.

Assigning User Permissions

Now that you've added people to the site, you can set the user permissions so that your team members can perform the tasks you want them to accomplish in the site. You can do this in one of two ways in SharePoint Online, and it's just a bit confusing if you've never worked with SharePoint before.

SharePoint enables you to assign permissions for specific individuals, or you can assign permissions by groups, and make sure that individual team members are part of the group you want to have the necessary access level. For example, you might give some team members the ability to view and change content, while others have only the permissions they need to review content posted in the site.

SharePoint offers six permission levels: View Only, Enhanced Contribute, Read, Contribute, Design, and Full Control. Table 3-1 defines each of these permission levels.

TABLE 3-1 User Permission Levels in SharePoint Online

Permission Level	Permitted User Action
View Only	View content but not edit it
Read	View and download content
Contribute	View, edit, add to, and remove content
Design	View, edit, add to, remove, approve, and customize content
Full Control	Has full control of the SharePoint site
Enhanced Contribute	View, edit, add to, and remove content, and approve items and manage lists

The simplest way to work with permissions for your team members is to begin with the basics: each new member you add to SharePoint is given Member privileges, which means the new member can read all content on the site and contribute to that content (through editing, adding, or removing material). So if you're fine with everyone being able to read and edit the site, you're good—no changes are required.

If you want to change the default permission for a specific user—either limiting the permission so that the user can only read the information, for example, or granting full control so that the team member can make all kinds of changes on the site (including adding and removing user accounts), you need to know how to modify permissions. Here's how to do that:

1. On the Admin Overview page, click Manage Team Sites in the Team Sites And Documents category.

2. On the Team Site Settings page, click Site Permissions in the Users And Permissions area.

3. Click Grant Users Permission Directly (shown in Figure 3-16), and then click the permission level you want to assign to the team member.

4. Type the text for the email message if you want to send one, and click OK. The team member is assigned the permission level you selected.

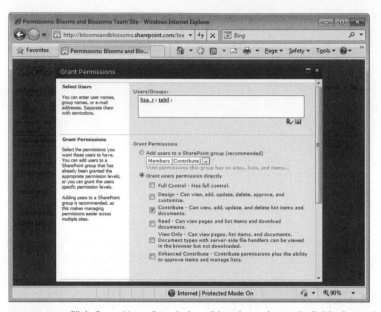

FIGURE 3-16 Click Grant Users Permissions Directly to choose individual permissions for the users you select.

GROUP TYPES AND PERMISSIONS IN SHAREPOINT

If you're working with large teams or coordinating the activities of more than one team, you might find the group method easier because you can simply assign team members to the specific group and then manage the permissions for everyone all at once. The groups SharePoint sets up by default are these:

- Members, who can read content and contribute to the content on the site

- Owners, who have full control of the site

- Tenant Users, who are given the permissions you assign to your domain group

- Viewers, who can read all content on the site

- Visitors, who can read the content on the site when they are granted access

- Website Designers, who are assigned design privileges

You can use these groups or create a new group with the permissions you want to provide to your team members by using the controls in the Users And Permissions area of the SharePoint Settings screen.

Configuring Lync Online

Your final task for setting up Office 365 for the rest of your team involves making sure Microsoft Lync Online is ready to help members communicate the way you need it to. Depending on the types of projects you work on and the ways in which you want your colleagues to connect, you might choose to turn on various features to help files and messages flow a little more smoothly.

Set External Communications

Begin in the Admin Overview page by clicking General Settings in the Lync area. The Lync Online Control Panel appears, as you see in Figure 3-17, providing options for you to allow or disable external communications (meaning that people outside your organization will—or won't—be able to contact your team in Office 365). In addition to setting up external communications, you can tailor the settings and permissions you've assigned to each user.

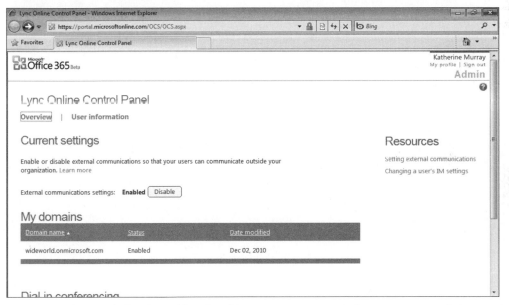

FIGURE 3-17 The Lync Online Control Panel enables you to set contact preferences, user permissions, and dial-in conferencing settings.

Modifying User Information

To change the settings for a particular user, click User Information in the Lync Online Control Panel. This link takes you to a page listing the various users on your account. Select the check box for the user with the information you want to change and click Edit User. As you can see in Figure 3-18, Lync Online displays a window showing the user's information so that you can change the settings that do the following:

- Allow the user to send files using Lync.

- Enable the user to hear audio and watch video.

- Let the user communicate with others outside your Office 365 team.

By default, all these options are enabled; to disable the capabilities, simply deselect the check box of the item you want to change.

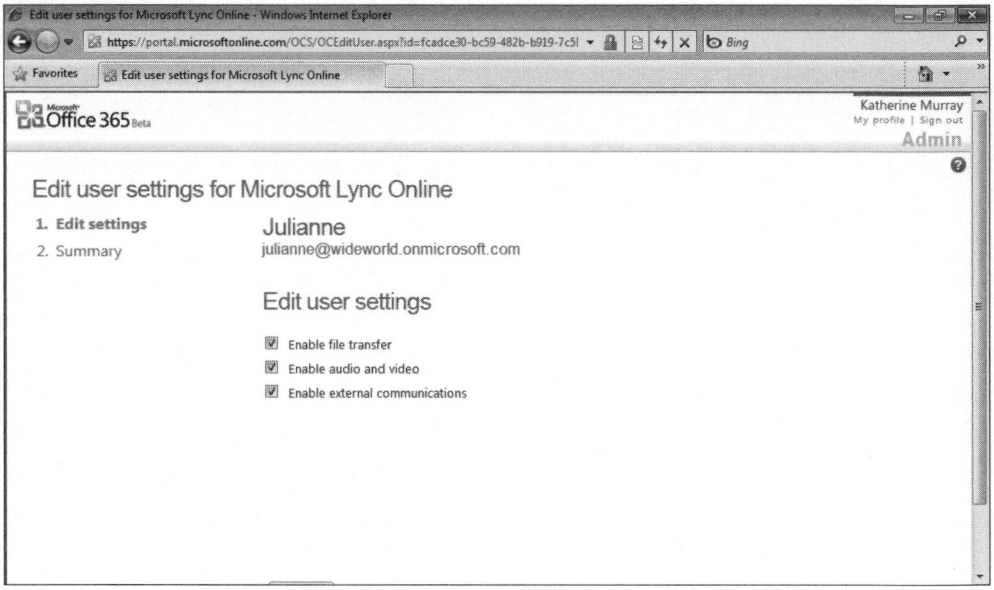

FIGURE 3-18 You can set program capabilities for individual users in Lync Online.

Setting Up Dial-in Conferencing

In the bottom half of the Lync Online Control Panel, you'll see information about dial-in conferencing. This feature enables team members to join an online meeting by calling in. Before you can set up dial-in conferencing in Lync, you need to have an account established with an audio-conferencing vendor. You can then add the information the vendor provides you—such as the call-in number and password—to each user account so that your team members can join audio conferencing when you host online meeting using Lync.

To enter the dial-in conferencing information, click the Manage link. The Edit Dial-In Conference Settings window appears. (See Figure 3-19.) You can add the dial-in conference information to a user account by clicking the user name and following these steps:

1. Click the Provider arrow, and choose the name of your provider from the list.

2. Type the call-in local number.

3. Type the call-in toll-free number.

4. Type the passcode for the account.

5. Click Save.

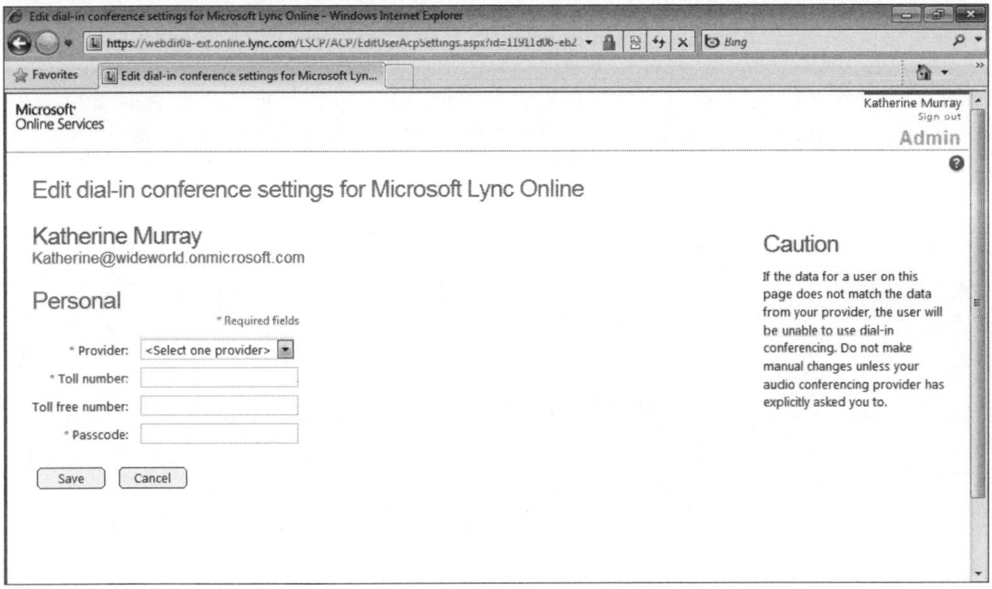

FIGURE 3-19 Enter the audio-conferencing access numbers and passcode for each user who will participate.

Managing Your Subscriptions

One of the beautiful things about Office 365 is that it's built on a model of efficiency. You can purchase only what you need—for only the team members you need—and keep your costs down and your support load light while moving toward the business-critical goals on your horizon. To help you manage who uses what and when they use it, Office 365 gives administrators the means to review, manage, and change the subscriptions to the services their teams use.

You'll find the tools you need for reviewing and managing subscriptions in the Subscriptions area on the left side of the Admin Overview page. Each of the three links offers you a different way to survey your Office 365 subscriptions:

- **Manage** provides you with a listing of all current subscriptions in use by your team.

- **Licenses** shows the number of licenses you have available (and are using) as part of your subscriptions.

- **Purchase** enables you to instantly add to the subscriptions you already have.

To view your team's subscriptions in Office 365, click the Manage link. The table shown in Figure 3-20 will appear. (Your subscriptions might look a bit different, of course.)

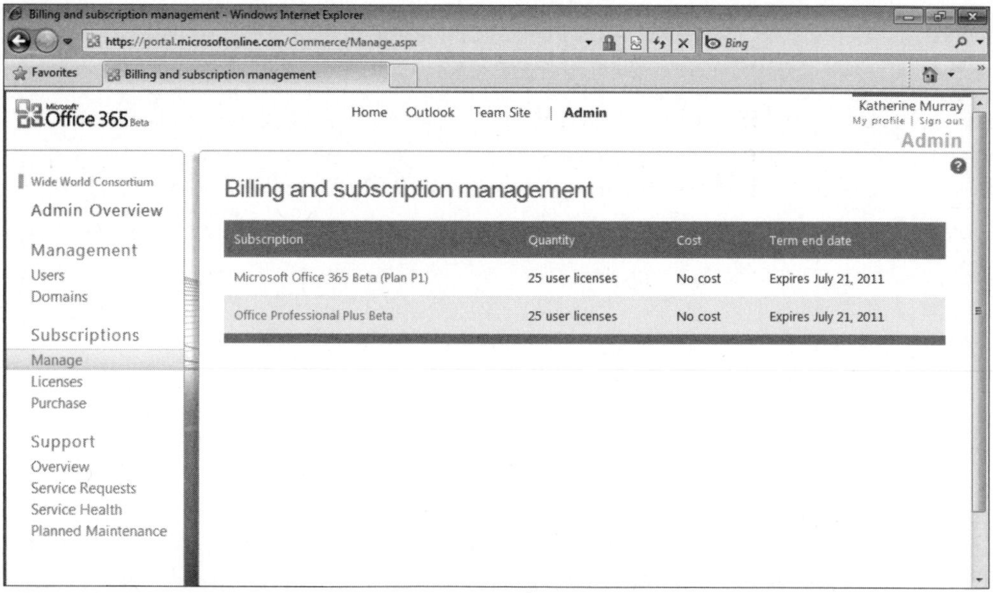

FIGURE 3-20 In the Subscriptions area, you can review the subscription and licenses available in your Office 365 account.

Note	The image in Figure 3-20 was captured during the beta program, which is why "No cost" appears in the Cost column.

When you click Licenses, Office 365 shows you the number of licenses currently in use by your team members, as well as the total number of licenses available to you. You can give users access to services by returning to the Admin Overview page and clicking Assign User Licenses in the Admin Shortcut area in the top center portion of the screen. Then click the user name and either select the check boxes of services you want to add or clear the check boxes of services you want to remove.

Tip ✓	If you need to pick up a few more licenses, remove user accounts you've assigned that you no longer need.

Finally, the Purchase window enables you to add to the subscriptions and licenses you have available in Office 365. This enables you to add on to what you need in real time, without requiring you to leave the site, purchase or download software, or jump through any of the hoops that installing new programs often requires. Nice!

Getting Help with Office 365

Even though Office 365 is built on what are likely to be some of your favorite and most familiar applications, learning the whole lay of the land—and creating the kind of setup you want—does involve a learning curve. Knowing this, Microsoft has created an engaged and active support community to help you get the help you need.

You'll find access to help throughout Office 365, whether you're working in the Admin area or not. For general help needs, you can click in the search box at the top of the right-most column and type a word or phrase that reflects what you're looking for. You can also click any of the links on the right—including the Community links—to find additional how-tos, ask a question in the forums, or read the Office 365 blog.

On the Admin Overview page, you also have the option of displaying the Support Overview page, where you can search for help in the community, see what people are saying in the forums about the different services, and get a bird's-eye view of your billing and service requests. (See Figure 3-21.)

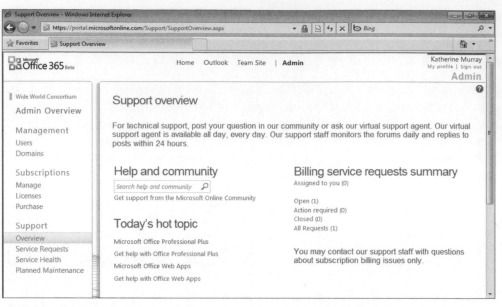

FIGURE 3-21 The Support Overview page gives you, as an admin, a big-picture look at various help offerings.

Other help tasks that fall to you as the administrator involve creating service requests for those times when you need professional assistance with the site, and checking overall system status to ensure there are no interruptions in service. These tasks are very important when you've got people logging in from all over the world and the web is your primary means of connection.

Creating Service Requests

Anyone who has ever spent time on the phone with technical support knows this universal truth: it is not fun.

First, you're probably frustrated because the software isn't working the way it should. Second, you probably have a deadline hanging over your head, which adds pressure. Third, as an administrator, you're at least in some capacity the one who has to figure this stuff out. So when you're having trouble with a program or you have a question you or your team members can't find the answer to, what do you do?

Begin by clicking Admin in Office 365 to access the Admin Overview page. Then click Service Requests in the Support area on the left side of the screen. In the Service Requests window, click New Request. (See Figure 3-22.) This opens a new Service Request window so that you can fill in the information you need in order to communicate your problem clearly to tech support.

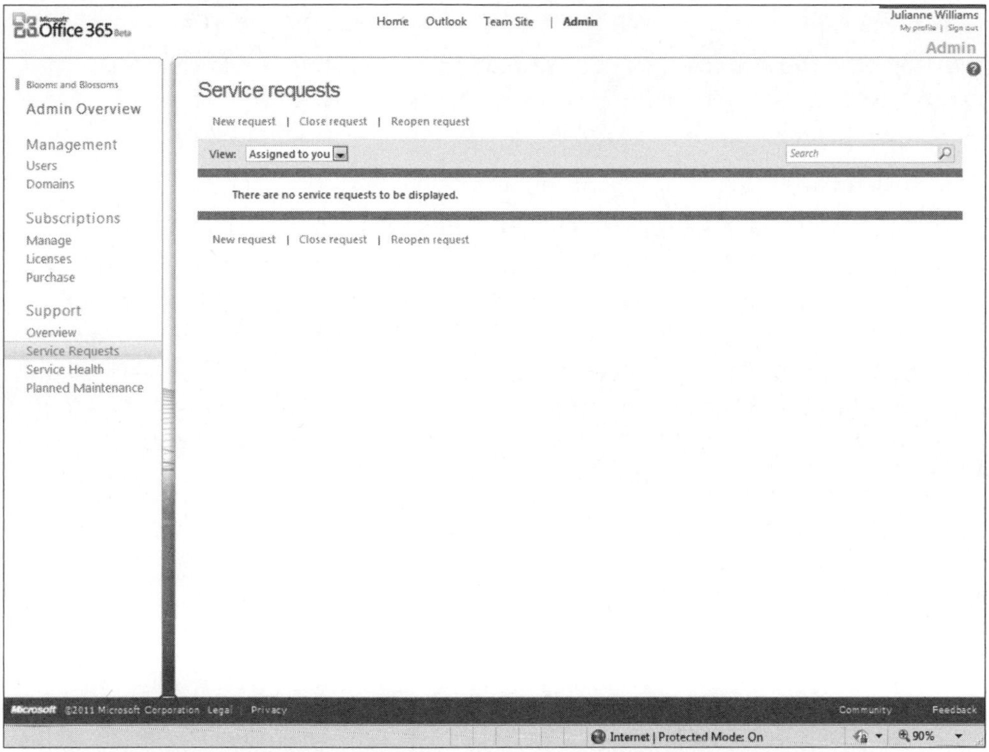

FIGURE 3-22 You can start a new service request by clicking Service Requests in the Support area of the Admin Overview page.

Here are the steps to get started filling out the service request form:

1. In the Identify Issue window, identify the problem as clearly as you can. Click the Service arrow, and choose the service you are having trouble with (Exchange, Lync, or SharePoint).

2. Click the Service Area arrow, and choose the category that reflects what you're having trouble with.

3. Click the Problem Description arrow, and choose your questions or issue from the list.

4. Click Operating System, and choose the operating system running on your computer. Similarly, choose the Office version and browser you use.

5. Click Next.

6. Enter a title that gives the technician an idea of the problem you're having.

7. Click in the Description area, and describe the problem fully.

8. In the Error Message area, provide any error messages you receive.

9. Click the arrow to the right of Have You Reproduced This Problem On More Than One Computer?, click either Have Not Tried, No, or Yes to let the technician know whether the problem exists on only one system or throughout your site.

10. Click Next.

It's often helpful for tech support personnel to see what you see when they are evaluating a problem you're having. You can capture a screen shot of any error message or problem you see on-screen and send the image to the technician. To capture the image, you can simply press Prt Sc while the problem is displayed on the screen and then paste the picture into your favorite image editor (such as Windows Paint); then save the file. Attach the file to your service request in the Attach File page by clicking the Attach A File link. Navigate to the file you want to attach, click Open, and when prompted, click Yes to affirm that you do want to attach the file.

The file appears in the center of the File Attachments page. You can remove the attachment if you'd like by clicking the Remove link that appears to the right of the attached file.

> **Tip** ✓ Of course, you aren't just limited to capturing a screen shot of the problem—you can use Problem Steps Recorder in Windows 7 to record the steps that reproduce the problem and then upload the file along with your service request.

Finally, send your service request to Microsoft by clicking the Submit button. Office 365 displays a Confirmation window, providing a summary of your request and providing a reference number. Click Finish to return to the Service Requests page.

Checking System Status

When you depend on a web-based service to provide connectivity to your team members and access to your programs and files, making sure the service is up and running correctly is a major concern. Recognizing this, Office 365 keeps you clued in about challenges and updates in the Office 365 system. If you're having trouble accessing a service, for example, your first step in solving the problem is to check the status of the overall system to make sure there aren't service glitches somewhere along the way.

To check the system status of Office 365, follow these steps:

1. Click Admin to display the Admin Overview screen.

2. In the Support area on the left side of your screen, click Service Health. The Service Health screen shows you the status of all the different services running in Office 365. (See Figure 3-23.)

3. Scroll down the list to check the status of all services.

4. Click the blue-and-white information icon to display the details about a particular service interruption.

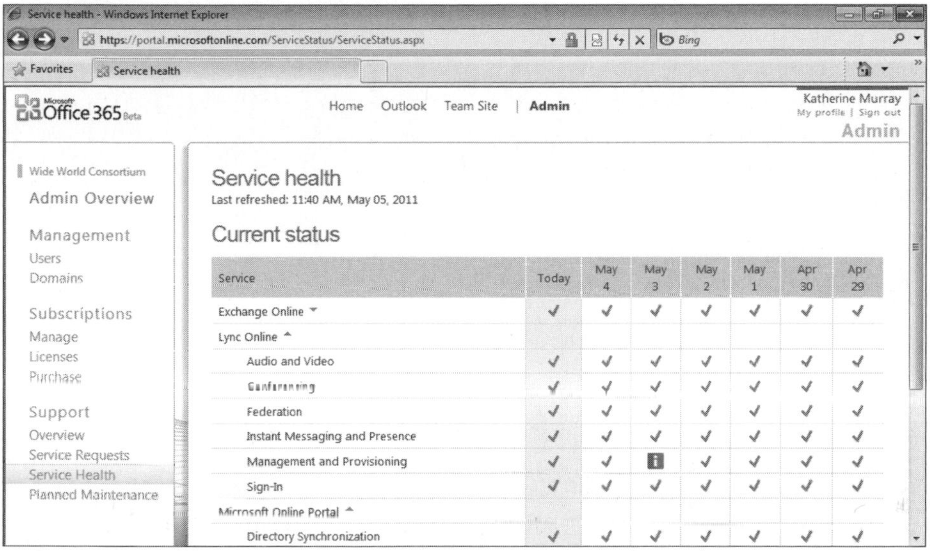

FIGURE 3-23 Check the system status of Office 365 to make sure that all services are up and running properly.

If you want to find out when the software will be going through planned maintenance upgrades, click Planned Maintenance on the left side of the screen. You'll be able to see when the next maintenance activities are scheduled, read details about the activity, and see the date and time the event is scheduled. This information will help you avoid scheduling site events that might be affected by the changes. For example, you might want to avoid scheduling an online meeting using Lync at the precise time the Lync service is set to undergo program maintenance.

◼ What's Next

In this chapter, you discovered the ins and outs of administration—at least as they pertain to your Office 365 account. You learned how to set up the space so that the people you want to have access can log in; you set permissions; you set up the various programs the way you want them to be used by your team members. You also found out how to manage service subscriptions and licenses and discovered how to check system status and get help. The next chapter starts Part II, "Teamwork in the Cloud," and shows you how you can get things moving on a team level in Office 365.

Teamwork in the Cloud

NOW THAT you've set up an Office 365 account, created user accounts for your team members and assigned permissions (if you're the administrator, anyway), the real fun begins! This part of the book shows you how to get your team working together by using various features of Office 365. The first chapter gives you a kind of appetizer plate of different services to sample, and the remaining chapters in this part show you specifically how to create a team site and begin sharing files of all types.

CHAPTER 4

What Your Team Can Do with Office 365

OK, YOU'VE GOT your Microsoft Office 365 account set up, and you've arranged for team members to get into the site. Now it's time to get inspired. Whether you are putting together a team to work on a specific project—like planning an amazing special event—or a team that will collaborate over time on many projects, creating a workspace your team can share and thinking about various things you'd like to accomplish together are two important steps in putting together a successful team.

This chapter discusses what you need to do to help your team be successful. Envisioning the type of team environment you'd like to create is a good place to begin. You'll be doing more brainstorming than actual site creation in this chapter—the specific steps for creating your shared worksite is the topic of Chapter 5, "Creating Your Team Site with SharePoint Online." This chapter shows you a variety of tasks you might want to accomplish with your team, ranging from sharing files to translating documents to broadcasting presentations and more. Depending on the nature of your work, you might need some features more than others—and this chapter will help you think through the tasks for creating just the kind of group experience you hope your team will have.

Starting with the End in Mind

Before you begin setting things up online to give your team the tools they need to get busy, it's a good idea to think through the goals for your team and envision the process—and benchmarks—you can follow to help the team reach those goals successfully. Envisioning the overall direction—even if you will be inviting the team's input on that—is a good way to set the foundation for the team's work. Here are some questions to get you started:

- What is the long-term goal of your team?

- When do you want to accomplish the goal?

- Will you have specific roles for various members of your team (designer, writer, editor, project manager, and so on)?

- Will you work collaboratively on specific pieces (for example, will an editor and a designer need to have access to the same document at the same time)?

- Will you have team meetings at regular intervals (weekly, biweekly, or some other regular schedule)?

Thinking through the ways in which your team will assign tasks, report on progress, communicate one-to-one and to the entire team, and find and work with important files will help the team work together more smoothly in Office 365. The rest of this chapter offers specific techniques you can use to prepare your team space to be a hive of productive activity.

BECOMING A TEAM

Throw a group of people together and give them a common goal and what do you have? A team.

How well that team works together, however, might have a lot to do with where the team is in its natural life cycle. In the 1960s, psychologist Bruce Tuckman came up with a phrase to describe the way teams come together. He described four stages—forming, storming, norming, and performing—as the process by which the team gets organized and begins to work together productively. Here's a quick look at the four stages of the process:

- **Forming**   In this first stage team members are just getting to know one another. They might be a little anxious, or very polite, wondering what will be expected of them and how the other team members will behave. The leader's role is important in this stage because it's the most clearly defined role and helps the rest of the group feel less anxious about what's to come.

- **Storming**   In this stage, people are starting to get to know each other and personalities start emerging. The leader might feel a little challenged as people jockey for position and assert what they do best. Storming can bring out personality clashes and struggles over authority. People might push back on deadlines, "forget" to do important tasks, or rebel against the group in others ways. Things might just not be a whole lot of fun as many skirmishes and struggles rise to the surface.

- **Norming**   As a result of the tumultuous nature of the storming stage, norming brings a sense of organizing for the team. The group begins to establish norms that enable members to know how and when things are submitted, who is in charge, what the reporting will look like, who to go to with problems, and so on. In the norming stage, team members are also getting to know each other better and might turn to each other for help with tasks or questions. As a result, the team begins to feel more like a team and starts to build trust and cooperation.

- **Performing**   This stage is the productive phase of the team. With the earlier stages out of the way and with the benefit of the organizing that went on in the norming stage, performing enables the team members to do what they need to do to meet the group goals.

Tuckman later added a fifth stage, called "adjourning," in which the group finishes its work, celebrates its successes, and disbands. Note that not all teams go through this process exactly this way—some skip steps, and some seem to get stuck in a particular stage and never get out of it. It's an interesting paradigm to keep in mind as you watch your own team come together, though, and it can be reassuring if you find your team in the tumultuous storming stage.

Creating a Shared Space

One of the challenges of working in the cloud is that, well, you're working in the *cloud*. It's a bit more difficult to look at someone across a desk and talk about something face to face (although you can use Lync Online and your webcam for some real facetime). Your weekly staff meetings in which each person gives an update of his or her part of the project are harder to pull off. People might be in or out of their office—how do you know?

Although working in the cloud poses particular contact challenges, it also offers many great benefits. The first advantage, of course, is that you can create a shared workspace where your team can access the files they need to complete their work. They can also use familiar programs, thanks to Office 365, and log in and complete their tasks whenever it's convenient.

Some additional benefits Office 365 offers help bridge the gap between your "real world" needs and your productivity goals. You can find out when others are online—there's the possibility for that "face-to-face" meeting—by using the presence technology available through Lync Online. And you can create a shared workspace—the familiar board room table—by designing a SharePoint Online site where you can post events, comments, files, and more.

Displaying the Team Site

SharePoint Online is the place where you'll find everything you need to create your shared site. To find SharePoint Online in Office 365, follow these steps:

1. Log in to Office 365 with your user name and password.

2. Click on the Team Site tab at the top of the window. The SharePoint Online team site appears, ready for you to modify things to suit your needs. (See Figure 4-1.)

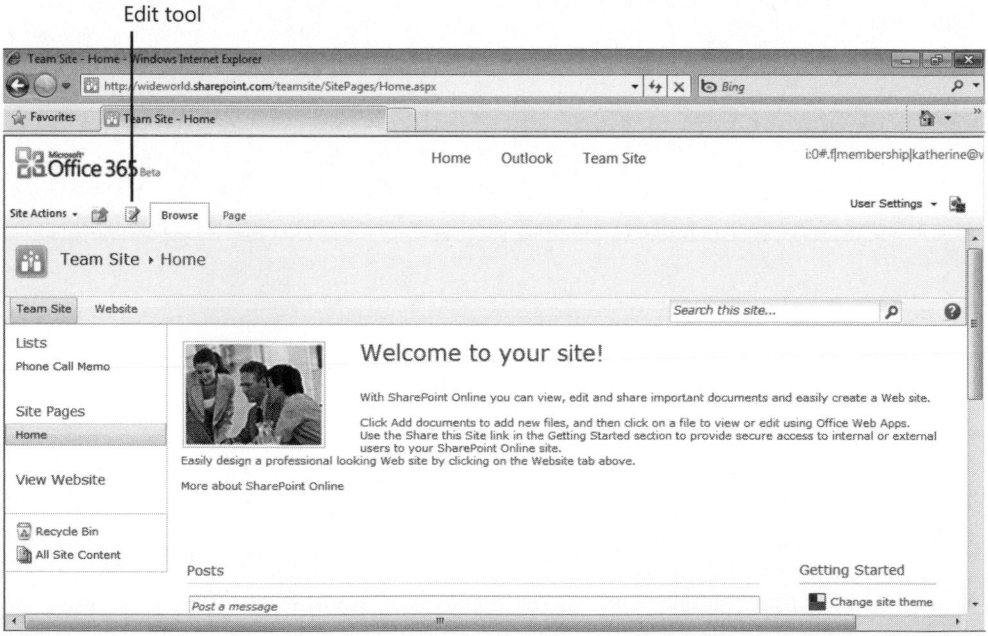

FIGURE 4-1 You can customize the SharePoint team site to include the type of content you want to share with your team.

Click the Edit tool (located just to the left of the Browse tab) to display editing mode. The ribbon at the top of the page changes to include a set of editing tools you can use to add pages, change the page layout, and add site elements, such as tables, pictures, video clips, document libraries, a calendar, and other web parts.

See Also You'll learn more about customizing your team site by adding web parts and other elements in Chapter 5.

PLANNING THE WORK OF YOUR TEAM

Knowing in advance what you want your team to accomplish will have some bearing on the types of elements you add to your team site. I'll cover this in more detail in Chapter 5, when you actually create the team site, but thinking through what you want to accomplish will plan the overall work of your team.

Here are a couple of ideas along this line:

- If your team is coming together to do a specific project—for example, the launch of a new exhibit—you might need to plan to include the following things in the site: shared calendars with regular team meetings; a document library for storing marketing materials and designs; announcements so that team members can see when new items are posted or updated; a way to view overall deadlines and your progress toward the goal; and online meetings with presentations and chat, to make sure everyone is headed in the same direction.

- If your team is working remotely over the long haul—perhaps you are a small business with offices on a couple of continents—your needs for your team site might be a little different. You still would benefit from a shared calendar and regular meetings, but you might also create document libraries for each member of the team, a public site you all work on, announcements and tasks, and other web parts that help you socialize as well as complete business-critical tasks independently and as a team.

Whether your team is working together for a short time or for an indefinite period, be sure to include the basics—calendar, document library, and announcements—as you start out. You can always add to the features of the site as you go along, when you notice what's missing that might make your teamwork a little smoother.

Working with Document Libraries

One great use of your team site is to share documents you all need as you work on your shared project. You can create multiple document libraries in SharePoint Online and store Word documents, pictures, media clips, and more—whatever your team needs access to.

You'll find what you need for creating a document library when you click the Edit tool in the Team Site and click the Insert tab in the Editing Tools tab. Click Document Library to display the tools for creating and working with libraries. (See Figure 4-2.)

FIGURE 4-2 Click the Insert tab in the Editing Tools, and choose Document Library and New Document Library to create a new place to store shared files.

Choose New Document Library to create the new space for your shared team files. Type a name for the new library, and click OK; Office 365 then inserts the new library on the current page. You can then click the Add Document link and upload the files you need to the new document library. (See Figure 4-3.)

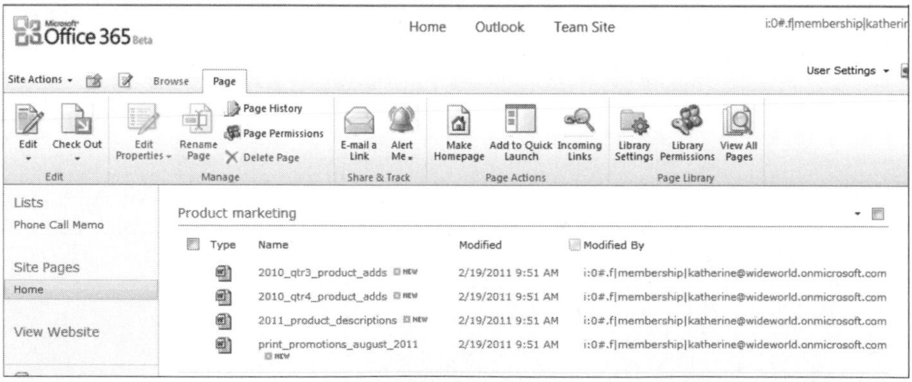

FIGURE 4-3 After you upload files to the document library, other team members can access and share the files.

Tip	Because the new document library is placed on the current page, you might want to create a new page before adding a document library. You'll learn how to do this in detail in Chapter 5, but the quick steps are to scroll down on the Home page and click Create New Page on the right side of the page.

Creating a Space for Announcements

Another thing you might want to do right off the bat with your team site involves creating a space where your team can share upcoming announcements related to your shared work. You might post news about upcoming meetings, post the results of surveys, or share ideas you want to discuss with the team. Like everything else in SharePoint Online, your announcement lists are completely customizable and you can add multiple lists to share different types of information—whatever best fits your team. (See Figure 4-4.)

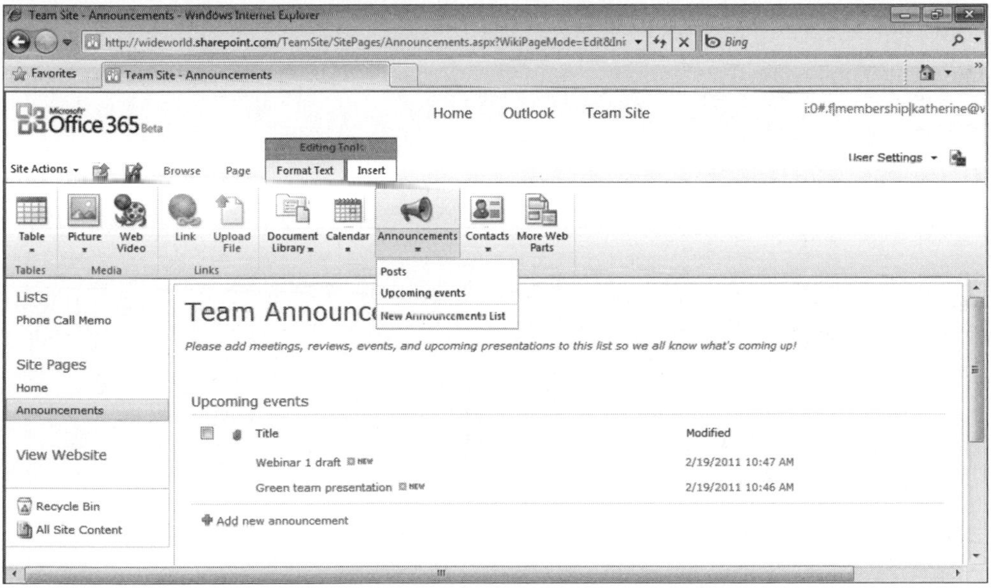

FIGURE 4-4 Create team announcements to let everybody on the team know what's next on your task list.

WHAT ELSE CAN YOU DO IN SHAREPOINT?

This section has given you a few ideas for the types of things you might want to do first with your SharePoint team site, but you can add all kinds of elements and customize the look and feel of the site to your heart's content. You can even create a public website (not simply a team site) where you share your creations with the world. Some other tasks you might want to do in SharePoint include these:

- Add files.

- Change page permissions.

- Change the site layout.

- Set alerts so that you know when content is updated or added.

- Rename the site.

- Add a site description.

- Customize the HTML for the site.

- Add pictures and tables.

- Create a new contacts list.

- Check files in and out.

- Add a calendar.

- Add special web parts to increase the functionality of the site.

- Edit the site in SharePoint Designer.

Sharing Calendars Securely

One of the challenges to working with a group of people you rarely see is that it can be tough to get everybody in the same place at the same time. For that reason, being able to share calendars so that your colleagues can see at a glance whether you're available for a team meeting is an important way to stay in touch.

With Office 365, you can easily manage your calendar and share it with other members on your team. (See Figure 4-5.) The appointments and meeting announcements you save and send are secure in your cloud environment while still being easily accessible to those with the permissions to share your information. You can also change your permissions at any time, so if you have team members who come and go, you can easily add others to your share list.

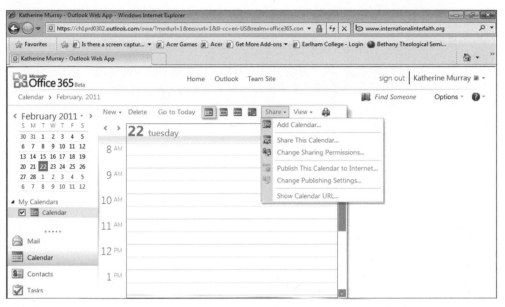

FIGURE 4-5 You can easily share your calendar in a secure environment using Office 365.

SCHEDULING FOR TEAM SUCCESS

So how often do you need to schedule team meetings, group meetings, project meetings, and post-meeting meetings? One of the nice things about working in the cloud is that you can avoid being meeting-ed to death, which is sometimes hard to avoid in the face-to-face business culture.

The number of times you meet—and the topics you meet about—will depend in part on the type of team you're creating, what your focus is, and who your leaders are. Truly collaborative teams might enjoy getting together for some creative time and status updates once a week or so. Teams that have a top-down management style might be more regimented, with mandatory team meetings once a week at a specific time. Of course some teams—especially high-performing sales teams—meet each morning to go over the plan for the day. So it's your call—and your need—that should determine how often you meet with your team.

Whatever timeframe you choose, try to be consistent with your meetings, at least while your group is going through the forming and storming stages. Once you get to norming, the meetings will sort themselves out, but having some kind of structure to hold to—such as, "We'll have a team meeting every Wednesday at 9:00 a.m. EST"—can help the group begin to get organized.

Tip

✓

When you're setting up meetings for the first time, remember that different team members might be in different time zones. If team members have set the time in Office 365 to accurately reflect their local time, the Office 365 Calendar should take the time difference into account when you set up the appointment. But if the team member hasn't set the local time, you might need to be extra careful when you set up those meetings to ensure that everyone logs in at the right time.

Translating Content on the Fly

When you work with colleagues who might be located anywhere on the planet, you might encounter language issues now and again. It's one of the realities of the global marketplace—translation tools are a feature you really do need in your cloud computing toolkit. Translation tools are actually part of Office 2010—in Word, PowerPoint, and Excel—and you'll be able to use them in Office 365 with teammates near and far. Using the translation features, you can easily translate words and phrases as you work on documents or converse with colleagues anywhere in the world.

For example, when you open a Word document in Office 365, click Edit in Word. The file opens in the familiar Word 2010 interface. You can then turn on the Mini Translator tool by clicking the Review tab and clicking Translate in the Language group. Click Choose Translation Language, click the Translation To arrow, and choose the language you want to use from the list. Click OK, and click Translate once again; this time click Mini Translator to turn the feature on. (See Figure 4-6.) Now you can highlight a word or phrase while you work and the Mini Translator tool will show you the translation in real time (and even pronounce it for you if you click Play). Nice!

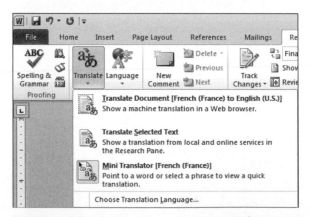

FIGURE 4-6 Select the language you want to translate to, and click the Mini Translator to turn on the translation feature.

MAKING SURE LANGUAGE ISN'T A BARRIER

If your team spans continents and cultures, it's a good idea to address language challenges right off the bat. If you're creating material for public use, you might want to strive for a standard that is easy to translate into different languages, which means you need to avoid local phrases that won't be easily translated later.

You can also have a conversation with your team about preferred languages and how you can all best understand each other, in email, online, and on the phone. You might choose one common language that most of your team members can use fluently, or default to English if that's a commonly known language.

If your team members use words or phrases you don't understand, ask them what they mean—this is much better than guessing or implying that you understand when you really don't. You might miss something important that way!

The Mini Translator tool offers translations for nearly 30 different languages, and additional languages are being added all the time. So use the Mini Translator regularly to convert words and phrases you don't recognize into content you can use.

Making Instant Contact with Team Members

Contact has been getting easier for most of us who work with technology over the last, oh, say 10 years. We used to write and deliver memos, make phone calls, and schedule meetings. Today we send email messages or—if that's too slow—we can send instant messages to others who are available online at the same time we are.

Instant messaging is nothing new, of course. Windows Live Messenger and other instant messaging programs have been around for years. The thing that's new is the ability to communicate seamlessly with team members from within your work environment. Early on, instant messaging was a bit of a challenge to secure, and large corporations most often just disallowed the use of instant messaging while they figured out the security piece. Now in Office 365, you can use Lync Online to easily and securely chat with colleagues in real time without worrying about who might be intercepting the messages you send. It's safe and secure and done within the Office 365 environment.

ONE-TO-ONE AND TEAM-BASED COMMUNICATIONS

When your group is just forming, you might be concerned that too much one-to-one conversation through instant messaging and email might leave the rest of the group out. Will the team become a *team* if people pair up and leave everyone else out?

Luckily, you can invite more than one person to instant messaging conversations, and you can also keep a log of your conversation so that you can share it with the full team later if you choose.

You can help the entire team connect and communicate by scheduling online team meetings regularly during the forming and storming stages. Beyond that, don't worry too much about one-to-one communications unless you're concerned that team members aren't getting their tasks done (and that can be an item on the next team meeting agenda).

Holding Online Meetings

Especially if your team is scattered all over the globe, being able to assemble everyone in one place at a given time is really important. With Office 365, you can use the Calendar tool to schedule your team meetings and Lync Online to easily meet online and make sure everyone is on the same page.

When you click Meet Now by clicking the Options button in the top right corner of the Lync window, Lync displays the Group Conversation dialog box and asks you to choose the type of audio you want to use for the meeting. By default, Lync uses its own integrated audio and video. (See Figure 4-7.) You can also ask participants to call you at a number you specify if you have a particular conference calling number you prefer to use.

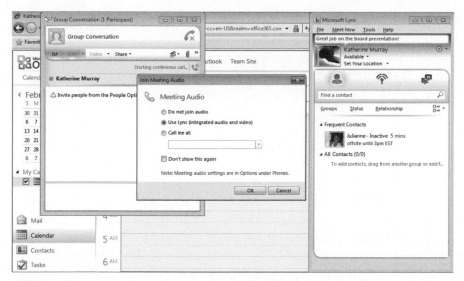

FIGURE 4-7 You can use Microsoft Lync to meet online with your team—either at your set meeting time or on the fly.

CALL IT A GROUP

Team meetings can help your team members feel like they're in sync—or they could be boring ho-hum meetings that members resent taking the time to attend. For best results, keep your meetings short and sweet—and keep them positive and focused.

Members will enjoy participating in something they feel good about or something that helps them solve problems they are experiencing. So you might want to set up your team meetings to follow a general process like this:

- Welcome to the group

- Team successes from last week

- Team focus for this week

- Individual reports

- Something funny (or a tip or positive customer experience)

- Goodbye for now

This whole process might take only 15 minutes, but if you follow it regularly, you'll get the work of the team done, celebrate some successes (which builds momentum), and help people feel like it was a good use of their time. Not bad for a little time in the cloud.

Broadcasting Presentations Online

The online broadcasting capabilities of PowerPoint 2010 is another big change that was part of Office 2010. But now, as an Office 365 user, you have the benefit of broadcasting presentations live to your team and your clients—no matter where in the world they happen to be. You can simply prepare your presentation with PowerPoint Web App (available in Office 365) and then prepare it for presenting online. This involves creating a web link you send in an email to others so that they can view the presentation live in their web browser. One of the present limitations of this feature is that any audio or video you've added to the presentation won't be visible over the web; but you can set up a conference call in addition to the presentation and talk your team members through it slide by slide.

Tip ✓	Even people outside your team or those not using Office 365 or PowerPoint 2010 will be able to view the presentation if you send them the web link, so this is a good way to share product or service information with clients and customers even if they aren't using Office 365.

WHAT MAKES A GREAT ONLINE BROADCAST?

The most important thing to keep in mind about an online broadcast you're preparing is that you want your message—and your goal—to be as clear as possible. Here are a few ways you might use the broadcasting feature with your team:

- You want to show everyone how to use the team site.

- You are sharing design options for your new product packaging.

- You want to share a presentation you plan to give at an upcoming company meeting.

- You want to invite team input on a presentation about your work.

- You are learning and sharing research about a specific topic that affects your work together.

A good online broadcast takes into account that the audience members have other things to do—and might be doing them while you think they're watching your presentation! So make sure that the presentation is engaging—presenting information very clearly and pausing at key points for audience questions or interaction.

Be sure to use an audio component—whether it's a traditional conference call or a call you set up through Lync Online—so that your team members can share their own ideas and ask questions as needed.

You can also prepare and share handouts and other collateral materials by posting them in your team document library in SharePoint Online or by emailing them to the team before the broadcast begins.

Creating and Modifying a Website

Not only does SharePoint Online enable you to create a team site where you can create document libraries, share announcements, set up meetings, and more, but it gives you the means to create a public-facing website that shares your information with the world. Having the team site—which is invisible to the public—and the public site together in one tool is a real time-saver and can help you focus clearly on the different tasks and communications you need to both manage your team and present your wares to the world.

You'll find the link for viewing your public website in the Website area at the bottom of the Home page. To edit the public website, however (not simply view it), you need to click Admin at the top of the Office 365 page and scroll down to the Website area. Click the Edit Website link to begin working with the content on your pages. By default, your website includes five pages: Home, About Us, Contact Us, Site Map, and Member Login. You can then customize the content on the page, add new pages, change the site theme or layout, or edit the website as you see fit. (See Figure 4-8.)

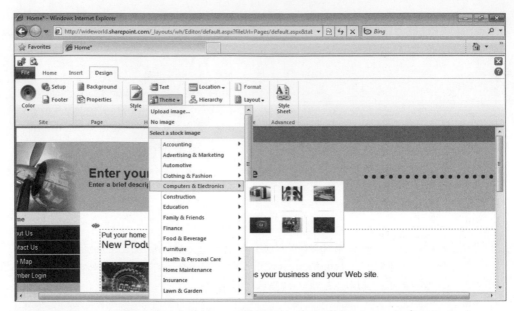

FIGURE 4-8 You can easily apply new themes and layouts to the website you create for your team.

TIP ✓ If you've worked with Office Live Small Business, you'll notice that the web tools are the same ones you used in that program. You can easily edit, format, and add web components to your pages using the simple web tools provided now in SharePoint Online.

See Also You'll learn all about customizing the content in the SharePoint Online website in Chapter 5.

▮ What's Next

This chapter focused on some of the tasks you can start with as you begin to pull your team together. The next chapter goes into greater detail about customizing your team site in SharePoint Online. You'll learn how to tailor the content just the way you want it for your team and create a site you'll share with the world as well.

CHAPTER 5

Creating Your Team Site with SharePoint Online

SHAREPOINT ONLINE is likely to be the heart of your cloud operation, helping you stay in touch with the team, share documents, post announcements and updates, and manage the various tasks that will be part and parcel of your projects. You do, after all, need a *space* where your team can come together in some fashion and share what you're working on.

The basic SharePoint Online site provided for you in Office 365 is just the beginning—you can customize the site to include all sorts of tools and web parts that suit the type of information you need to manage and the results you want to create. You can also use SharePoint Online to create a forward-facing website that enables you to share your work with the world.

The point is to create a site that looks and feels like a home base for you and your team—a virtual office space where you can find the files you need, chat with your colleagues over coffee, get updates on important tasks easily, and feel you're in sync with the group. The last chapter introduced you to some of the tasks you might want to accomplish in your team site; this chapter shows you how to add text and images and rearrange the furniture so that it fits just the way you and your team like to work.

Planning Your Team Site

If you've ever been on any kind of team, one fact you know to be true is that no two teams are created equal. Each team has its own personality—some are friendly, some are focused, some are all business. Teams have different goals—such as preparing for a big event, writing the curriculum for a new training project, or producing an annual report. Teams also have different kinds of leadership, ranging from a kind of rotating, team-based leadership to a top-down style with a "my way or the highway" type of person at the head.

The type of site you create in SharePoint should reflect the work style that fits your team best. If you like to keep everybody in the loop about upcoming deadlines and recently completed tasks, make sure you display announcements and updates in a prominent place. If you just want to get down to business and provide a common space for files you all use, you can add a document library right there on the home page of your team site.

Creating a Simple Team Site—Fast

You can spend a lot of time—in fact, there are whole books written about—designing a SharePoint site to reflect just the types of information you want it to offer. But designing your site can be as simple as throwing some words and pictures on a page, if that's what you choose. If you just want a shared space to post information—and your team will be together only for a short time—that amount of effort might be just right for what you need. If this is what you're looking for, and you are an Admin user, you can create an Express Site in SharePoint Online.

The fastest way to create a functional SharePoint site is to use the Express Site options. This enables you, for example, to quickly create and share information about the project your team is working on. This site is based on a ready-made template that includes a document library, where you can store your files, and an announcements list.

To create an Express Site, follow these steps:

1. In Office 365, click Team Site at the top of the screen.

2. In the team site, click the Site Actions arrow in the top left of the ribbon.

3. Choose More Options.

4. In the Create window, click Site and scroll to and click Express Team Site. (See Figure 5-1.)

5. Enter a title and the URL where you want the site to appear.

6. Click Create. The new site is added beneath the existing top-level team site of your site collection, and you can begin to add your own content and customize it to meet your team's needs.

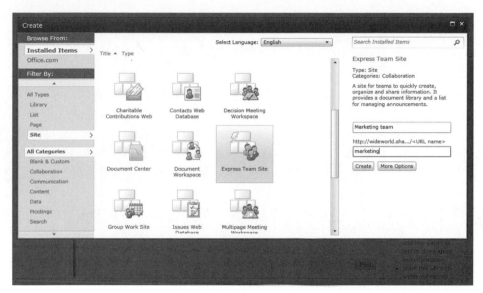

FIGURE 5-1 Click Express Team Site to create a new team site quickly.

Putting Some Thought into the Team Site Design

If you're envisioning a team that will work together for a while, one that really needs to communicate well, have access to the latest versions of files, and be able to see at a glance what the various members of the team are working on, putting some thought into the design of the site will help you create a cloud experience your team members will be likely to appreciate and use. You might want to get together team members (on the phone or using Microsoft Lync) to discuss the following questions:

- What are your team goals?

- How long will your team be together?

- Will you focus on one project or multiple projects?

- Will you have regular team meetings?

These types of function questions will help you determine what types of web parts and tools you'd like to add to your team site. If your team will be together over the long haul, creating multiple projects, you might want to envision a site with multiple pages that can each contain the files and updates related to one specific item you're working on.

> **Tip** ✓ When it's time to think about the site you want the public to see, asking similar kinds of questions about function can help you plan the content you want to include. For example, what do you want your clients or customers to be able to do on your site? Will they download a report? Sign up for your latest catalog? Submit an idea? Your answer to those questions will help you think through the types of elements you want to build into your site design. You learn more about how to design the site clients and customers will see in Chapter 12, "Designing Your Public Website."

Thinking through the overall look and function of your site also gives you the chance to throw a few design touches into the mix. You can easily choose—and change—site themes that coordinate the color scheme used throughout the site. You might want to choose a look that corresponds with your company logo, for example, or select a color and layout style that best reflects the type of content you'll be creating.

As you can see in Figure 5-2, SharePoint's Editing Tools Insert tab offers you the tools you need to add all sorts of elements to your team pages. You can insert the following elements by using the ready-made tools already placed on the ribbon for you:

- Tables
- Pictures
- Links
- Files
- Document libraries
- A calendar
- Announcements

FIGURE 5-2 SharePoint's Editing Tools Insert tab offers a number of tools you can add to the pages in your team site.

Tip ✓	And if you want to add special functionality to your pages, you can click the Insert tab in the Editing Tools tab and click More Web Parts. You can add specialized tools to your page that enable you to gather information from your team, track the location of various team members, get info about the latest updates, post media, and much more. Check out the section, "Adding Web Parts" later in this chapter for the specifics on these great site tools.

Choosing a Site Theme

One of the first choices you're likely to make as you develop your team site will have to do with how you want the site to look. SharePoint Online makes it easy for you to apply a coordinated color scheme—which carries through all tools you add to the site—that creates a kind of distinctive look and feel for your team space.

We know a lot more about color choices than we used to, especially when it comes to creating a work environment with the right feel. Cool colors—like light blue or green—create a kind of relaxing atmosphere; you might use these colors when you're working on a high-stress project and want to help everybody maintain their equilibrium and not stress out. For low-energy teams that need to be cranked up a notch, use vivid colors like reds and oranges to stimulate attention and get some of those creative juices flowing.

By default, the Office 365 color choice is set to Default (no theme), which gives you a very basic, clean-cut look for your team site. To change the default theme to one with a bit more color definition, follow these steps:

1. Display the site by logging in to Office 365 and clicking Team Site.

2. Click Site Actions.

3. Choose Site Settings.

4. In the Look And Feel area, click Site Theme.

5. In the panel on the right in the Select A Theme window (shown in Figure 5-3), click the names of different themes to see the color combination on the preview grid on the left side of the screen. The fonts selected for headings and body text also change to show your selection.

6. When you have selected the theme you like, click the Apply button at the bottom of the list.

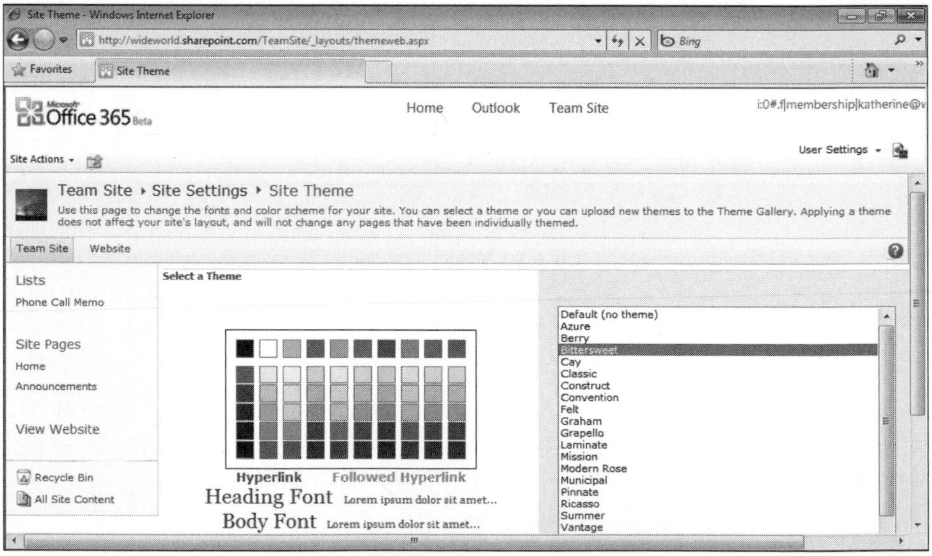

FIGURE 5-3 Choose from a variety of color palettes that control the color of hyperlinks, headings, and body text on your site.

> **Tip**   ✓   If you create an additional team site and you want to change the theme for that site (but not the top-level site), click the tab for the new team site before you click Site Actions.

Office 365 processes your changes and displays the team site with the new theme selection in place.

You can change your site theme as often as you like until you settle on a style you want to keep. You might want to choose a theme that corresponds to your company logo, your product packaging design, or some other set of colors that have some relevance to what you're trying to do. Or, as an exercise designed to help your team feel more involved in the process, you could ask the team to vote on the color selections they like best.

For best results, and a cohesive team, however, get your theme choices established early and keep the same look and feel for the duration of your project. Too much changing right off the bat can make your team feel scattered, like the workspace has no real definition. A solid choice at the beginning and consistency throughout the project helps establish stability and a sense of identity for the team.

> **Note**   Only those with Admin privileges will be able to make the theme changes, however, so you might have to choose different themes over a series of days and have team members vote for the themes they like best.

Changing the Text Layout of Your Page

The way your page is laid out is another important choice that contributes to the overall look of your team site. The layout also affects the way tools appear in the columns on the page, which of course affects how easily (or not) your team can find what they need. There's no single overarching text layout feature that affects all the pages you create; instead, you need to choose the layout for each page independently.

If you've been browsing the Web for any length of time, you have no doubt seen all kinds of layout styles, and some work better than others, depending on what publishers want to accomplish with their sites. Some are packed with information three or four columns wide; others are more open and might have a huge graphic front and center on the page, with a little text underneath. Many sites that are designed around sharing bits of information use some kind of columnar format to do that—you might have a navigation column on the left, a center column with primary articles, and an "extra" column on the right. That, of course, is just one example—notice as you browse other sites what you like and what you don't. And bring that knowledge back to your SharePoint Online experience when you're creating the user interface for your team.

To choose the layout you want to apply to the current page, follow these steps:

1. Select the team site page you want to edit, and click Edit to the left of the Browse tab.

2. In the Editing Tools Format Text tab, click Text Layout in the Layout group.

3. Click the option in the Text Layout list you want to apply. (See Figure 5-4.)

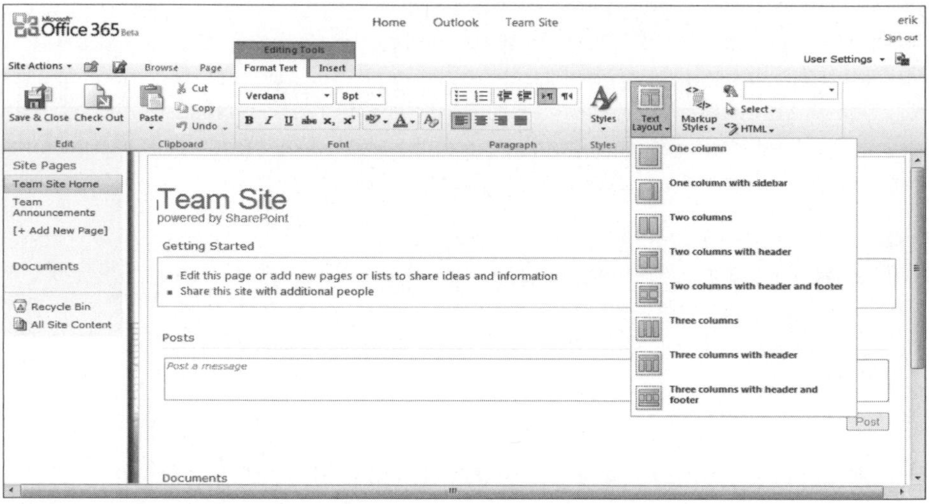

FIGURE 5-4 In Editing mode, click Text Layout in the Editing Tools Format Text tab to change the layout of the current page.

The layout is applied to the page, and your existing content is rearranged to fit the new layout. You can change the layout you've selected at any time by choosing Text Layout again and selecting a different option. You can also hide, remove, or modify individual text boxes that have content in them by clicking the arrow in the upper right corner of the text box and choosing Minimize, Delete, or Edit Web Part. (See Figure 5-5.)

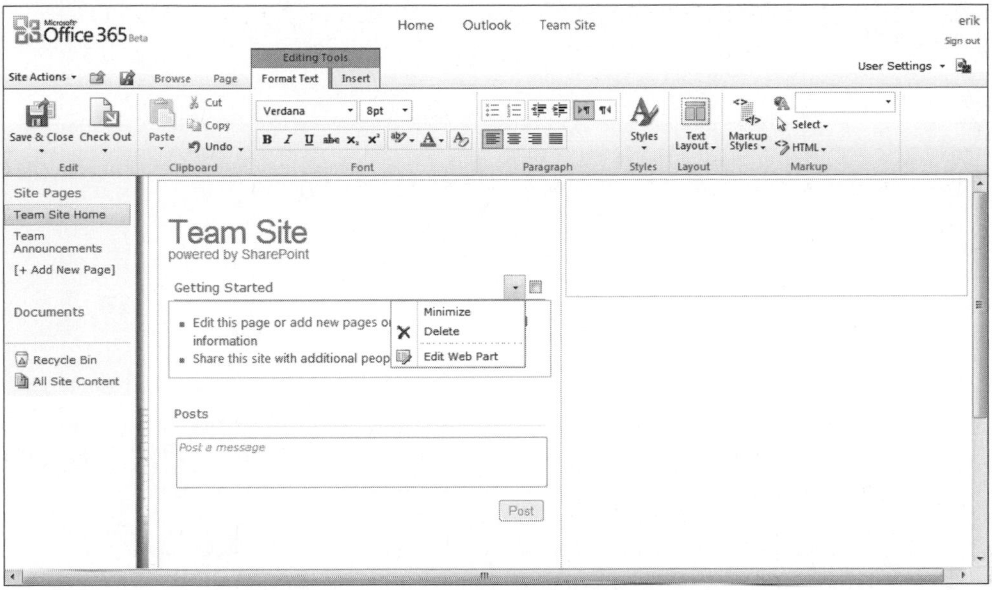

FIGURE 5-5 You can hide, remove, or change a text object by clicking the down arrow in the upper right corner of the text box.

You can go ahead and add introductory content to your page by clicking in the text box and adding a heading and opening paragraph. Use the Formatting tools in the Font group to apply the format you want to the text.

Posting an Update

One thing you might want to do—and something you can do at any time (whether you've chosen your theme and layout yet or not)—is post a note to let your team members know what's going on. By default, your team site Home page includes a Posts area, just beneath the Introduction area at the top of the screen.

To add a new note, click in the notes area and, in the List Tools List tab that appears, click New Item in the New group at the far left end of the ribbon. Click New Item, as shown in Figure 5-6.

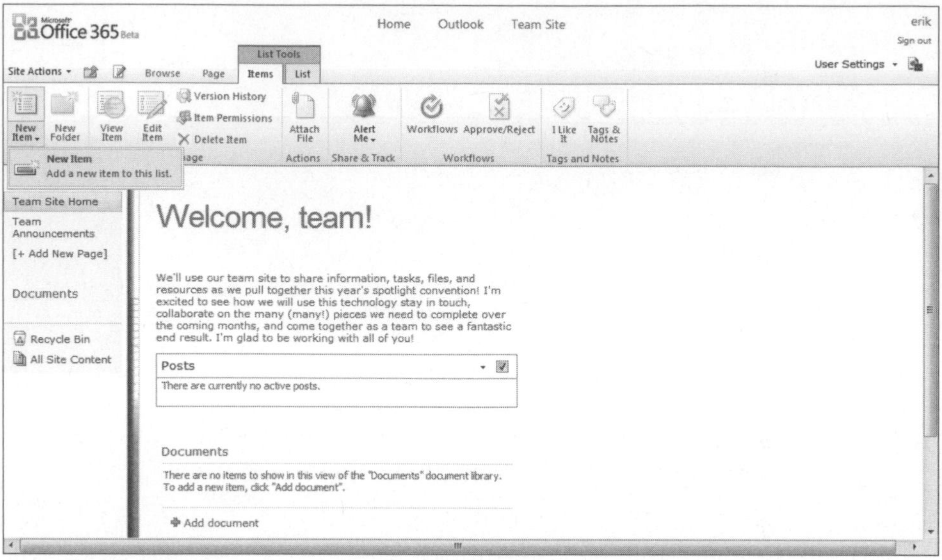

FIGURE 5-6 Click the Posts area, and click New Item to add a post to the page.

In the Posts - New Item dialog box that appears (shown in Figure 5-7), type a title and the body content for your post. If you want the post to automatically expire, click the calendar symbol to the right of the Expires box and choose the date on which you want the note to expire. Click Save to add your post to the page. The information appears on the page below the post box so that your entire team can see it when they log in.

FIGURE 5-7 Enter a title and body for your note, and click Save.

Tip

✓

This is a small idea, but it can add up to a big benefit—the posts you add, and add consistently, can really set the overall tone for your team site. If your notes are always reminding people about upcoming deadlines, folks might dread your notes after a while. But if you mix up your notes with reminders, news, and celebrations, remembering to give team members props when they accomplished a goal or finished a task, people will enjoy logging in and seeing the latest posts—especially if they are being recognized for something!

Note

If you want to edit the post you've just added, you can do so easily. Click the post, and the List Tools List tab appears on the ribbon. Click Edit Item in the Manage group. The Post appears in the View tab. Click Edit Item once again, make your changes, and click Save.

Adding and Formatting Pictures

And, of course, even if you're working on a ho-hum project with lots of ho-hum data and not-very-exciting personalities, you can always spruce up your space by sharing images—of products, people, buildings, flowers, or other fun or interesting images related to your team or project. Adding pictures to a page gives the page energy and life, even if the pictures aren't the most exciting in the world. Statistics show that people read and retain information better when they have images on the page to help rest their eyes (and reinforce the content). So think through ways to include some visuals on your page—even if they are just product pictures or the company logo.

So whether you have a functional reason to include photos—such as showing the latest product images you'll use in your catalog, or adding corporate head shots so that people can see each other in the site—or you simply want to decorate a little bit, the actual process for adding pictures is simple:

1. Display the page of the team site you want to change, and click to position the cursor where you want to add the picture.

2. Click Edit to the left of the Browse tab.

3. Click the region on the displayed page where you want to insert the picture.

4. Click the Editing Tools Insert tab.

5. Click Picture. (See Figure 5-8.)

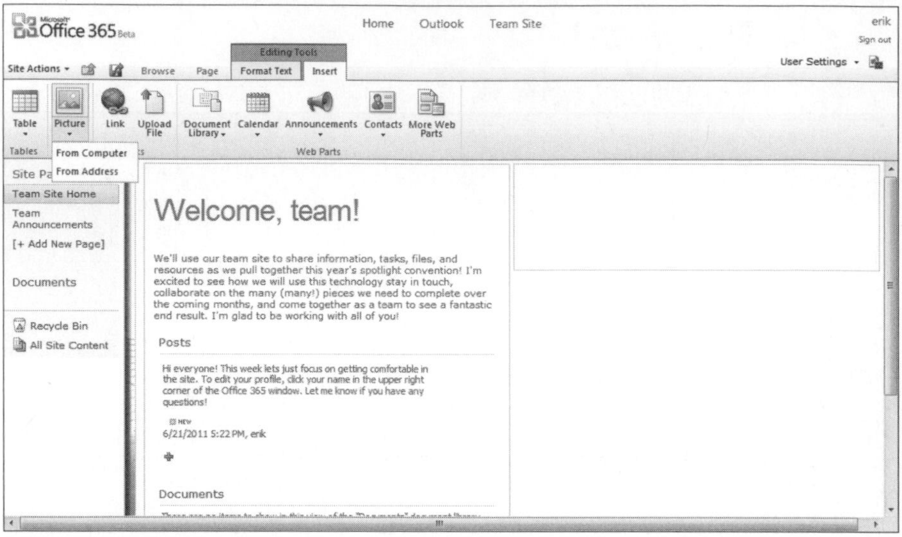

FIGURE 5-8 Click the Editing Tools Insert tab, and choose Picture to begin the process of adding art to the site.

6. Choose From Computer if you want to place an image that you have saved on your hard drive. Choose From Address if you want to use a picture from another website.

7. In the Select Picture dialog box (shown in Figure 5-9), click Browse and navigate to the folder containing the file you want to use. Click the file, and click Open.

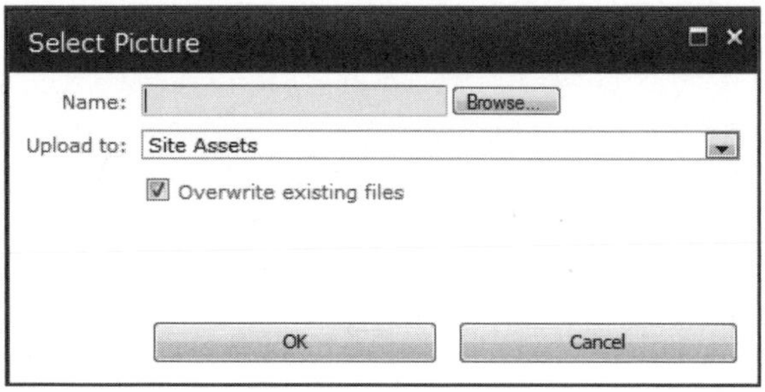

FIGURE 5-9 Click Browse, and navigate to the folder on your computer where the picture you want to use is stored.

8. Choose the folder you want the picture to be uploaded into, and click OK.

9. In the Site Assets dialog box, type a title for the image (which also serves as alternate text for readers who can't see the visual), and click Save. (See Figure 5-10.)

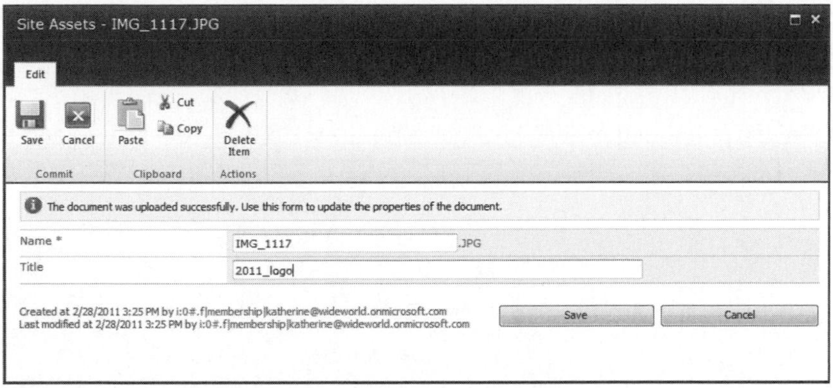

FIGURE 5-10 Enter a title for the picture in the Site Assets dialog box.

The picture is added to your page, and the editing tools appear so that you can fine-tune the way the image looks on your page.

> **Note** The Site Assets folder is probably fine for storing your pictures unless you want to create a specific folder related to your current project. If you have already created another folder and want to save the uploaded image to that folder, click the Upload To arrow and choose the folder you want. Then click OK.

Editing Your Picture

If you've done any website work in the past, you probably remember how much of a pain it was to get images in the site that look just the way you want them to. And if you really wanted to change a few picture basics—like maybe add a border, change the size of the image, or realign it on the region of the page where you placed the picture—you needed to remember the commands so that you could manipulate the picture by hand.

Well, not any more. With Office 365, once you place the picture on the page, the Picture Tools Design tab displays the tools you need to make those sorts of changes easily. With just a few clicks and keystrokes, you're done. Here are the simple steps:

1. Click the image you just added to the page. The Picture Tools Design tab appears. (See Figure 5-11.)

2. To change the way the image aligns with the text on the page, click Position and choose the option you want from the displayed list.

3. To add or remove a border, click Image Styles and click your choice.

4. To resize a picture, click in the Horizontal Size or Vertical Size box and type the new measurement for the image (in pixels). If you want to preserve the aspect ratio of the picture, leave the Lock Aspect Ratio check box selected.

5. When you're finished making changes, simply click outside the picture and the tools disappear.

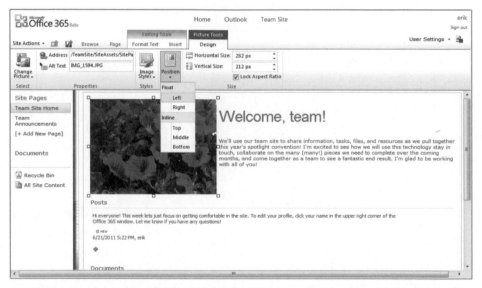

FIGURE 5-11 Use the tools on the Picture Tools Design tab to enter the alternate text, change the position, or resize the image.

Tip ✓ The Change Picture tool on the Picture Tools Design tab is a real timesaver once you've got an image on the page in the size and position you like. You can just swap out a picture by clicking Change Picture, navigating to the folder where the image is stored, selecting it, and clicking Open. The new picture is placed in the same position as the previous one, and the same settings are applied to the new image. Nice!

Adding a New Page

When you first begin working with your team site, of course, SharePoint Online has started the process for you by giving you both a team site and a public-facing website that you can use to share information with your clients and prospective customers. But part of thinking through the overall plan for your team site means envisioning what other pages you want to include. Depending on the type of team you're creating—and the type of work you all need to do together—your site will need different types of pages.

So what kind of pages will you want to add? In a later section, you'll learn about web parts, but you might want to create different page for different functions. For example, one page might contain your marketing strategy, a document library of marketing files you use, some marketing images, and a post area where those on your team who are focusing on marketing can update the others about their project tasks. Another page might be a general team page, in which you use social media type updates, announcements, and more to help the team stay in sync. Another page might have a log of deliverables—which pieces need to be reviewed when.

To add a page to your team site, follow these steps:

1. Click the [+ Add New Page] link in the navigation bar on the left side of the screen. (See Figure 5-12.)

2. In the New Page dialog box, type a name for the new page and click Create.

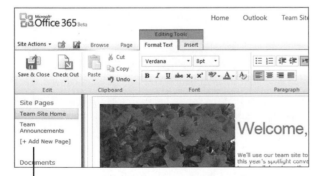

Click to add a new page.

FIGURE 5-12 Click [+ Add New Page] in the navigation panel on the left to add a new page to your team site.

Office 365 then creates the page with the new name you entered and displays the blank page, ready for you to add your content.

■ Entering and Editing Content

Adding content to your page really is as easy as clicking and typing. You can, of course, format the text to your heart's content—similar to the techniques you use every day in Microsoft Word—and you can copy and paste information into Office 365 as you would any other application.

When you first add a new page, Office 365 displays the blank page and positions the cursor in the top area of the screen, ready for you to type your first bit of text. You can simply click the tool you want in the Editing Tools Format Text tab to change the format of your text.

When you open an existing page, you need to click the Edit tool, to the left of the Browse tab, to display the page in editing mode. The Editing Tools tab appears so that you can make the changes you want to make to the page. You might want to

- Change the font size, style, or color.
- Format the text and set paragraph alignment.
- Choose specific text styles for the content.
- Apply markup styles to the text you add.
- Identify the language you used for the content you've added.

The following sections touch on some of these editing tasks. Many of you already know how to do these tasks from your work with other word processing programs.

Formatting Your Text

The basic steps involved in typing and formatting the text, headings, captions, and other content on your page is super simple. When you click in a text box on a page in your team site, the Editing Tools tab appears, showing the Format Text tab by default.

To format text you've already typed, simply select the text and then choose a new setting in the Font group in the Format Text tab. You can change the font, size, and style (bold, italic, underline, strikethrough, subscript, and superscript), apply highlighting of various colors, change the color of the text, or clear all formatting current applied to the text.

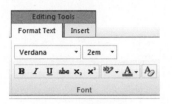

Adding Text Styles

SharePoint Online includes a number of text styles you can apply to the text on your pages. Click Styles in the Layout group to display a menu of style options. You'll find the styles shown in Figure 5-13. To apply one of the styles to existing text, simply highlight the text and choose the style. You can also apply a style before you begin typing by clicking to position the cursor and then choosing the style.

FIGURE 5-13 You can apply a text style to your text before or after you type.

Applying Markup Styles

Because you're working on the web with Office 365, having a tool that enables you to apply markup styles directly to your text is a good thing. This helps you style your team site pages the way you would prepare your website pages using HTML markup styles.

If you've done any work with markup languages in the past, you might recognize the styles shown here:

Again, you can apply the markup styles to the text *after* you add it or before you type it. Either way, the styles will be embedded in the HTML for the site and will be recognized and displayed properly no matter which browsers your teammates might be using.

Coding for Language

On the far right side of the Markup group of the Editing Tools Format Text tab, you'll find the Languages tool. You can use this tool to add a markup tag to your content that tells the browser which language is being used. For example, if you have a word or phrase in Italian for your teammates in Italy (shown in Figure 5-14), you can select that phrase, click the Languages arrow, and choose Italian from the list. This tells the browser the language being used so that it is represented properly in team members' browsers if the web browser supports this.

FIGURE 5-14 Apply language markup when you have words or phrases in other languages on your page.

<table>
<tr><td>Tip
✓</td><td>If you need help in the translation department, you can display a file in an Office 2010 Web App and then open it in Word, Excel, PowerPoint, or OneNote on your computer to get access to the new Mini-Translation tool, which enables you to translate words and phrases on the fly. What's more, you can translate the text and then copy it from the application and paste it right onto your SharePoint Online page. Pretty slick.</td></tr>
</table>

Adding Web Parts

Web parts are exciting interactive tools you can use on your team site to add all sorts of functionality to the pages. The Editing Tools Insert tab contains the Web Parts group with ready-made Web parts you can insert directly on your page. These web parts can do the following:

- Add a document library to your page.
- Insert a new or existing calendar on the team page.
- Create or add an announcements list.
- Add a list of contacts to the page.

The More Web Parts tool includes a number of specialized elements you can use to expand the functionality of your site. Depending on what you want to do with your site, you can add Web parts that do the following things:

- Deliver content that is relevant to individual users.

- Add a site assets list.

- Show the whereabouts of your team members.

- Post upcoming events.

- Add a phone call memo tool.

- Add an image viewer or a slideshow web part.

- Insert a web part that delivers Microsoft Silverlight content.

- Add a user task list.

- Create a list of team members in the site.

To add a web part to a page in your team site, begin by displaying the page on which you want to add the part. Then follow these steps:

1. Click in the region of the team page where you want to add the web part.

2. Click the Editing Tools Insert tab.

3. Click the web part—for example, Document Library—you want to add to your page. (See Figure 5-15.)

4. If you have more than one document library already created, a list appears so that you can choose the one you want to add. You can also choose New Document Library if you want to create a new one.

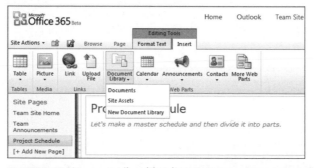

FIGURE 5-15 You can easily add web parts to your team page using the Web Parts tools in the Editing Tools Insert tab.

Sharing Your Site

Even though your SharePoint Online team site is meant to be a secure environment for you and your team to work in, you can invite other team members to join you once you get the site going. To share a team site with someone else, follow these steps:

1. Select your team site from your Office 365 home page.

2. Click Site Actions on the far left side of the ribbon.

3. Choose Share Site.

4. In the Share Your SharePoint Site window (shown in Figure 5-16), enter the email addresses of the team members you want to add to the site. You can click Check Names, to the right of the text fields, to ensure that you are choosing participants in your company address book.

5. Alternately, you can click the Users In This Group arrow and select the group you want to use to find the visitors or members you want to invite.

6. Modify the Subject line if you like, and type a message in the bottom text field.

7. Click Share to send the invitation to your contacts.

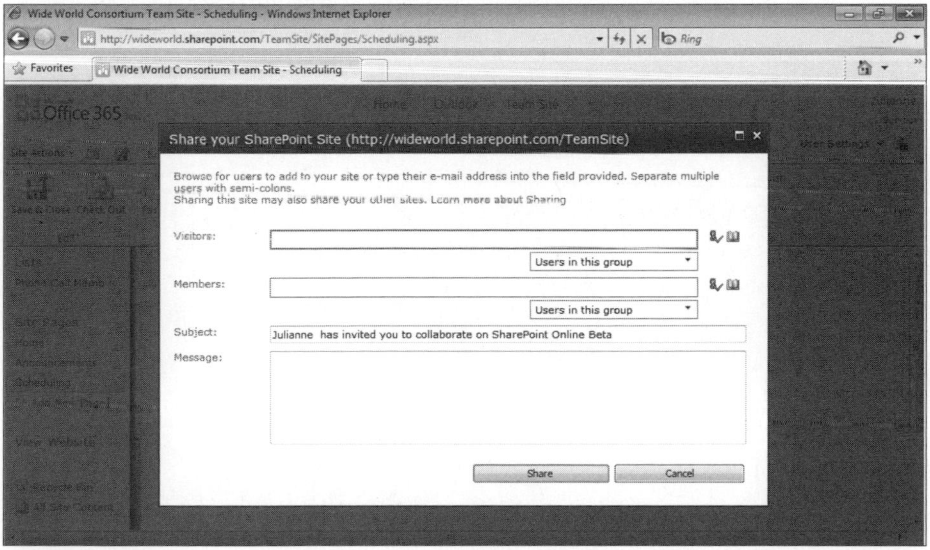

FIGURE 5-16 You can invite others to join you in the team site by choosing Share Site from the Site Actions list.

When the people you invited receive the e-mail invitation, they will be able to click the link in the message and log in to the site.

What's Next

This chapter gave you a close look at a number of the tasks you'll want to accomplish soon after creating your team site. Whether you want to keep it simple or create an elaborate design, you can enhance the form and function of the site by choosing a theme, customizing the format, adding pages and content, inserting and editing pictures, adding web parts, and more. In the next chapter, you learn how to add files to your SharePoint team site, share them with others, and check them in and out for your use.

CHAPTER 6

Posting, Sharing, and Managing Files

HAVING AN ONLINE PLACE to gather is important, especially if you hope your team will gel into a productive group with members who enjoy each other's company and work well together. But you can create groups in all kinds of places—blogs, social media sites, and even in your favorite instant messaging tools. Why do you need a tool as sophisticated as SharePoint Online to give your group that extra something it needs to succeed?

The file management capabilities of SharePoint Online enable you to create document libraries, share documents and pictures, check files in and out, and work with files in a way that will help your team be as productive as possible. This chapter shows you how to set up, manage, and work with team files in SharePoint Online.

What Is a Document Library (and Where Is It)?

When you first begin using your SharePoint team site, you'll find a basic page already created for you—but that's it. If you want to add a document library—a place to store, organize, and manage the files you'll share with your team—you'll need to add it yourself. This section shows you how to think through, create, and add files to document libraries in your site.

PLANNING YOUR LIBRARIES

What kinds of files will your team share? This depends on the types of projects you're creating. If you're preparing a marketing report, for example, you'll probably work with files like these:

- A set of notes about the project

- Minutes from meetings about the project's design

- The schedule for delivery

- Images of products that will be included

- A document with the text for the report

- A worksheet showing the budget for the project

- Reviewers' comments or review forms

And this might just be the tip of the iceberg. Your project might be much more complicated, or you could have several projects going on at once—in which case, you might want to create different document libraries on different pages to contain the files related to the various projects.

One of the beautiful things about document libraries is that they enable you to cut down on the number of versions you have available for an individual file. Suppose that you write a draft of the text for the report and then post it to the site. Another team member can edit it; someone else can do a content review; the designer can apply the template and theme you want to use; a manager can do a line-by-line review—*all using the same file*. This means you won't have six different versions of the file that someone will need to merge into the most recent copy. Using the file check-in and check-out feature in SharePoint, team members can each make their changes to the file in the file library so that all changes are incorporated in one file and you don't run the risk of using the wrong file when it's time to finalize the project.

Creating a Document Library

In the previous chapter, you walked through the process of adding a document library when you added a web part in SharePoint Online. You can create a document library on any page you'd like, anywhere in your site. The trick is to begin on the page where you want to add the library. Then follow these steps:

1. Click the link in the navigation panel on the left that will display the page you want to use.

> **Tip** ✓ Alternately, you can create a new page for the library by clicking [+ Add New Page] and entering a name for the new page. Click Create to add the page.

2. Click Edit to the left of the Browse tab.

3. Click the Editing Tools Insert tab.

4. Click Document Library in the Web Parts group, and choose New Document Library.

5. In the Create List dialog box, type a name for the document library and click OK. (See Figure 6-1.)

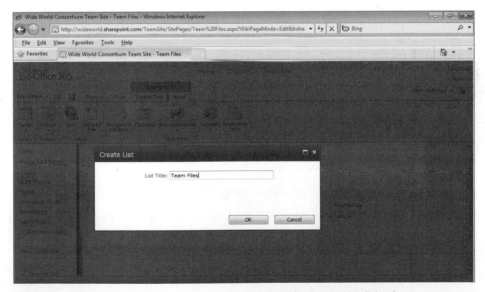

FIGURE 6-1 Create a new document library, and name it in the Create List dialog box.

You can name the document library just about anything you want and include spaces, punctuation characters, and even items that are no-nos in other names, such as percentage symbols and exclamation points. The name of the document library will also appear in the Document Library list in the Web Parts group so that you always have the option of adding the library to another page if you like.

Adding Documents

Now to make the library functional, you need to add some files. You can do this by uploading files one at a time, or you can upload multiple files at once. When you're first creating the document library, you might want to add all the files you've saved using the multiple upload feature, and then as you expand the files later, add them one at a time. This section describes both processes.

Posting Single Documents

Here are the steps for uploading a single document:

1. Begin by clicking the Add Document link beneath the document library. (See Figure 6-2.)

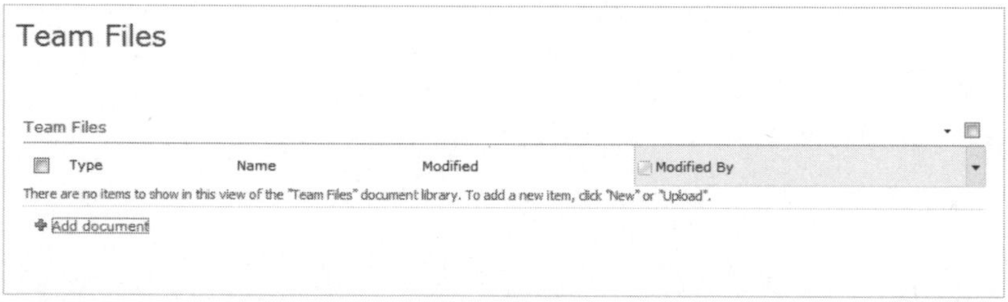

Team Files

Type	Name	Modified	Modified By

There are no items to show in this view of the "Team Files" document library. To add a new item, click "New" or "Upload".

✚ Add document

FIGURE 6-2 Click Add Document to begin adding documents to your library.

2. In the Team Files – Upload Document dialog box (shown in Figure 6-3), click the Browse button.

3. Navigate to the folder containing the file you'd like to add. Click it and click Open.

4. Click OK to close the Upload Document dialog box.

   The file is added to the list, and the type, name, date the file was last modified, and name of the person who modified the file are displayed in the document library.

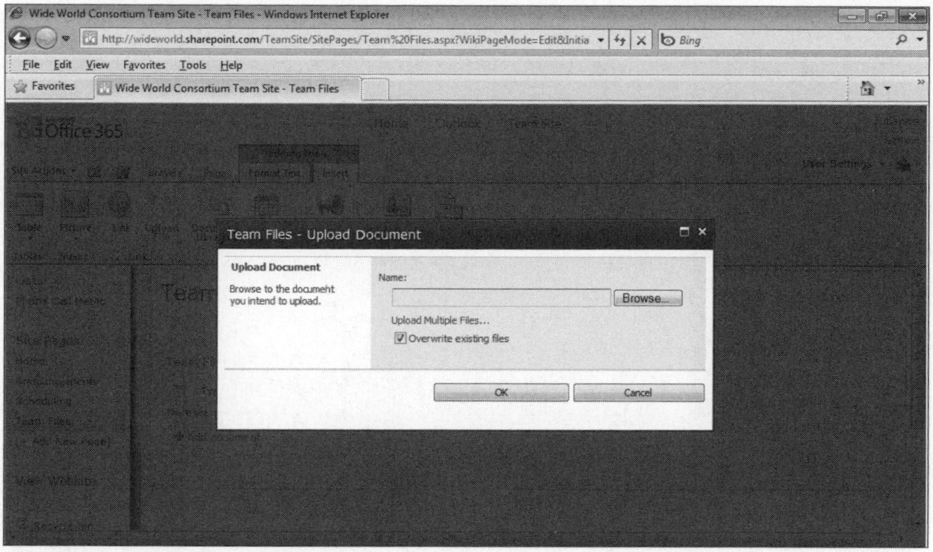

FIGURE 6-3 You click Browse in this dialog box to upload a single file.

Adding Multiple Documents

If you have a number of files you want to post to your document library, you'll find it easier to upload them all at once. Here is how to do that:

1. Begin by clicking the Add Document link.

2. In the Team Files – Upload Document dialog box, click Upload Multiple Files. The Team Files – Upload Multiple Documents dialog box appears. (See Figure 6-4.)

3. Using the folder tree on the left, you can drag the files you want to upload to the blue area in the top of the dialog box or click the Browse For Files Instead link to display the Open dialog box.

4. If you choose to browse for files, navigate to the folder containing the files you want to add and select them.

5. Click Open to add the files.

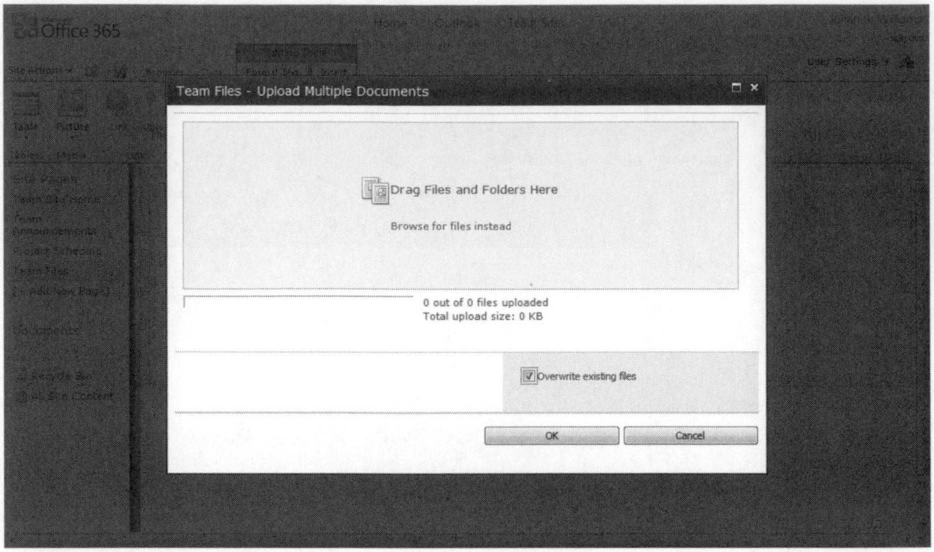

FIGURE 6-4 The dialog box that appears when you click Upload Multiple Files in the Team Files – Upload Document dialog box.

Tip ✓	By default, the Overwrite Existing Files check box is selected so that any files you upload will overwrite files with the same name that are already in your document library. You'll find that it's a good practice to keep this check box selected so that versions of specific files are kept to a minimum in your site and reduce the risk of someone on your team working with an outdated version of the file. You'll have to communicate this policy in advance to the team, though, so that all members understand that new versions of files will overwrite older versions with the same name.

Organizing Document Libraries

Keeping your documents named and organized effectively will go a long way toward helping your team find what they need when they need it. You can help this process along by choosing specific naming conventions for the various files you post. You might ask everyone to name files with their initials and the date in the file name, or assign specific codes for different departments to use so that they'll be able to recognize their own files easily.

In addition to ordering files by the naming conventions you choose, you can also arrange files based on the information in the document library table. What's more, you can customize the columns in the document library to include information that you feel is most relevant to your project.

Ordering Files in Your Document Library

By default, the document library shows four columns: Type, Name, Modified, and Modified By. You can sort the files by hovering the mouse cursor over the column you want to sort by; when the down arrow appears, click the arrow to display a list of sorting options.

For example, if you want to sort the Name column so that the files appear alphabetically from A to Z, hover the cursor over the left side of the Name column header. Click Ascending (as shown in Figure 6-5), and the files are alphabetized in the document library.

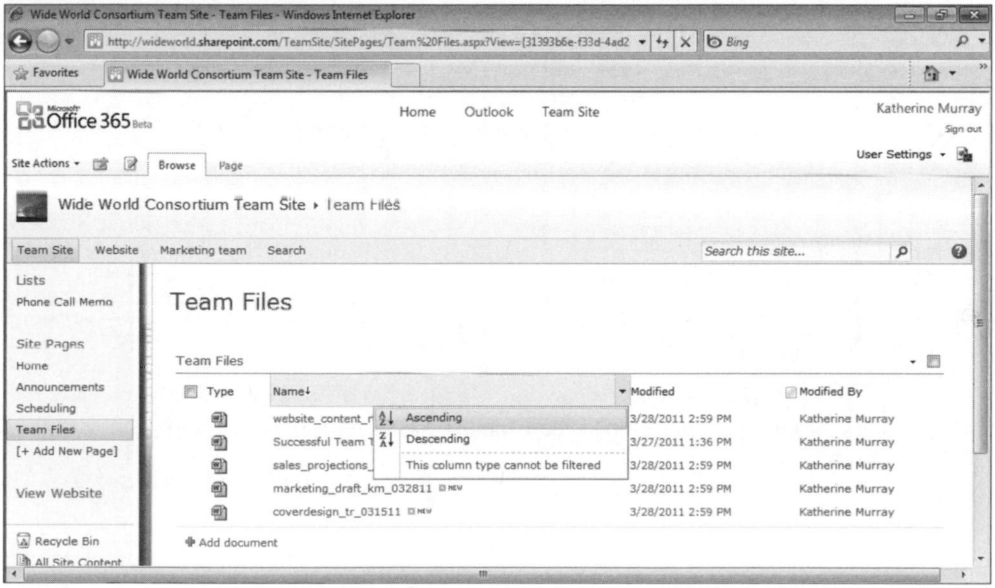

FIGURE 6-5 You can sort the files in the document library so that they are easy for your team members to find.

Modifying the Current View

You can easily create your own kind of document library with the columns that best fit the information you need to know for your specific project. For example, you might want to add a column that shows who a file is checked out to and list the departments that are responsible for the various files.

Begin the process of modifying the current view of the document library by clicking the top row of the document library table. The Library Tools Library tab becomes available. Click Modify View and a list of options—which include Modify View and Modify In SharePoint Designer (Advanced)—appears. Click Modify View. (See Figure 6-6.)

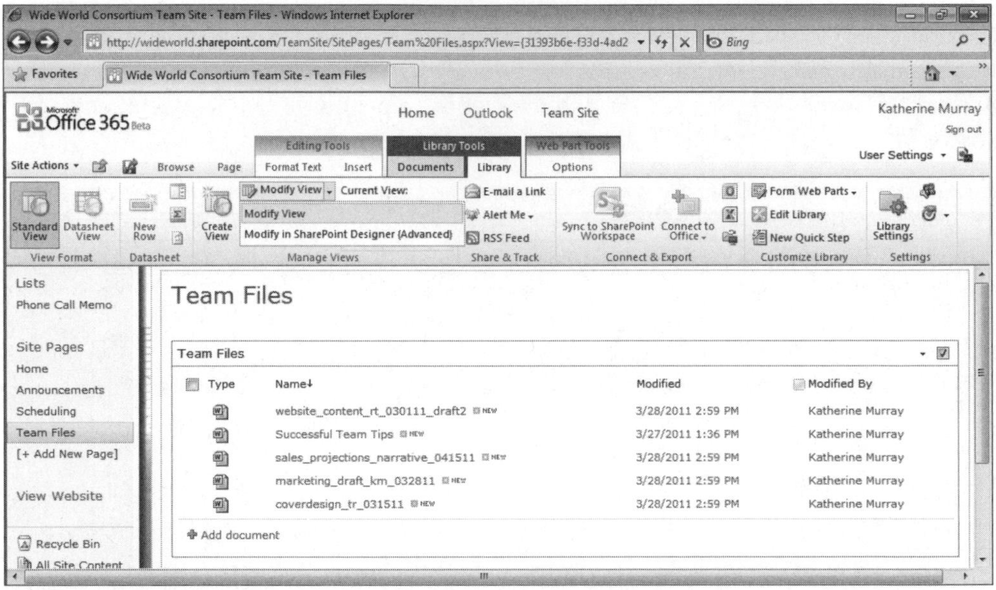

FIGURE 6-6 Click the document library, and choose Modify View in the Library Tools Library tab to modify the library.

You can change many things about the way your files appear in your document library. Clicking Modify View displays a screen that offers you a number of settings you can tailor to change the way the library appears. As you see in Figure 6-7, the choices on this screen enable you to do the following:

- Choose the columns you want to appear in the document library.

- Increase or decrease the number of columns displayed.

- Choose the columns by which the information will be sorted.

- Filter the items shown in the document library according to criteria you specify.

- Add a button that enables team members to edit the document library.

- Display check boxes next to individual items so that members can select multiple files.

- Group similar files.

- Add totals for items in the document library columns.

- Apply a style to the document library.

- Choose whether or not files are displayed in folders.

- Set a limit for the number of items that can be displayed in the document library list.

- Set the way you want the document library to appear when viewed on a mobile device.

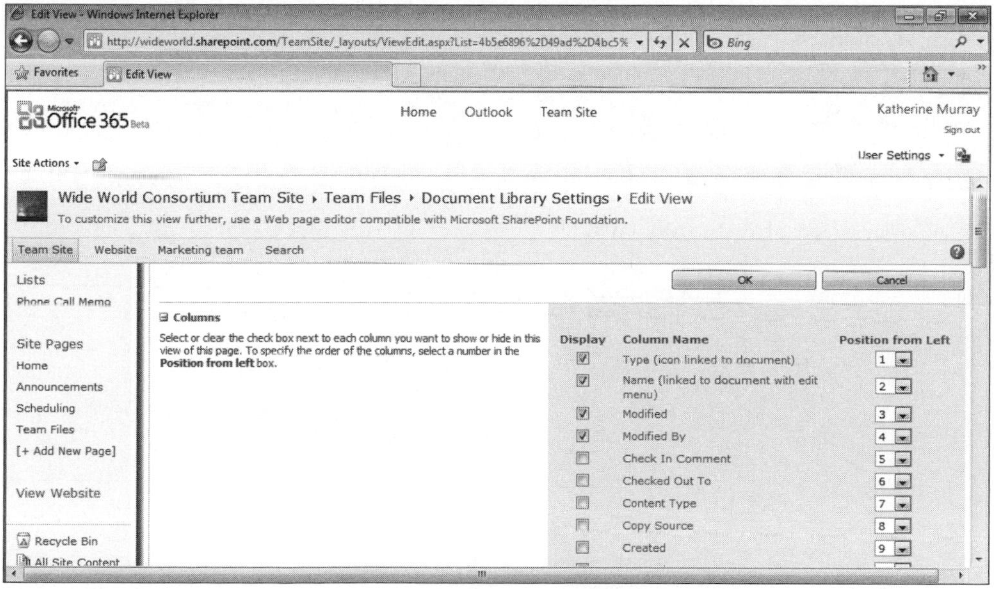

FIGURE 6-7 You can modify the current view of your document library and change the columns, style, number of items allowed, and more.

You can change the columns in the document library by displaying some and hiding others and by rearranging the order of the columns as they appear in the table. First select the check boxes in the Display column of the items you want to appear. Then, in the Position From Left column, click the arrow and choose the number that indicates the position in the table you want the column to have.

The Sort selection is another setting you can use to ensure that the files appear in the order that makes the most sense for your project. You can choose a primary sort and a secondary sort—this means the files will be sorted by the primary sort first and then by the secondary sort. For example, if you choose Checked Out To as the primary sort, your document library will list all documents by the person they are checked out to. If you select Title as the secondary sort, the documents will be listed alphabetically by title within the Checked Out To grouping.

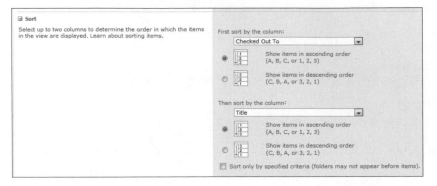

Filters enable you to choose which items will appear in the document library list. For example, you might filter the files so that only files posted in the last month appear in the list. Or you could show only files that have been posted by certain members of your team.

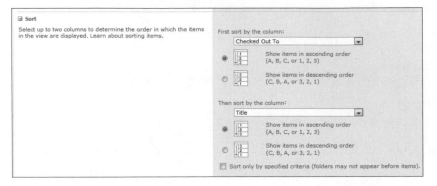

Another item you might want to experiment with as you're setting up your document library is the Style feature. SharePoint Online starts out displaying the library in default view, which is a simple design with no color shading at all. The other styles available in Modify View are Basic Table, Document Details, Newsletter, Newsletter No Lines, Shaded, and Preview Pane. Table 6-1 tells you a little more about the various designs you'll get when choosing the various library styles.

TABLE 6-1 Choosing a Document Library Style

Library Style	Description
Basic Table	The same view as Default view
Document Details	Shows each file in its own box with its file name, date modified, and modified by information
Newsletter	Lists files separated by lines, with an Edit button for each entry
Newsletter, no lines	Lists files without lines separating them, and includes an Edit button
Shaded	Displays shading in every other row of the document library
Preview Pane	Lists the files on the left, and displays the information for each file as you point to it

After you make your modification changes in Modify View, simply click OK to return to your document library and take a look at the changes you've made. If you aren't happy with the changes or want to try something different, simply click the top of the document library again to display the Library Tools tab and return to Modify View to make your additional changes.

DO YOU NEED TO USE SHAREPOINT DESIGNER?

Office 365 is designed to be easy to use and customize without a lot of technical know-how. You don't have to be a programmer to get the best use of all the features available to you. That's a good thing.

But what if you're comfortable designing websites and you'd like to have a little more design control over what goes where on the page? SharePoint Online enables you to open your page and work with the design directly in SharePoint Designer if you choose. You'll find this option in the Modify View list and also as an option in the Site Actions list.

SharePoint Designer is available as a free download from the Microsoft Download Center at *www.microsoft.com/downloads*, so if you try it and decide not to use it after all—no harm done. You might just find, however, that it's easy enough to use that you enjoy tweaking your team pages and having a bit more flexibility than the web-based design tools offer you.

Adding a New Column to the Document Library

Maybe the basic layout of the table is fine and you want to leave much of the information the way it is. But suppose that it's missing a column that shows which department created the file. You can add a new column easily by clicking the document library to display the Library Tools Library tab. Then click Create Column in the Manage Views group.

When the Create Column dialog box appears, as shown in Figure 6-8, type a name for the new column and choose the item that reflects the type of information you'll be storing in that column. For a department name, the default setting—Single Line Of Text—works fine. But you can also add a picture (perhaps a team member's profile picture) using the Hyperlink Or Picture setting, or create a menu of choices using the Choice item.

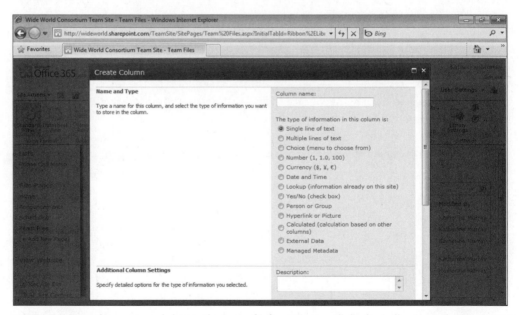

FIGURE 6-8 Enter the name, and choose the type of information you'll display in the new column.

In the Additional Column Settings area, you can type an additional description and choose whether you want to require that the new column contain information. You can also limit the number of characters entered in the column, add the column to the default view, and enter a formula if you want the data in the column to be validated.

Creating a New View for Your Document Library

Although you might not need to get too fancy with the ways you store your files in SharePoint Online, the program includes a large variety of features you can use to customize the information displayed in the table. You can create your own views and create the document library style that best fits your needs.

Note that the view you create for your document library isn't an either/or choice, however—it's both/and. You can have a regular document library view as well as a datasheet and calendar view, all using the same data. For example, Figure 6-9 shows a datasheet view that has been created for the document library you saw earlier in this chapter.

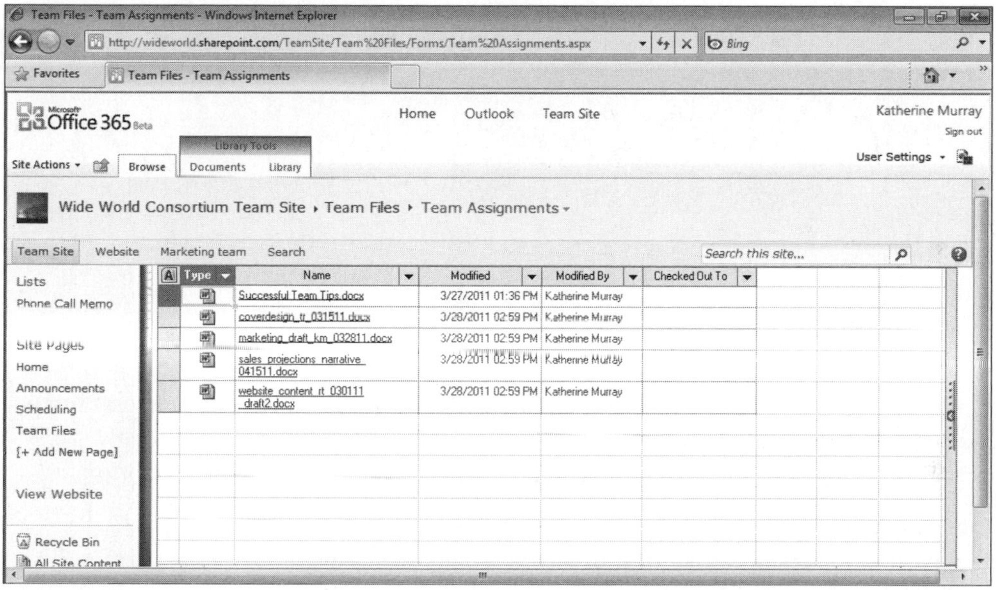

FIGURE 6-9 You can create a new view to show your files in different ways.

To create a new view for your document library, follow these steps:

1. Click the top of the document library to display the Library Tools tab.

2. Click the Library tab.

3. In the Manage Views group, click Create View.

4. In the Choose A View Format area, choose the type of view you want to create (Standard, Calendar, Access, Datasheet, Gantt, or Custom view).

5. Type a name for the new view.

6. Choose whether you'll share this view with the public or view it yourself.

7. Specify other settings related to the view type you selected, and click OK.

Switching Views

After you create new views, you need to be able to switch among their display easily. Here again, you go to the Library Tools Library tab, in the Manage Views group. Click the Current View arrow to display a list of available views, and click the one you want to see. It's that simple.

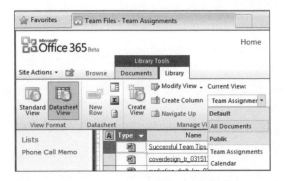

Working with Document Library Files

After you post your files in the document library, you can easily add to them, edit them, check them in and out, download copies of them, and set alerts so that you know whenever a new version of the file is posted to the space.

The Library Tools Documents tab appears when you click one of the files in your document library. The various groups—New, Open & Check Out, Manage, Share & Track, Copies, Workflows, and Tags And Notes—give you different sets of tools to use for editing, managing, saving, updating, and working with versions of the file. (See Figure 6-10.) Having these various tools to choose from helps you and your team members keep your files well organized so that everyone can stay as productive as possible by always working with the latest version of the file.

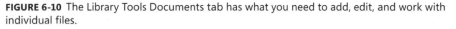

FIGURE 6-10 The Library Tools Documents tab has what you need to add, edit, and work with individual files.

In addition to using the tools in the tab, you can display a list of action choices by hovering the cursor over a file and clicking the arrow that appears on the right side of the Name column. These choices enable you to view or edit the properties of the file, edit the content of the file, check the file out so that you can work on it, create an alert so that you're notified when the file is changed, move the file to another location, manage permissions for the file, or delete the file.

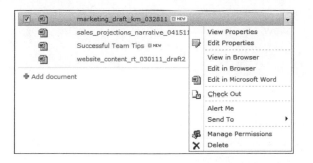

Adding a New Library Folder

Although you can set the number of files listed in the document library, at some point it becomes counterproductive to scroll through a list of 50 files, trying to find just the one you need. Similar to the way you manage files on your home or office computer, you can use folders in SharePoint Online to group files and make it easy to find the file you need.

To add a folder to a document library, follow these steps:

1. Display the page with the document library you want to change.

2. Click the library to display the Library Tools tab.

3. Click the Documents tab.

4. Click New Folder in the New group.

5. In the New Folder dialog box, type a name for the new folder and click Save.

The new folder appears at the top of the file list with the name you specified. You can change the settings for the folder (for example, rename it) or remove it by pointing to the folder name and clicking the arrow that appears on the right side of the Name column.

> **Tip** ✓
>
> You can connect the folders you create in SharePoint Online to Microsoft Outlook so that you can easily synchronize your files whether you're working in your team site or not. Click the folder you want to link, and click the Library Tools Library tab. When you click Connect To Outlook in the Connect & Export group, Outlook asks you to verify that you want to connect this SharePoint Document Library to Outlook. Click Yes, and the login window for Office 365 appears. Enter your user name and password, and Outlook downloads the file from the linked folder. A folder showing your team site name appears in the SharePoint Lists area at the bottom of the Navigation Pane in Outlook.

Starting a New Document

You'll learn more about working with Office 2010 Web Apps in Chapter 8, "Working with Office 2010 Web Apps," but you can easily begin and work with documents directly from the SharePoint document library. This makes it super simple to check on something in a file, talk about changes while you're online with your team, or just dive in and begin creating what you're thinking about while you're thinking about it.

To start a new document in SharePoint Online, click the document library and click New Document in the New group on the far left side of the Library Tools Documents tab. Click New Document, and a new blank document opens in Microsoft Word. A message box appears reminding you that some files may be harmful and asking you to verify that you want to download the file. Click OK and then click Enable Editing to begin working in the new document. These protection features are part of Office 2010 and are designed to safeguard you against potentially harmful files you might download from the Internet. After you enable editing on the document from your team site, however, Office adds the site to your trusted locations and you shouldn't need to click Enable Editing again.

> **Tip**
> ✓
>
> You can also upload an existing document from your computer to the document library by clicking Upload Document in the New group of the Library Tools Document tab. When you click the tool, you have the choice of uploading a single document or multiple documents, using the same Upload Document dialog box you used earlier in this chapter.

Viewing File Properties

File properties are simple to use in SharePoint Online. You can easily view and change the file properties—which include essentially the file name and the title—by selecting the check box of the file on the far left side of the document library and clicking either View Properties or Edit Properties in the Manage group on the Library Tools Documents tab.

In the Properties dialog box that appears when you click Edit Properties, you can rename the file or type a new title. (See Figure 6-11.) Additionally you can delete the file if you'd like by clicking Delete Item.

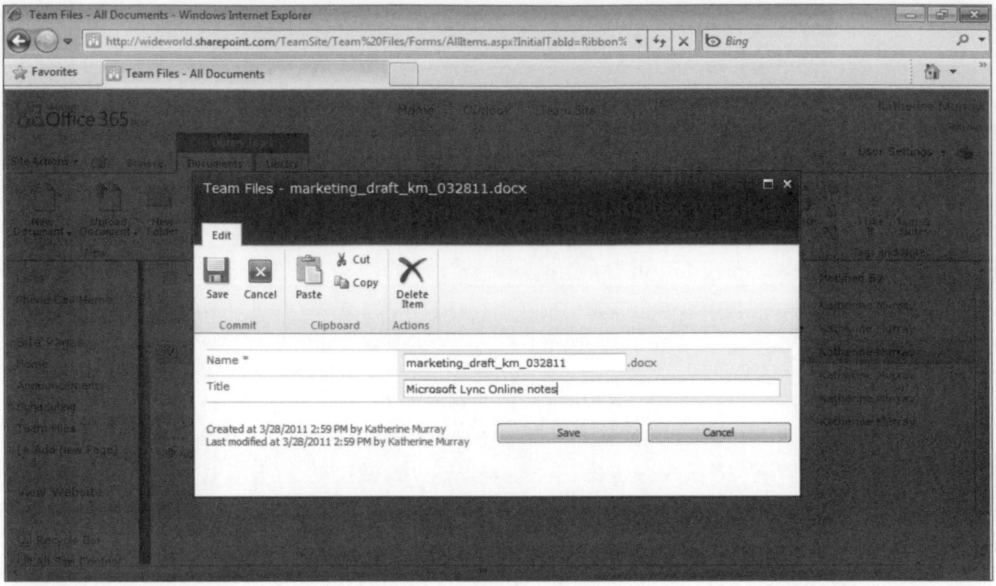

FIGURE 6-11 You can easily view and edit file properties to rename, retitle, or delete the file.

Checking Out and Checking In Files

When you're working as part of a team and sharing a workspace, having a mechanism in place that ensures people are always working with the most recent versions of shared files is very important. SharePoint Online does this by enabling you to check files out, work on them, and then check them in so that other members of your team can continue the work.

When you want to check a file out, follow these steps:

1. Select the check box of the file you want to check out.

2. In the Library Tools Documents tab, click Check Out in the Open & Check Out group.

3. A popup box warns you that you're about to check out the file. Select the Use My Local Drafts Folder check box if you want to store the file in a folder used to synchronize it with your online files.

4. Click OK.

Note	If you select the Use My Local Drafts Folder check box, you might see a message telling you that this feature will not work with Internet Explorer until you add your SharePoint Online site to your Trusted Sites Zone in Internet Explorer. If you get this message, cancel the checkout operation for now, make the change in Internet Explorer, and restart Internet Explorer. Then come back and check out the file as you originally intended.

You can then edit and save the file normally, and when you're ready to check it back in to your team site, click the File tab and choose Info. At the top of the center area of the Info tab in Backstage view, you can see that the file is still part of the online team site. At the top of the center column, the Office application lets you know that the file is currently checked out, and it gives you the option of either discarding the checked-out status (which means your changes won't be made in the file online) or clicking Check In to return the file to the team site. (See Figure 6-12.)

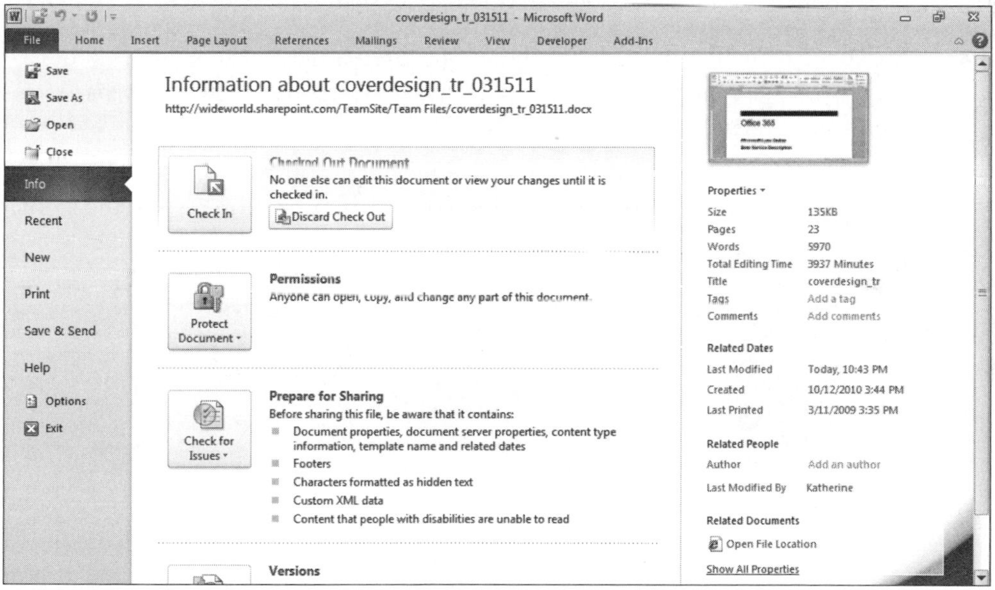

FIGURE 6-12 You can check in the file directly from the Office application you're using.

After you check in the file, other team members can see the changes you've made and work on the file themselves if necessary.

Setting Alerts

Another reality of working collaboratively on a team is that you must know who is uploading what document when. Especially if you're concerned about the deadlines you're facing, knowing that documents are being posted on time helps keep your stress level down and your team moving forward.

You can set alerts in the site so that you receive a message whenever specific files are updated or when changes are made to the team site in general. To set alerts, follow these steps:

1. Display the document library where you want to set alerts.

2. Select the check box of a file if you want to be alerted about a specific document.

3. Click Alert Me in the Share & Track group of the Library Tools Documents tab.

4. Choose Set Alert On This Document.

5. In the New Alert dialog box, enter the names of people you want to receive the alerts, and then choose the delivery method. (You can enter your email address or your mobile phone number if you prefer a text message.)

6. Choose the type of changes you want to be alerted about (all changes, changes made by others, changes made on a document you created, or changes made on a document you last modified).

7. Choose whether you want to get alerts immediately, receive a daily summary, or get a weekly summary. You can also choose the time of day you receive the alerts.

8. Click OK to save the alert.

> **Tip** ✓ You can view and modify alert settings you create by choosing Alert Me in the Share & Track group of the Library Tools Documents tab and selecting Manage My Alerts.

■ What's Next

Organizing, managing, and working with your files successfully is likely to be a major part of your work in SharePoint Online. This chapter showed you how to set up the document libraries in your site so that they include the information you want them to display, are easy to use and manage, and give you easy access to the types of tasks you want to accomplish with your files. The next chapter takes you a step further in SharePoint Online by showing you how to keep your team moving in the right direction by creating and managing workflows.

CHAPTER 7

Adding and Managing Workflows

WHETHER YOU KNOW IT or not, you use workflows all the time. They might not be written down, and others might not follow the same process (which might or might not cause you lots of headaches), but there is some kind of flow to the work you're doing. Whether you're publishing an annual report, getting a mailing out, launching a new Web site, or trying to support a sales force, the tasks you complete in your day fit into a larger work process that can be mapped and organized.

Workflows in the traditional sense are logical structures that help you know who does what when in the work process. When you're working with a team, workflows can help keep a project on track and help you see easily which team member is responsible for tasks at any given time. SharePoint Online in Office 365 makes it easy for you to create and apply workflows to the team projects you create. This chapter shows you how to create and use a workflow to keep your team engaged and working smoothly together.

Introducing Office 365 Workflows

Your SharePoint Online team site offers all kind of features and tools you can use to keep your team on track. Creating workflows for processes you use often—especially if they involve customer interactions or important project tasks or documents—can help you reduce the amount of time you spend worrying about getting things done.

To add a workflow to your team site, you need to first create a library or a list that includes a Choices column (which enables you to set the state of each item in the workflow). The basic idea is captured in the following steps:

1. You create a list of the tasks you need to accomplish to reach completion on a particular goal.

2. You create a workflow for that list that enables you to indicate when a task has been completed and whose involvement is needed next.

3. The workflow can notify that team member automatically by email to let him or her know it is time for his or her task in the project.

4. When all tasks are marked as finished, the workflow is complete.

> **Note**   You might want to use the Issues Tracking list template in SharePoint Online to create a list you can use with a workflow. You can also use the Custom List or a document library to create a customized list that you can use as the basis for the workflow, but for the workflow to work properly, you must include at least one Choice field that enables you to set multiple options. The Choice field is where you set the three different states (Active, Resolved, and Completed) the workflow uses to track the progress of the tasks.

The workflows you create help you easily coordinate the people, tasks, and deadlines on your different projects. By enlisting SharePoint Online to help you track the project's status, you can make sure things stay on schedule and that the right people are involved at the right points.

HOW WILL YOU USE WORKFLOWS?

A workflow does require a little forethought and planning when you set it up, but it can save you time and trouble if you have a number of people all working on different parts of the same process. You could use workflows to

- Follow a call for customer service from the initial contact to the resolution

- Track client inquiries about a new product

- Organize the process you use to create the annual report, from brainstorming to finishing the product

- Ensure that each new employee receives training from various members of your team

Whether you want to track tasks or files in a library, SharePoint Online makes creating and updating the workflow a simple matter of changing the status of tasks as you complete them.

Creating a New Workflow

A workflow is a process you attach to a list of steps you want to accomplish or a series of document tasks you want to complete in a certain sequence. When you want to create a workflow, you begin by creating the list or library you'll use as the basis for the workflow:

1. To create the list or library the workflow will use, click Site Actions, choose View All Site Content, and click Create. Click Library or List, and choose Issue Tracking List. Type a name for the list or library, and click Create.

2. Click on the List Tools List tab, and click the Workflow Settings tool in the Settings group. (See Figure 7-1.)

FIGURE 7-1 After you create an Issue Tracking list, click Workflow Settings in the Settings group of the List Tools List tab.

3. Click Add A Workflow.

4. In the Add A Workflow screen, leave the workflow template (Three-state) selected as shown in Figure 7-2. Type a name for the workflow, such as Tech Support Tracking.

5. In the Task List area, you can choose a task list you want to associate with the workflow or elect to create a new task list. If you don't have any other task lists created in the site, SharePoint Online defaults to creating a new list.

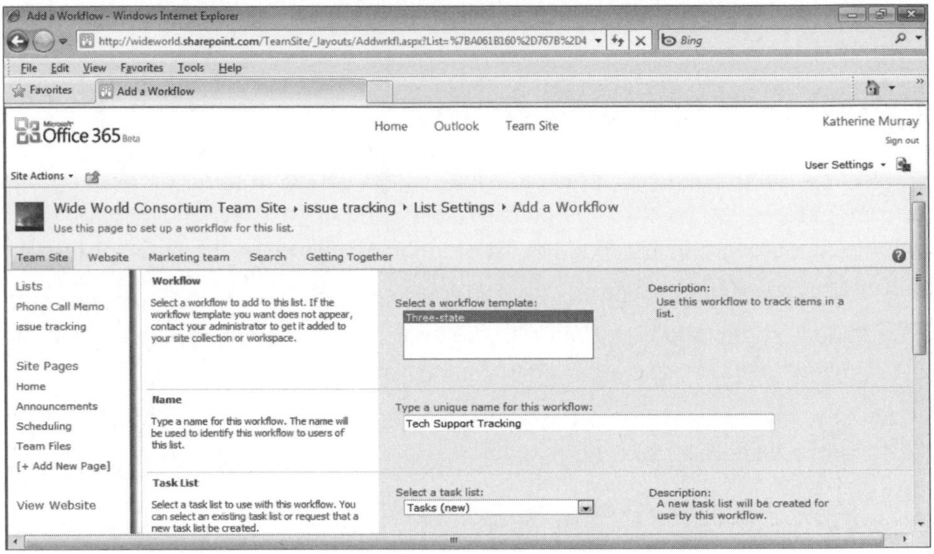

FIGURE 7-2 Type a name, and choose a list for the new workflow.

6. In the History List area, choose the name of the workflow history list you want to use from the list. Again, if you haven't created one previously, SharePoint Online will add one by default.

7. Choose how the workflow will be started by selecting the option box that best fits your process. By default, any user who has editing privileges is able to create a new workflow. You can limit this to only users with Manage Lists Permissions by selecting the check box if you like.

> **Tip** ✓ You can have SharePoint Online create a workflow automatically whenever a new item is added to your Issue Tracking table by selecting the Start This Workflow When A New Item Is Created check box.

8. Click Next.

Setting Workflow States

The Workflow states enable you to indicate the progress you're making on an issue in your workflow. The states you create might vary, depending on the type of work you're doing. For example, if you're tracking a grant proposal process, you might create workflow states that relate to the three main steps in your grant submission process:

- Research completed

- Letter of inquiry submitted

- Grant proposal submitted

If you're tracking technical support issues, you might create states such as the following:

- Active request

- In progress

- Completed

Or if you're tracking sales calls, your states might look like this:

- Request received

- Appointment scheduled

- Completed

In the Workflow States area, begin by choosing the field you'd like to set up as your Choices field. In the example shown in Figure 7-3, the issue-tracking table includes three fields that offer multiple choices, which means they can be used for the workflow.

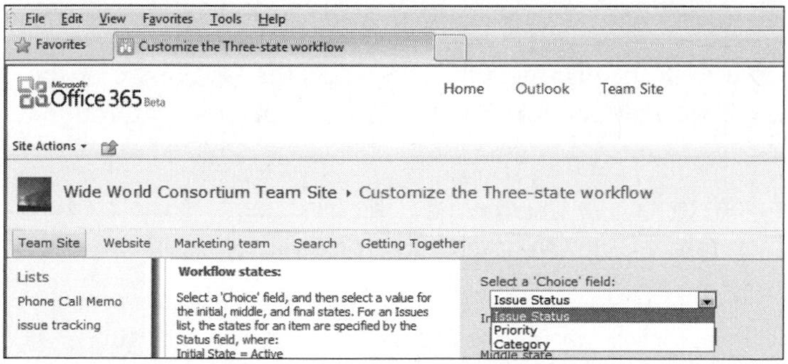

FIGURE 7-3 Choose a field that contains the values you want to use to track items in the workflow.

 **Tip** If you want to customize the values available in the workflow choice field, you must first change the values in the field itself before you begin working on the workflow. You can change the field values for a multiple choice field by adding a custom column and selecting the Choice type. You'll find the Create Column tool in the Manage Views group of the List Tools List tab.

Specifying Task Details

Your next step involves telling the workflow what you want to be generated when the workflow is created. In this section, you specify which fields you want the custom message to include; enter a task description; choose whether you want to include the date the task was modified, created, or assigned; and determine who to include in the details of the task. To complete this section, follow these steps:

1. Click in the Custom Message text box, and type the title text you want to be generated when the workflow is created. (See Figure 7-4.)

2. In the Include List Field selection, click the arrow and select the name of the field you want to be added to the Custom Message entry.

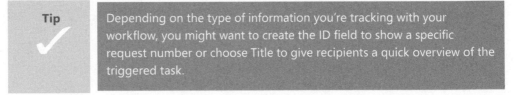 **Tip** Depending on the type of information you're tracking with your workflow, you might want to create the ID field to show a specific request number or choose Title to give recipients a quick overview of the triggered task.

3. Next type the text you want to be displayed that describes the task, and click the Insert Link To List Item if you want recipients to be able to click directly through to the task.

4. Choose whether you want to include the due date, the date the item was created, or the date the item was modified in the notification message.

5. If you want those receiving the list to see who the task is assigned to or who created or modified the task, click the Task Assigned To arrow and click your selection. If you want to assign the task to a specific person, click in the text box and type the name of the team member to whom you want to assign the task; then click Check Names to have SharePoint Online add the person's full email address to the box.

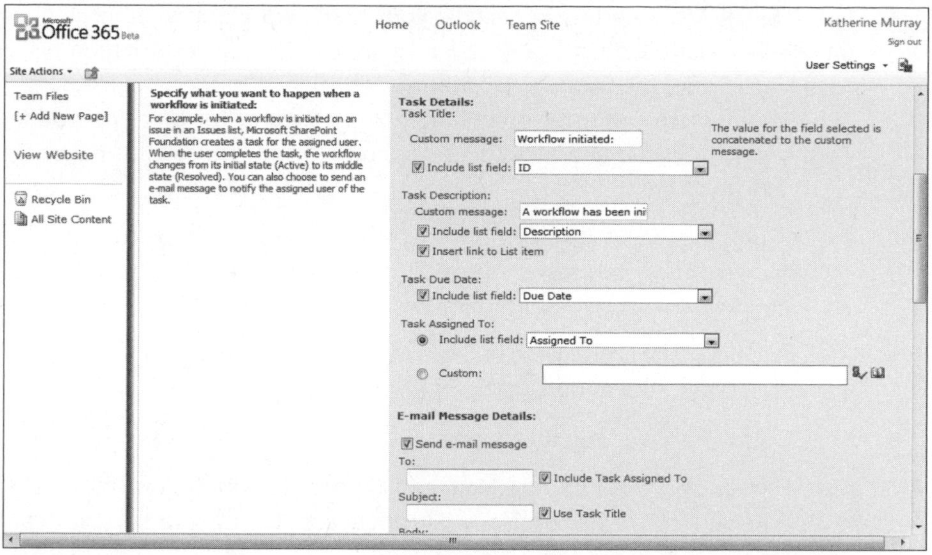

FIGURE 7-4 Enter the details for the workflow to determine what happens when specific tasks are completed.

If you want to locate a specific user but don't remember the user name the team member uses in Office 365, click Browse to the right of the Custom field in the Task Assigned To area. In the Find box of the Select People dialog box, type the first few characters of the person's name and press Enter. SharePoint Online searches the user list and displays the found user in the preview box on the right. To select the user, click the person's name and click OK.

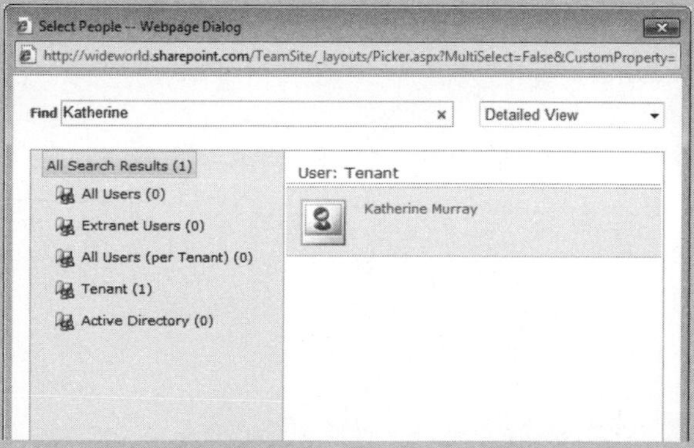

6. In the E-mail Message Details section, you tell the workflow whether to generate an email message automatically and, if so, which pieces of information you want to include. Select the Send E-Mail Message check box to send the message, and either type the information in the To and Subject fields or leave Include Task Assigned To and Use Task Title selected to include those information items automatically.

7. In the Body area, leave Insert Link To List Item selected if you want only to send the link to the triggered task. Alternately, you can type a message to let the recipients know what you want them to do with the task.

8. Repeat steps 3 through 7, choosing your options and specifying behaviors that are carried out when the middle task in the workflow is triggered.

9. Click OK to finish creating the workflow.

After you finish creating the workflow, you're taken back to your Issues Tracking list. The workflow will be applied to your project when you create the next task in the process.

Editing Your Workflow

If you want to change the workflow settings you have selected, click the Issue Tracking list in the left navigation panel. Display the List Tools List tab and then follow these steps:

1. Click Workflow Settings in the Settings group on the far right side of the ribbon.

2. Choose Workflow Settings.

3. In the Workflows screen (shown in Figure 7-5), click the name of the workflow you want to change.

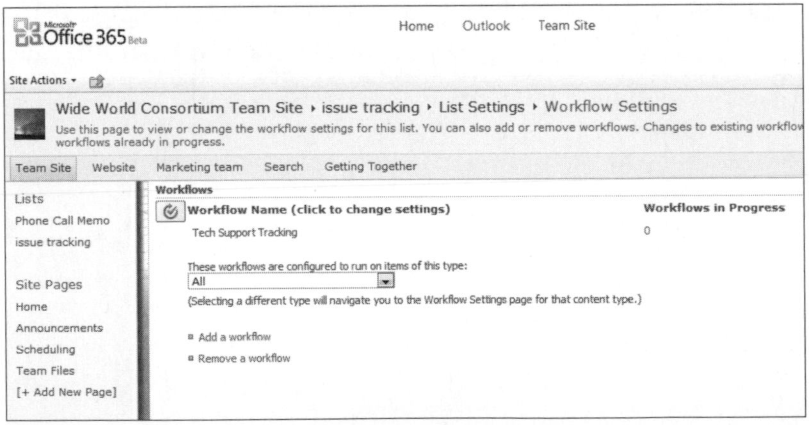

FIGURE 7-5 Display Workflow Settings, and click the name of the workflow you want to change.

The workflow settings appear so that you can make changes to your previous settings and resave the workflow with your current changes intact.

Using a Workflow for Your Project

If you selected the Start This Workflow When A New Item Is Created check box when you first created the workflow, the workflow is initiated automatically as soon as you create a new task. You can see the workflow in action by clicking Issue Tracking (or the customized name of the list you created) in the left navigation panel and reviewing the tasks in the list. In the right-most column, named for the workflow you created, the task shows the status of the workflow as In Progress. (See Figure 7-6.)

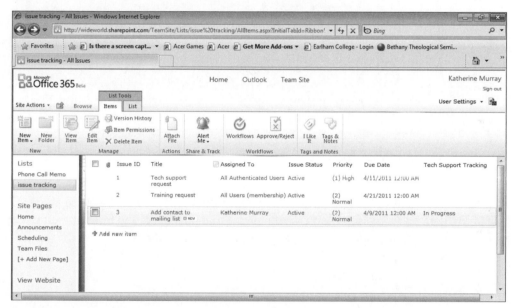

FIGURE 7-6 The Issue Tracking list shows that the workflow has been initiated.

Checking Workflow Status

You can click In Progress to display the Workflow Information screen, which gives you an overview of the active workflow. You can see who created the workflow, the date on which it started, the item in process, and the tasks affiliated with the workflow. (See Figure 7-7.)

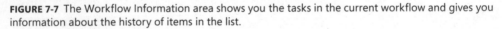

FIGURE 7-7 The Workflow Information area shows you the tasks in the current workflow and gives you information about the history of items in the list.

Completing a Workflow Task

When you finish a task that is part of the workflow, you can mark it as completed by clicking the list name in the left navigation panel. In the displayed list, select the check box of the item you've finished and click the arrow that appears to the right of the task name. A list of options appears, as shown in Figure 7-8. Click Edit Item.

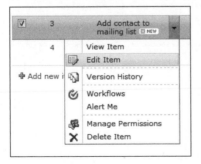

FIGURE 7-8 Click Edit Item to display the settings you need to mark a task as complete.

In the task window (similar to the one shown in Figure 7-9), click the issue and choose the option that shows the task has been completed. Scroll down and click Save to save the change. The window closes, and the task list is redisplayed, with the task status updated to show the task has been completed.

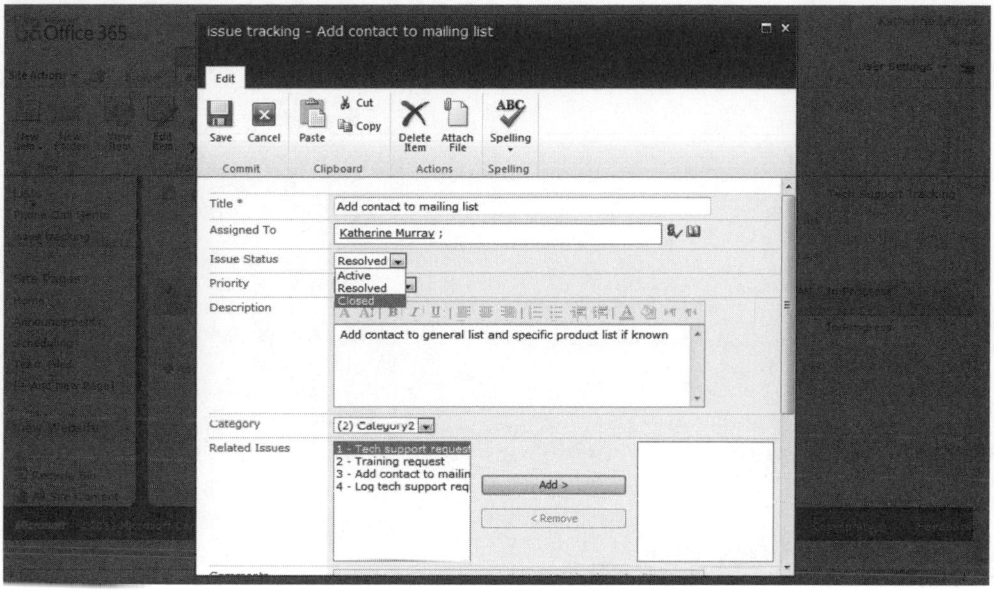

FIGURE 7-9 Change the Issue Status setting to show that the task has been completed.

Tip You can also display the task window so that you can change Issue Status by clicking Edit Item in the Manage group of the List Tools Items tab.

As workflow tasks are completed, SharePoint Online notifies the team members involved in the next stage of the process by sending email messages (if you selected that option when you were creating the workflow). At any time in the process, you can click Outlook at the top of the Office 365 window to view your email and see whether any notifications have been received.

Depending on the information you said you wanted to include in the notification, the email message might include only the link to the next task, or it might include a custom message, the task title, and other information you might need to display and complete the task. (See Figure 7-10.)

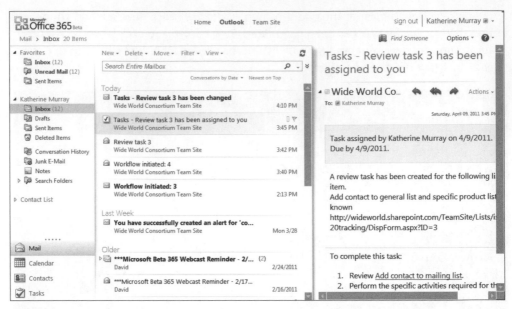

FIGURE 7-10 You can change Outlook in Office 365 to view any workflow notifications you have received.

Stopping a Workflow

Depending on the types of tasks you manage, it's very possible you'll need to create some tasks that are independent of other workflows you might have running. Perhaps you have one workflow that tracks tech support requests and others that organize your training process. When you want to create a task that is independent of a workflow—for example, you want to design a marketing strategy—you can create the task and then stop the workflow for that particular item. Here's how:

1. Click New Item in the New group of the List Tools Items tab.

2. Create the task as normal, entering the task information in the task window. Click Save.

3. In the task list, click the status of the task that is listed in the column on the right side of the window.

4. In the Workflow Information window, click Terminate This Workflow Now.

5. In answer to the prompt window, click OK, and the workflow is removed for that task.

Tip ✓	For best results, use this technique immediately after creating a task so that you don't run the risk of deleting tasks that follow this item in your workflow.

Managing Workflows

When you have created a number of workflows and they're all running at the same time, you need to be able to review, manage, and update the workflows as needed. Using SharePoint Online, you can display all your current workflows at once—and access them easily to tweak their settings—by following these steps:

1. Click the name of the list you created for the workflow (in this case, Issue Tracking).

2. Click the List Tools List tab.

3. Click the Workflow Settings tool in the Workflows group, and choose Workflow Settings.

4. Current workflows appear in the Workflows list. You can see the number of workflow tasks that are currently logged for each workflow. To review the settings for one of the current workflows, simply click the workflow name.

Note that any changes you make when a workflow is in progress will not be reflected in the current tasks already created.

What's Next

When you're working with a number of different people and coordinating efforts from multiple locations, it's helpful to have a way of tracking the major tasks of your project so that you're sure critical pieces are getting done. This chapter showed you how to add workflows to a list or library to help keep things on track. The next chapter introduces you to Office 2010 Web Apps.

CHAPTER 8

Working with Office 2010 Web Apps

FOR YEARS, WE'VE BEEN purchasing Microsoft Office suites, installing them on our local PCs or servers, and using our favorite applications to accomplish tasks, create documents, and keep things moving. But times are changing. Work is getting more flexible. We're no longer tied to a particular computer on a single desk, in the same office space, day in and day out (thank goodness). Now we can do our work on the move—in a plane, in a coffee shop, on the convention floor, or on the way to a soccer match.

Along the way, Microsoft Office has been evolving to keep pace with the changing way we work. With the release of Office 2010, Microsoft introduced Office 2010 Web Apps, which includes versions of Word, Excel, PowerPoint, and OneNote that you can easily use from any point on the globe you have web access. This means you can create, edit, revise, and share files while you're on the go, using the same familiar software you use on your desktop system. And now Microsoft brings Office 2010 Web Apps into Office 365 so that you can create and work with files that you can easily share with your team. One other great perk of working with Office 2010 Web Apps is that you don't have any software to support or upgrade; that's all done behind the scenes so that you can keep focused on the tasks at hand. And if you don't have Internet Explorer, don't worry—Office Web Apps run on Firefox and Safari browsers. That means that whether you're logging in on a Mac, PC, or kiosk at a hotel or airport, you'll find the same reliable Office interface and be able to review, edit, and save the files that are important for your work.

This chapter walks you through using Office 2010 Web Apps in Office 365. As you'll see, creating, editing, and sharing files with your team is a simple process, and Web Apps include all the major tools you use in your favorite Office desktop applications.

A First Look at Office Web Apps

As soon as you log in to Office 365, Office Web Apps are within clicking distance. Just below the Team Site area, you'll see the four Web App icons: Word, Excel, PowerPoint, and OneNote. (See Figure 8-1.) To create a new file using Word, PowerPoint, or OneNote Web App, just click the icon of the program you want to use and type a name for it. The new file will be created in the Documents library of your team site. (Excel Web App works differently—you specify the file name when you turn on the Autosave feature.) If you want to access a file that has been created and shared in the Office 365 team site, click the Shared Documents link in the Team Site area of your Office 365 home page or click the Documents link of any team site.

Click to see documents that are already posted in Office 365.

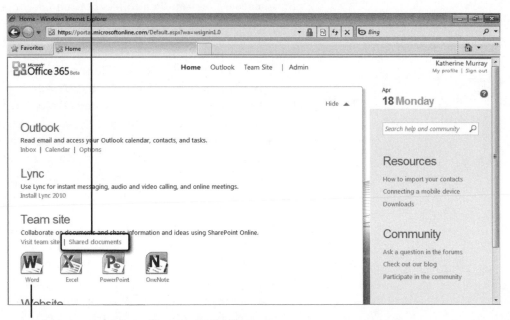

Click to start a new file in one of the Office Web Apps.

FIGURE 8-1 Open a new document using Office Web Apps from the Office 365 home page.

Introducing Office Web Apps

First introduced as companions to Office 2010 applications, Office Web Apps enable you to create, review, edit, and share files from any place you have access to the web.

Office Web Apps are designed to be a lighter offering than the more robust Office applications installed on your PC, but they provide you with the tools you need to keep your work flowing. Specifically, using Office Web Apps, you can

- Create new files in Word, Excel, PowerPoint, and OneNote.

- Review and format the content in your files.

- Add tables, illustrations, and Clip Art. (See Figure 8-2.)

- Clip and share notes easily.

- Collaborate with others as you edit and review files.

- Edit, update, and deliver presentations anywhere you have web access.

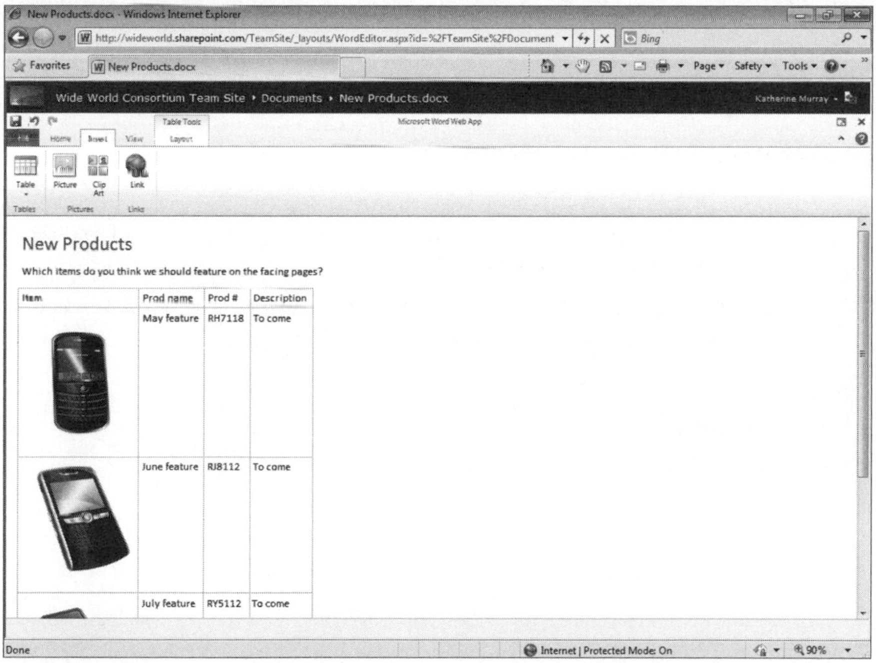

FIGURE 8-2 You can add tables, pictures, clip art, and links to a document in Word Web App.

Using Office Web Apps, you can open, edit, and save files that are posted in your SharePoint document library or you can work with files from your own desktop or laptop

PC or Mac. Working with the file in the way that best fits your project is another way Office 365 provides just what you need when you need it.

VERSIONS OF OFFICE WEB APPS

If you were using Office 2010 prior to working with Office 365, you might know that Web Apps have been available for both personal and business users of Office 2010 for some time. For personal use, you can work with Office 2010 Web Apps when you use files in your Windows Live SkyDrive account. (Windows Live SkyDrive is a free utility available as part of Windows Live services that enables you to store and share files in a central location online.)

If your company uses Office 2010 Professional Plus, which includes SharePoint Workspace 2010, you can use Office Web Apps through your SharePoint access. In Office 365, Microsoft brought together the best of both worlds, giving businesses from small to enterprise-level, as well as individual team members, access to the familiar Office applications they use every day to finish business-critical tasks.

How Office Web Apps Work

As you learned in Chapter 3, "Administering an Office 365 Account," one of the beautiful things about Office 365 is that there's very little software for you to support. Instead of trying to figure out what an error message means or what you can do to correct it, Microsoft takes care of the technical back end of things by keeping your software up to date, offering a comprehensive help system, and giving you a number of options for getting answers to your questions.

Office Web Apps are based on this ease-of-use idea, giving you just what you need to view and edit your Office files by using your favorite web browser. You can start a new file for Word, Excel, PowerPoint, or OneNote directly from your Home page in Office 365, or you can click Documents in your SharePoint team site to begin a new file with one of the Office Web Apps. (See Figure 8-3.)

The file you create appears in your browser window, where you can use a number of tools to add content, format the information, insert elements like tables and pictures, and share the file with others. Although you can do simple edits in Web Apps, they're designed to be a bit "lighter" than the full Office applications; so for in-depth editing, you can open the file in the application that is stored on your PC or Mac.

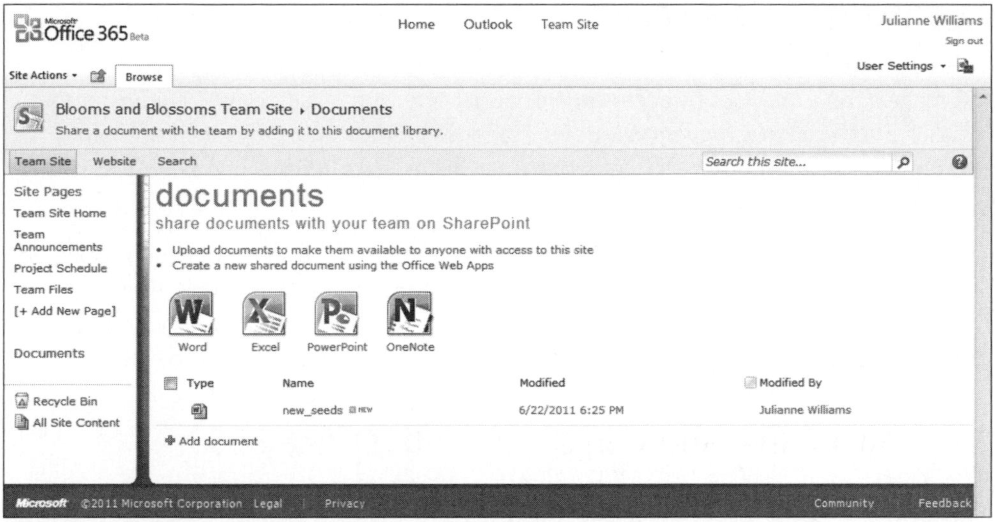

FIGURE 8-3 You can click Documents to display Office Web Apps when you're working in your SharePoint team site.

BETTER FLOW WITH SILVERLIGHT

Silverlight is a free web browser plug-in available from Microsoft that improves video quality, streamlines performance, and allows for enhanced interactivity in the Internet applications you use. Silverlight is available as a plug-in on Internet Explorer, Firefox, Chrome, and Safari browsers and is also available for Windows Mobile phones.

You don't have to have the Silverlight plug-in installed to use Office Web Apps, but it does improve performance in the following ways:

- Word pages and PowerPoint presentations load faster.

- Text looks clearer when you magnify it.

- The Find On This Page feature works more accurately.

- In PowerPoint, animations are smoother and slides scale to the browser window size.

To find out more about Silverlight or install it on your computer, visit *www.microsoft.com/silverlight*.

Web Apps on Your Phone

Office 365 also works with your phone and enables you to get updates, review files, and make simple changes by accessing your SharePoint team site through your phone browser or Office Hub (only on Windows 7 phones). Office Web Apps in SharePoint are supported on Windows Mobile phones, as well as BlackBerry, iPhone, iPod Touch, Android, and Nokia S60 phones.

The screens that you view on your phone have been optimized for display on mobile devices, so finding your way around the team site is similar—but simpler—than the browser-based approach you're familiar with. For more information about working with Office 365 on your mobile phone, see Chapter 9, "Going Mobile with Office 365."

What You Can—and Can't—Do with Office 365

Knowing that users often need to access files on the go—perhaps to review a report with a client, check recent sales data in a worksheet, or update the spelling on a slide—Office Web Apps give you tools to review your files and make simple changes from any point you have web access.

Although the programs are robust enough to help you create, edit, and share simple files, they do not include many of the specific tools that are available to you in the Office programs you run on your computer. For example, high-end protection features, such as Information Rights Management (IRM), are not available in Office Web Apps. For increased security, Microsoft recommends you use the full version of the software available on your desktop or laptop computer.

Additionally, although you can view tracked changes in a document that has been posted to a SharePoint document library and opened in Word Web App, the web program doesn't include any functionality that will enable you to work with the tracked changes. To work with tracked changes, you need to use your desktop version of the software.

Here are some other differences you should be aware of:

- Format Painter isn't available in Office Web Apps.
- You can't add symbols or shapes or use the equation or date and time feature in Office Web Apps.
- Word Web App doesn't allow you to edit objects such as SmartArt.
- Translation features and the thesaurus are also not available.
- The Spelling Checker is available only in Word, PowerPoint, and OneNote.

- Macros are not enabled in any of the Office Web Apps.
- You can't use inking or embed media files in a notebook in OneNote Web App.

Creating, Saving, and Closing a New File

You can create a new file easily by clicking the Office Web App icon of the file type you want to create. The new file opens in the browser window (shown in Figure 8-4, with Excel Web App displayed), and the ribbon offers the tools you need to get started.

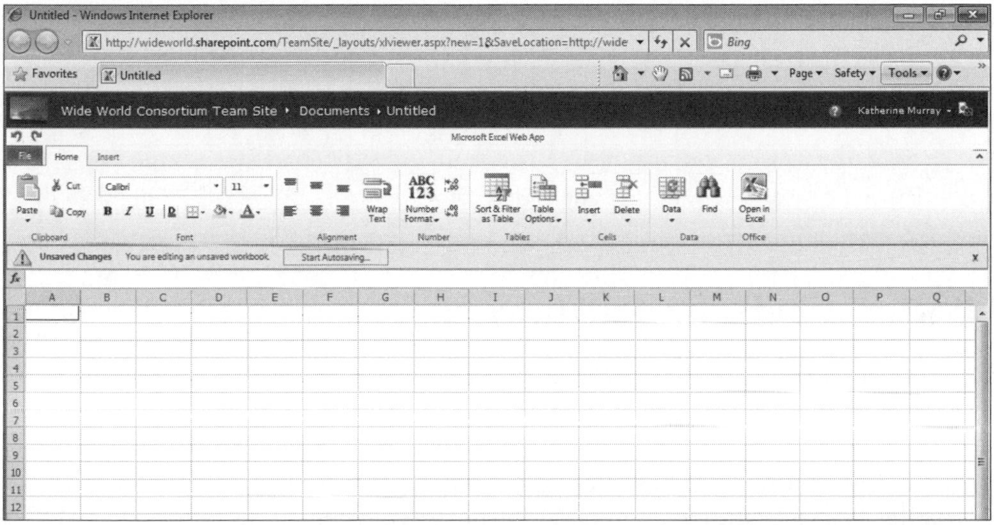

FIGURE 8-4 After you click the Excel Web App icon, the new worksheet appears in your web browser.

Tip	In Excel Web App, you'll notice that the Unsaved Changes banner appears at the top of the new worksheet. Click Start Autosaving to display a dialog box in which you can enter a file name, and then click OK.

You can now enter information by clicking in the cells and typing, copying, and pasting information, or creating tables for your workbook data.

When you're finished working with an Excel workbook, a OneNote notebook, or a PowerPoint presentation using Office Web Apps, click the File tab and click Close when you're ready to close the file. Because these Web Apps autosave your information, you don't need to do anything to save your changes.

When you're finished adding content to a Word file, save and close the document by following these steps:

1. Click the File tab in the Web App.

2. Click Save.

3. Click File again, and click Close.

This saves the changes you made in the Word file and closes Word Web App. You are returned to your SharePoint document library, where you can create, view, or work with other files.

> **Note**   Excel autosaves the changes you make to the worksheet, but interestingly enough, there is no way to close the worksheet beyond simply navigating away from the page. Excel Web App saves the worksheet for you, though, so clicking the Back arrow to return to your Home page or document library won't cause any loss of data.

■ Working with an Existing File

In Chapter 4, "What Your Team Can Do with Office 365," you learned how to create document libraries and post files so that your team members can get to them easily. When you want to work with a specific file—for example, perhaps you want to review the sales projections your manager just posted—you can choose whether you want to view or edit the file in the Office Web App. When you are working on a file, it is locked so that other users can't change the file while you're working on it. After you close the file, it is made available to your teammates for editing. Here are the steps:

1. Click Team Site at the top of your Office 365 Home page.

2. Display the document library where the files are stored.

3. Click the arrow to the right of the file name. (See Figure 8-5.)

4. Click one of the following:

    ■ View In Browser, if you simply want to review the file

    ■ Edit In Browser, if you want to be able to make changes in the file

    ■ Edit In Microsoft Word, if you want access to all editing tools in the full version of Word and you have Office 2010 installed on your computer.

    The file opens in your browser window, and you can edit or review the file as you'd like.

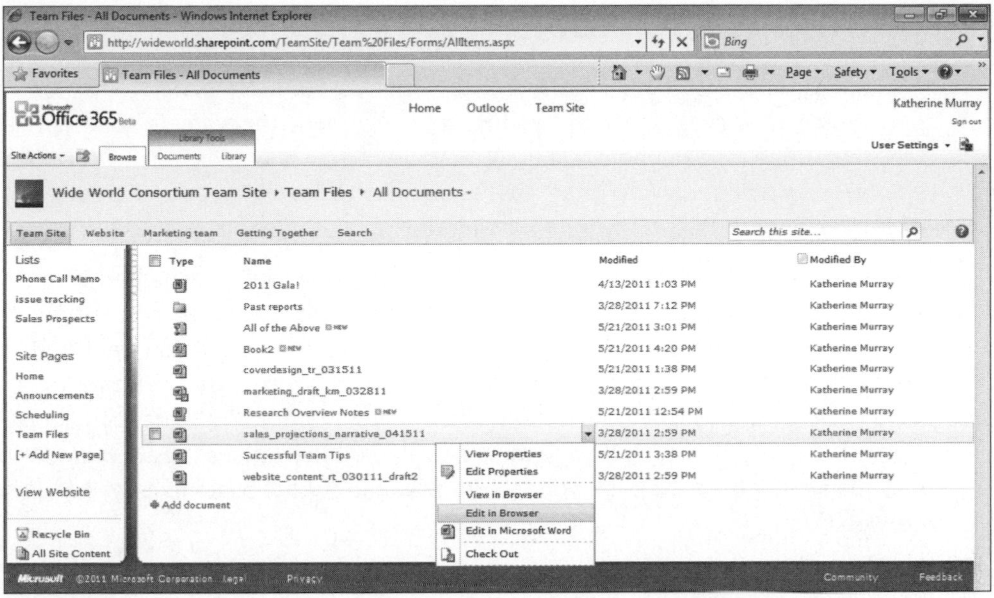

FIGURE 8-5 You can choose to view or edit files from your SharePoint document library.

Note   Even though the example in Figure 8-5 shows Edit In Microsoft Word as one of the options available, Word is listed only because the selected file is a Word document. If you select an Excel worksheet file, the option displayed is Edit In Microsoft Excel.

FILE SIZE LIMITS: OFFICE 365 HAS TO DRAW THE LINE SOMEWHERE

Office 365 does set a limit on the size of your file uploads. No single file can be larger than 50 MB, which might not seem like much if you're used to creating large documents with lots of photos, tables, and illustrations or PowerPoint presentations with plenty of media—audio and video.

Administrators do have the power to increase the upload size, but doing so requires a little behind-the-scenes wrangling. So if you bump into the size issue repeatedly, let your friendly Office 365 tech support person help you increase the limit. Access Office 365 help by clicking Admin on the Office 365 Home page, clicking Overview in the Support area on the left side of the browser window, and clicking Get Help With Office Web Apps.

■ Choosing Your Tools

The familiar Office 2010 ribbon offers you specific sets of tools related to the task you're performing. If you've just added a picture to a document, for example, tools appear in tabs that are related to photo editing. Whether you're working online in Office 365 or editing a document on your local PC, the tools the Office 2010 application gives you are directly related to the tasks you're working on.

When you're working with an Office Web App, the same tool management approach enables you to have just what you need on the screen at any given point in time. You'll find fewer available tools in Office Web Apps, however, because if you want to do some heavy-duty editing, you can open the file in Microsoft Word, Excel, or PowerPoint; make any necessary changes; and save the file back to your Office 365 SharePoint library. Figure 8-6 gives you a sense of the tools available on the various tabs in Word Web App. As you can see, the tools allow you to add, edit, and format content, as well as switch between views.

FIGURE 8-6 Office Web App offers different sets of tools depending on which tab you click on.

Levels of Editing in Office Web Apps

As you can see, Office Web Apps are designed to be partners in crime to your favorite desktop Office applications. You won't be using them all the time, for everything, because there are a number of features you probably like and need that will be available only in your desktop applications. But Office Web Apps are perfect for those times when

- You need a quick sign-off from a manager on new content you've added to a report.

- You want to share notes with a colleague about a new product you're developing.

- You need to get an update on sales reports or review a project budget before heading into a meeting.

- You want to share a product presentation with others to help them prepare for an upcoming sales call.

In other words, you use Office Web Apps when you need straightforward processing power and the flexibility of an "access anywhere, use anytime" tool.

But—never fear—if you begin doing a few light tasks with an Office Web App and then realize you really do need a bigger set of tools for some more in-depth work, you can easily move your file to your desktop application with a click of the mouse.

Viewing Your File in Office 365

For example, suppose that you open a PowerPoint presentation you want to review by clicking View In Browser in the SharePoint document library (as described in the previous section). The presentation appears in the web browser window, and you can press PgDn to move through the various slides. (See Figure 8-7.)

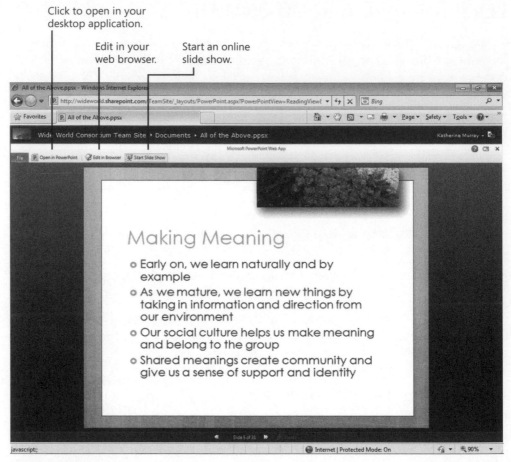

FIGURE 8-7 When you're viewing a file in your web browser, you can click the tools at the top left to edit the file in your desktop application or in the browser window.

Editing in Your Web Browser

When you click Edit In Browser, the Office Web App changes to provide more tools in the ribbon and to enable you to select and work with objects—text, pictures, tables, and more—in the file. As you can see in Figure 8-8, you can revise and format the content in the file after you click Edit In Browser.

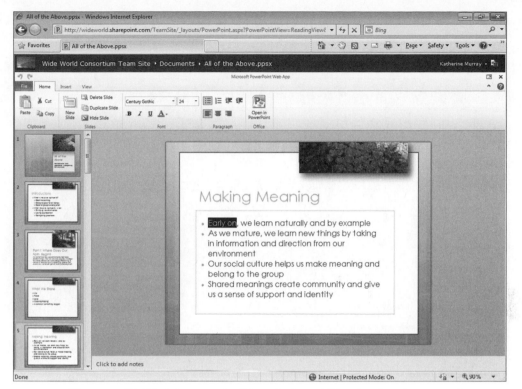

FIGURE 8-8 When you click Edit In Browser, the ribbon displays additional tools and you can select content on the slide.

Taking It to the Desktop

If you decide that the work you want to do is a little more involved than the tools in the Office Web App can handle, you can easily click the option to open the file in your full desktop application. When you click Open in PowerPoint, for example, Office 365 may prompt you to enter your Office 365 user ID and password, and then the file opens in the full PowerPoint program that is installed on your computer. (See Figure 8-9.)

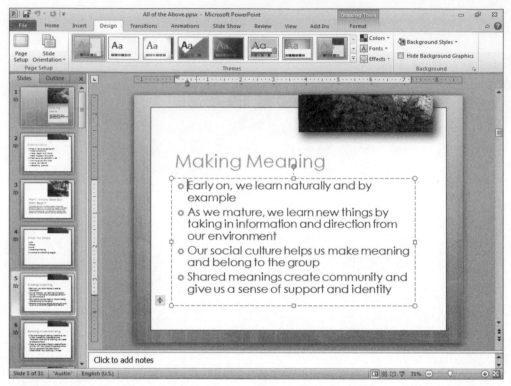

FIGURE 8-9 When you open the file in PowerPoint, the full range of application tools is available to you.

After you make the changes you need in the file, you can save it back to the SharePoint team site by clicking on the File tab and clicking Save. You can see from the file path at the top of the Info tab that the file will be saved back to your team site. (See Figure 8-10.)

Now that you know the basics of opening, viewing, and editing files in Office Web Apps, the rest of this chapter takes a look at some specific tasks you might want to try in Office 365.

File location shows the file will be saved to the team site online.

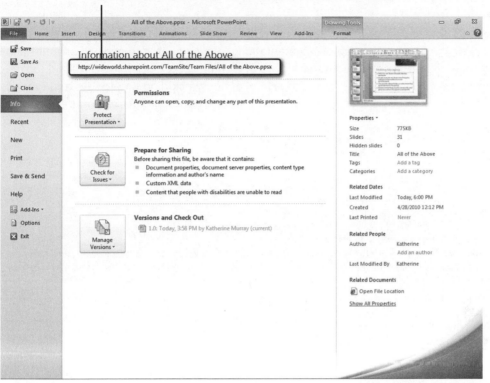

FIGURE 8-10 Save the file back to the team site by clicking on the File tab and clicking Save.

Co-authoring with Office Web Apps

One of the challenges of working remotely—especially if your team is scattered all over the country, or the globe—is that collaboration can be difficult. Think about it. If you're in the office and you need to make a team decision about a new design for the spring catalog, you can all gather in the conference room, spread the designs out on the table, and talk about your likes and dislikes.

In a cloud environment, weighing in as a group on a specific project takes a little more planning, but now, thanks to Office 365, it can be done more easily. Using the co-authoring features available in Office Web Apps, you can work alongside team members in the same file, working on complementary sections and chatting in real time—via Lync Online and instant messaging—while you're doing it.

Editing in the Browser

The way Web Apps behave when you're using them to co-author files varies slightly depending on which program you're using. For example, when two of you are editing a document in Word Web App or a presentation in PowerPoint, one person can edit the document in the Web App, but the second person must click Open in Word. and the second user will see a dialog box with several options, including one to save and sync the edits with the server when the first used is no longer using the file. (See Figure 8-11.)

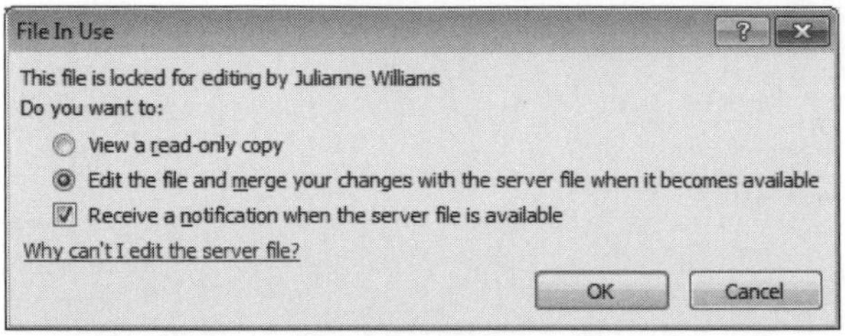

FIGURE 8-11 When you are the second author opening a file in Word Web App or PowerPoint Web App, you are given a choice of viewing the file only or making changes and saving them to the server later.

After the first user closes the document, Word lets you know you can save your changes to the server as well by clicking Save. (See Figure 8-12.)

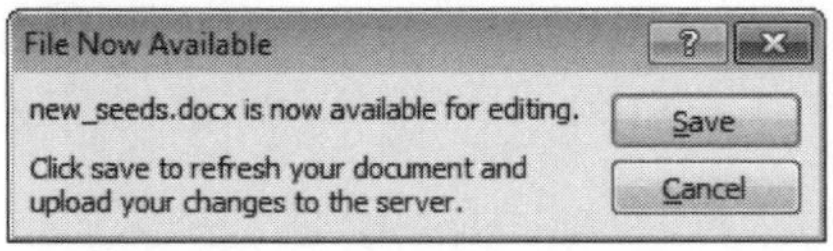

FIGURE 8-12 Word or PowerPoint lets you know when the first co-author has closed the file so that your changes can be synced with the server.

Excel Web App behaves differently, enabling two co-authors to be working in the same file in their browser windows. To edit a worksheet using Excel Web App, you can open the file and click Edit In Browser, whether you're the first author or an additional co-author. Excel displays the number of authors working on the file in the lower right corner of the worksheet window. You can click the notification to see who else is working on the file with you. (See Figure 8-13.)

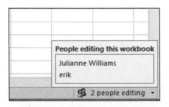

FIGURE 8-13 You can click the co-author symbol in the lower right corner of Excel Web App to see who else is working in the file.

OneNote is a different animal altogether, making co-authoring a simpler process. Co-authors can simply open the OneNote notebook in Outlook Web App, make changes, add content, and take notes to their hearts' content, and OneNote syncs the information seamlessly so that other authors' additions appear as you go.

Another Way to Co-author in Office 365

You can also co-author documents using Office 2010 applications by editing them in your own version of the software on your desktop or laptop computer. The connection is maintained with the server, and you can see who else is working in the file and collaborate effectively. Here's how to open one of your Office 365 documents so that you can co-author a file working in the Web Apps on your own computer:

1. In the Office 365 Home page, click Team Site.
2. Display your SharePoint document library.
3. Click the arrow to the right of the file name you want to edit.
4. Click Edit in Microsoft Word.
5. The document opens in Word. Edit the file as usual.

Word lets you know when other authors are working in the file, and it marks the changes made by another author when you click on the File tab and either choose Save or press Ctrl+S to save the file. (See Figure 8-14.)

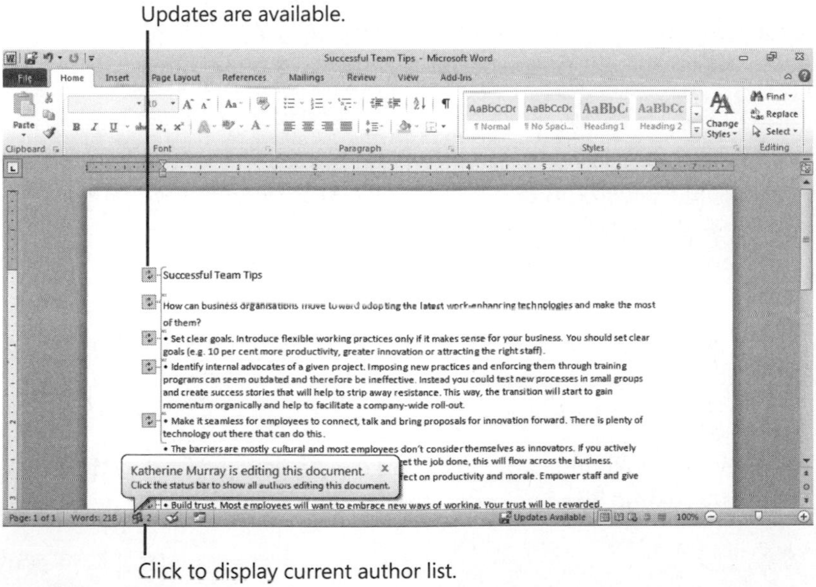

FIGURE 8-14 Word lets you know where the file has been updated and provides a list of current authors.

When new authors open the file while you're working on it, Word displays a pop-up message and shows you the number of authors working in the current file. (See Figure 8-15.)

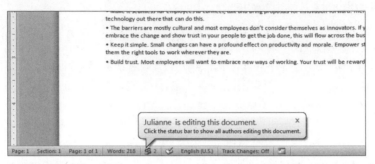

FIGURE 8-15 Office 365 lets you know when another author logs in to co-author the current file.

When you finish making changes in the document, simply click File and choose Close. If any changes have not been saved, you'll be prompted to save the file. You can return to the SharePoint document library and view the file and see that all changes are reflected in the file.

Reviewing and Editing Excel Worksheets

Similar to the process of opening, viewing, and editing other files in your SharePoint document library, you can open an Excel worksheet in Excel Web App. Click the arrow in the SharePoint document library to view or edit the file in your browser.

Although the features in Excel Web App are limited, you can add data, create formulas, use functions, and sort, filter, and recalculate the data in the workbook. You'll find everything you need for entering, formatting, and adjusting rows and columns on the Home tab.

> **Note**   At this time, Excel Web App in Office 365 does not support the use of charts, although you can add charts to the version of Excel Web App that is available through Windows Live SkyDrive.

In addition to using the workbooks and data tables you create, you can work with PivotTables you previously created using your desktop version of Excel 2010.

You can download a snapshot of the data and formulas in your worksheet by clicking on the File tab and clicking Download A Snapshot, as you see in Figure 8-16. This view gives you a sense of the contents of your workbook without applying the formatting to the file.

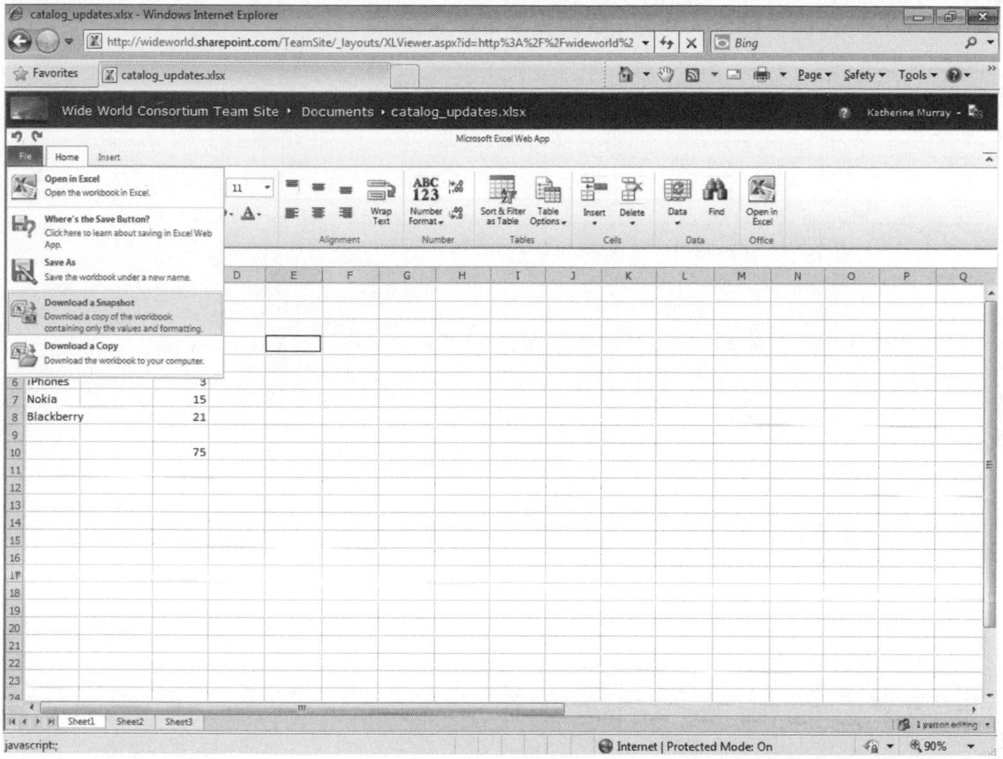

FIGURE 8-16 After creating and editing Excel data, you can download a snapshot of the information you've entered.

Working with OneNote Notebooks

When you create a OneNote notebook in OneNote Web App, the program creates a shared notebook by default, meaning those with the necessary permissions (which the site Admin sets in the User settings) are able to view, edit, and save notes in the shared notebook. The notebook opens in your browser window with sections and pages listed in the navigation pane on the left. You can type in the page area and format the text as you'd like. You can also click Tag and choose the tag that will help you locate the content later. (See Figure 8-17.)

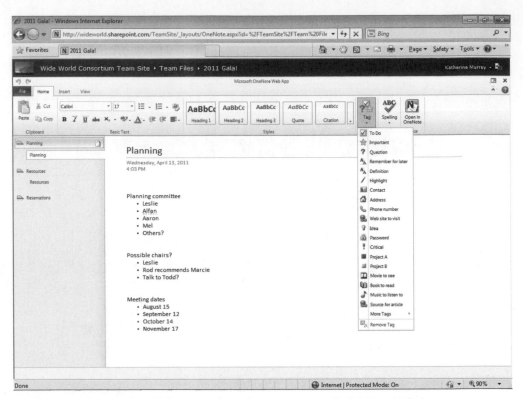

FIGURE 8-17 You can easily add, format, and tag the notes you save in OneNote Web App.

The tools on the Insert tab give you the option of adding new pages and sections, inserting tables, incorporating pictures and clip art, or adding links to your notes pages. On the View tab, you can choose between Editing View and Reading View, review information about various page versions, and click Show Authors to see which authors added the various notes on the page. (See Figure 8-18.)

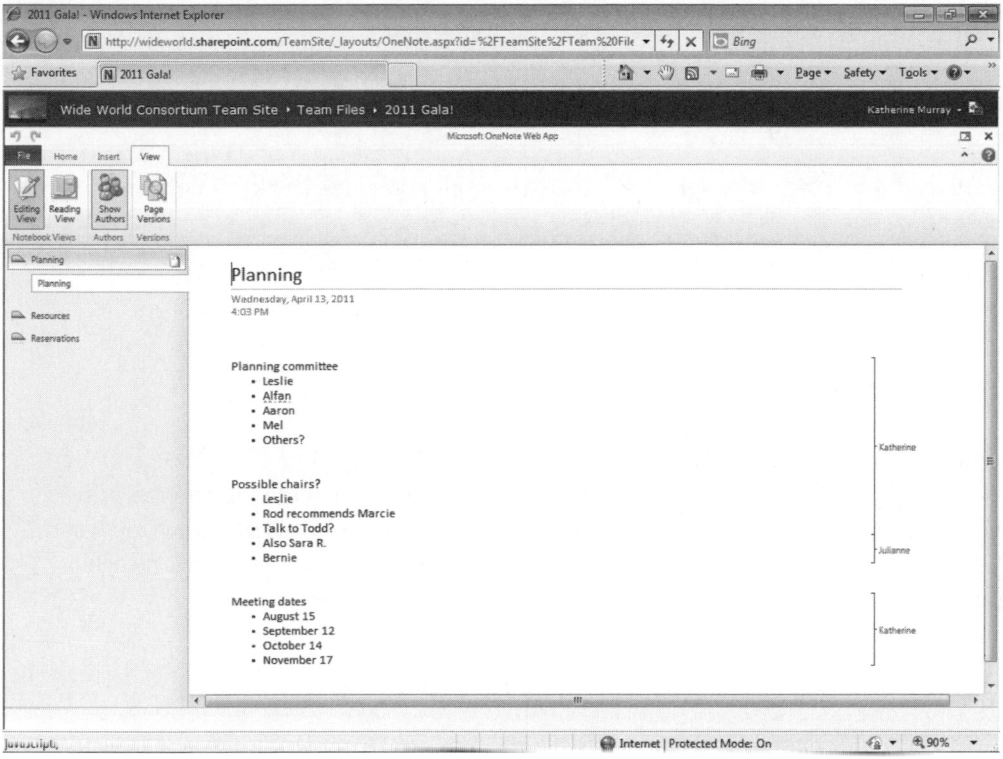

FIGURE 8-18 Click Show Authors to display the names of contributing authors along the right side of the notes page.

PROTECTING ONENOTE NOTEBOOK SECTIONS

If you like the idea of sharing your notebook with the team but you'd like to keep a section or two password protected for your eyes only, you can do so. Open the OneNote notebook in OneNote 2010 on your computer (by clicking Open in OneNote on the far right side of the Home tab), and then right-click the section tab of the section you want to password protect. Choose Password Protect This Section, and click Set Password. Type a password and confirm the password you entered; then click OK. When you exit the notebook, it is synced back with your Office 365 shared documents.

Now when you or one of your team members opens the notebook in OneNote Web App, the rest of the shared notebook will be available. However, when someone clicks the password-protected section, that person will not be able to open the section. If the user clicks Open In OneNote, a message appears informing the user that the section is password protected. The user is then prompted to press Enter and type the section password. The user can enter the password—if she knows it—and click OK to edit the section, or she can click Cancel and close the notebook.

What's Next

In this chapter, you explored Office Web Apps and discovered how to create and work with files from Word, PowerPoint, Excel, and OneNote, both in the Office Web App versions and in your desktop applications. The next chapter shows you how you can use your mobile device to work with files and stay in touch with your team in Office 365.

Going Mobile with Office 365

LET'S FACE IT. Who wants to sit indoors, stuck at a desk on a beautiful spring day? And wouldn't it be nice to make the most of the 30 minutes you spend sitting in the doctor's office by getting some work done on your phone? Office 365 makes accessing and working with your files easy and seamless, thanks to its flexible, connect-anywhere design. If you're not quite finished reviewing a file and it's time to hit the road, you can access the document and finish it later using your mobile phone.

You can use Office 365 with your smartphone to view, edit, and share the Word, Excel, PowerPoint, and OneNote files you have posted in your SharePoint team site. This chapter introduces you to the various ways you can use mobile devices to access your Office 365 files. You'll see the oh-so-beautiful Windows Phone 7 used to demonstrate some examples in this chapter, but Office 365 works with a variety of phones, including BlackBerry, Android, iTouch, and Nokia smartphones.

MANGO: IT'S NOT JUST FOR BREAKFAST ANYMORE

As this book was being written, Microsoft released a bit of information about the next Windows Phone operating system, codenamed Mango. This new release will add features that make sharing files easier and more seamless when you're interacting with Office 365. Mango also supports Lync functionality so that you can take your instant messaging and presence on the road with you while staying in sync with Office 365.

How Will You Use Your Phone with Office 365?

One of the major design objectives for Office 365 was that it be easy to access and easy to use on all sorts of devices—PCs, netbooks, laptops, tablets, and mobile devices. The idea is to ensure that wherever you are you can access your team site and work with your files, using whatever device gives you the web access you need.

Smartphones today are increasingly able to browse the web in a convenient, quick manner. Even the best phones a few years ago had long wait times while graphics downloaded and rarely offered interfaces that were custom designed for the mobile phone. Today, developers design specifically for the small screen of the mobile device, and they optimize the navigation and site functionality to make finding what you need as easy as possible.

On Windows 7 phones, users can access their Office 365 account directly from the Office Hub, a feature that brings together the mobile versions of Word, Excel, PowerPoint, and OneNote. This means you won't have to use your web browser to access your Office 365 account—instead, you can connect directly to SharePoint and use these Office applications to view and work with your Office files with a few simple taps.

Office 365 optimizes the screen for mobile devices, which means you can find, open, and work with the files you need easily on your mobile phone. Using your phone, you can

- Check email, contacts, and calendar items.

- Access your team site to review announcements and posts.

- View and edit Word documents stored in your SharePoint team site.

- View and work with Excel worksheets available in your document libraries.

- Review and work with PowerPoint presentations.

- Update, edit, and share OneNote notebooks.

No matter what kind of work you want to get done while you're on the road, you can easily open, view, edit, and share your Office 365 files and stay in touch with your team along the way.

Receiving and Sending Email on Your Phone

In Chapter 2, "Getting Started with Office 365," you learned how to set up your Office 365 email so that you can view it and respond to it on your mobile phone. The process varies depending on the type of phone you have. After you've set up the phone to work with Office 365, you can view your email simply by tapping the email icon on your Start screen.

If you've set up your Office 365 mail as your primary mail account, the Outlook icon on your Windows Phone 7 start screen shows the number of emails waiting for you to review, as shown in Figure 9-1. (If you've set up a different email account as your primary account, that account will appear by default in the Outlook icon, providing of course it is an Outlook-based account.)

FIGURE 9-1 Your Windows Phone 7 shows you the number of emails awaiting your attention.

To read your email, tap the Outlook icon. The messages appear in a list on your phone. (See Figure 9-2.)

FIGURE 9-2 Tap the Outlook icon to review the list of available messages.

Next, tap the message you want to see, and it opens on your screen, pictures and all. (See Figure 9-3.)

— Click to display
email options.

FIGURE 9-3 The email message opens in your phone display.

You can tap the three dots in the lower right corner of the phone display to see email options that enable you to reply to or forward the message. To respond to the message, tap Reply and type the message you want to send on the keyboard that appears in the phone window. Then tap the Send button to send the message.

When you're ready to delete email messages you no longer need, tap the area of the screen to the left of the message in the Inbox screen. A check mark appears to the left of the message. You can scroll through the list and tap to add check marks to all the messages you want to delete. Tap Delete at the bottom of the Inbox window to remove the messages. (See Figure 9-4.) If you'd rather file the messages for safekeeping, you can tap Folder and choose the folder in which you'd like to save the selected messages.

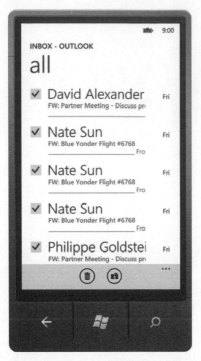

FIGURE 9-4 Tap to select the messages you want to remove, and then tap Delete.

Tip ✓	To learn more about mastering your Windows Phone 7, see *Windows Phone 7 Plain & Simple*, by Michael Stroh (Microsoft Press, 2010).

Tip ✓	Thanks to the flexibility of Office 365, you can use the iPhone and iTouch—as well as your Mac computer—to access, edit, and update the files in your SharePoint team site. Using your iTouch to connect to Office 365 is similar to both the Windows 7 and Windows Mobile 6.5 phones in that you can use your phone's web browser to access your Office 365 account.

Using the Office Hub on Your Windows Phone 7

The Office Hub is a built-in feature on the Windows 7 phone, enabling you to access your Office files and SharePoint sites easily from one starting point. You might find the Office Hub tile on your Windows Phone Start page or on the Apps list. If you don't see the Office Hub tile on the Start page, flick left or tap the arrow to display the Apps list. (See Figure 9-5.) Tap Office to display the Office Hub.

Tip ✓	You can add the Office Hub to your Start page by touching and holding the Office Hub icon on the Apps page. A popup option appears, and you can tap Pin To Start to add the icon to your phone Start page.

FIGURE 9-5 If you don't see the Office Hub on your Windows Phone 7 Start screen, flick the screen to the left.

When you tap the Office Hub, an overview page appears, offering you a number of ways to work with the files in your SharePoint team site on Office 365. Flick the page twice to the right to move to the SharePoint page. (See Figure 9-6.) Tap Open Link, and type the web address of your team site or document library in the web address field that appears (for example, http://wideworld.sharepoint.com).

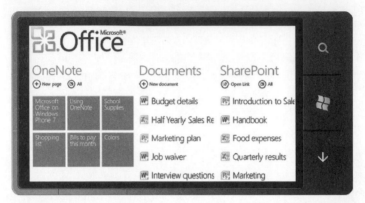

FIGURE 9-6 You can move directly to your team site through the SharePoint page in the Office Hub.

> **Note** While Office 365 was still in beta, Windows Phone 7 couldn't access an Office 365 SharePoint site directly; instead, users needed to use Internet Explorer on their phones to access their team sites. If you get an error when you try to log directly into your Office 365 account from the SharePoint Online area in the Office Hub, you'll see an Open button that will open the site in your phone's web browser. Tap the button, and your Windows 7 phone does the connecting for you.

Tap the link that takes you to the document library in your SharePoint Team site, and you'll see the list of files stored there. (See Figure 9-7.) You can work with the files at the size you see them on the mobile screen, or you can magnify the display by using the pinch gesture to grab and enlarge the area you want to see more clearly. Table 9-1 gives you a quick introduction to the terminology used for different touch gestures on a Windows 7 phone.

FIGURE 9-7 Your team document library displays files that you can open and work with on your phone.

TABLE 9-1 Touch Gestures on Your Windows 7 Phone

Gesture	Explanation
Tap	Touch the screen once quickly.
DoubleTap	Touch the screen twice quickly.
Hold	Touch and hold your finger on the mobile screen.
Drag	Touch the screen, and move your finger in any direction.
Flick	Drag your finger across the screen, and lift it without stopping.
Pinch	Put two fingers on the screen, and press them together or move them apart.

Last-Minute Word Editing on Your Mobile Device

After you tap the document you want to view, the file opens in the appropriate Office application streamlined for your phone. For example, in Figure 9-8, the Word document opens in the mobile version of the Word. If the document includes multiple pages, you can review the document and move from page to page by tapping the arrows at the top of the screen.

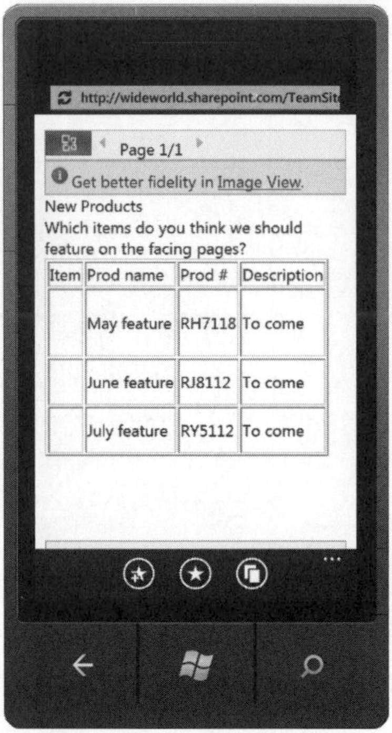

FIGURE 9-8 Word is optimized for your mobile phone so that text is easy to read on the small screen.

If your document includes pictures, you'll see a message bar that says, "Get better fidelity in Image view." Tap the Image view link to display the images in the document.

Tip	If you later want to hide images once again so that you can read the text more quickly, tap the Word program icon and then tap Text Display to suppress the display of the images and view only the text.

Editing a Word Document on Your Phone

The editing tasks you can perform on your mobile phone are a bit limited, but you can still get a lot done. You can read through a new report, for example, and make simple edits by correcting spelling, changing words, and adding content. You can change the format of text by boldfacing, italicizing, or underlining it, and you can highlight text and change text color. What's more, you can add comments to the document—which is great if you're reviewing a piece that's being created by your team—and send it on to other team members for their review as well.

That's quite a lot of work you can do while you're on the road! Here are the how-tos for editing your document on your phone:

1. Tap the Word program icon in the upper left corner of the display. The file options appear.

2. Tap Download A Copy. (See Figure 9-9.)

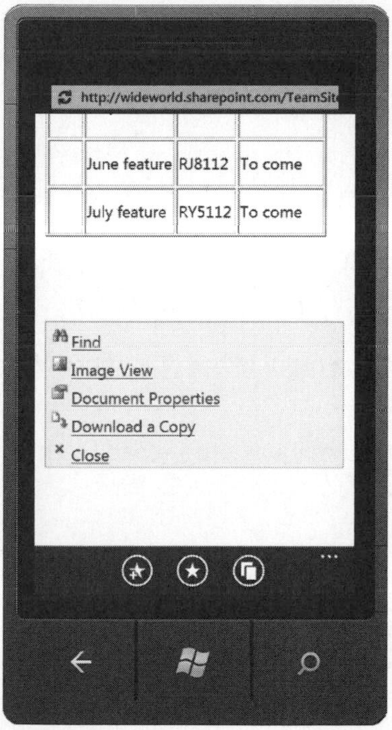

FIGURE 9-9 Tap Download A Copy to begin editing the document on your phone.

3. Tap the file icon when prompted.

4. Tap Edit to begin to edit the content. (See Figure 9-10.)

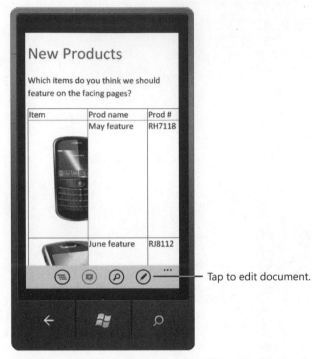

— Tap to edit document.

FIGURE 9-10 Tap Edit to display Windows Phone 7 editing tools.

5. Tap the arrows or flick the screen to move to the place in the document where you want to make the change.

6. Tap a word or space to position the cursor, and then use the keypad to enter new text or correct existing text. (See Figure 9-11.)

Tap to position cursor

Tap to insert a word

Type new content

Delete previous character

Start a new line

Change text format

FIGURE 9-11 Edit existing content, or add content to your document using the Windows Phone 7 keyboard and prompt text.

Adding Comments

If you're taking a quick look at documents while you're on the road, chances are good that you are reviewing existing documents, reading over something somebody else added, or tweaking a draft you've been working on for a couple of days. In other words, you probably won't be writing long tomes on your phone from scratch. If you're eye-balling a piece for a team member, being able to add your own comments becomes an important feature. Actually, this is helpful anytime you're working on a team, so you can easily see how others feel about the ideas being presented and incorporate the changes in the final document if you choose.

On Windows Phone 7, you have the ability to add comments to your documents when you're working in editing mode. Open the document on your phone as described in the previous section, and tap Edit. Across the bottom of the screen, you'll see the series of four tools: Outline, Comment, Find, and Format. (See Figure 9-12.)

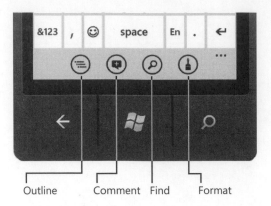

Outline   Comment Find   Format

FIGURE 9-12 You can tap Comment to open a comment window and add your notes to the file.

The first screen that appears after you tap Comment asks you to enter your user name so that your note can easily be identified by others who view the file. If you choose to do this, tap in the User box, type your name, and tap Save.

Your document is then displayed, with an open comment box attached to the word at the cursor position. Use the keypad to type your comment and then tap outside the comment box to close it. The word appears highlighted in a kind of conversation bubble, so others can see easily that there is a comment attached to the text. They'll be able to view the comment by tapping the highlight. (See Figure 9-13.)

| Tip ✓ | You can undo or redo editing and formatting operations while you're working on your phone. You'll find the tools in the Options screen, which you can display by tapping the three dots in the lower right corner of your phone display. Tap Undo to reverse the last operation or Redo to repeat your previous task. |

FIGURE 9-13 The highlighted conversation bubble lets others know there is a comment attached to the text; tap it to display the comment.

Formatting Text

Another simple editing task you might want to do on your phone involves basic formatting. If you're looking over a section about a new product, for example, and you decide that you want to boldface all the places where the product name is mentioned, you can simply tap the product name and then tap Format in the editing tools along the bottom of your phone. The Format window appears, as you see in Figure 9-14. Tap the format you want to apply—Bold, Italic, Underline, Strikethrough, Superscript, or Subscript—and the text changes in your document.

FIGURE 9-14 Tap the format you want to apply to the selected text, or turn on the formatting feature, enter your new text, and turn the feature off.

Similarly, you can highlight words by selecting the text, tapping Format, and tapping the highlight you want. You can turn on the highlight by choosing the settings before you enter new text so that anything you enter appears highlighted. (This is the best technique if you have long passages you want to highlight.) Then turn off highlighting so that the format returns to normal for subsequent entries. (See Figure 9-15.)

Of course, the other tool in the Format window is a no-brainer. You can change the actual color of the text by tapping Format and tapping a new color in the bottom of the Format window.

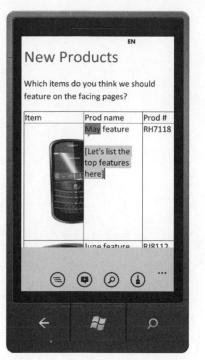

FIGURE 9-15 Add highlighted text so that others on your team can find the new content easily.

Saving and Sending Your Edited Document

After you make all these changes to your document, you need to save them and perhaps send the file to your colleagues. Tap the options button (the three dots in the lower right corner of your phone screen) to display additional file options. (See Figure 9-16.)

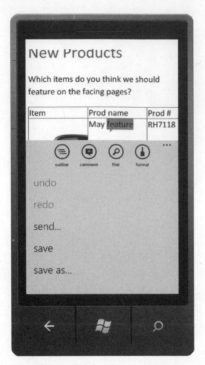

FIGURE 9-16 Display file options to save and send the document to others.

Tap Save to save the document as-is, Save As to save the document under a new name, or Send to send the document without saving a copy on your phone. Windows Phone 7 prompts you to complete the options, and the file goes happily along to your other teammates for their review.

When you're ready, tap the Word icon to display the file options and tap Close to return to the documents in your SharePoint team site.

Reviewing and Updating Excel Data

Working with an Excel worksheet on your mobile device is similar with regard to the basic tools and features you'll use on your phone to review, edit, and format the data in the worksheet file. As you would expect, the display looks different, and the range of commands available to you are different than the ones you'll find in Word. But in general, you'll notice the same, optimized, clean screen display and a set of editing tools that help you review, update, and pass along the worksheet when you're ready.

You begin by opening the worksheet by tapping the file name in the document list on your SharePoint document library screen. When the worksheet opens on your phone, you can tap the arrows at the top to move through the sheet and review it (if necessary) or flick down the page to see additional data. (See Figure 9-17.)

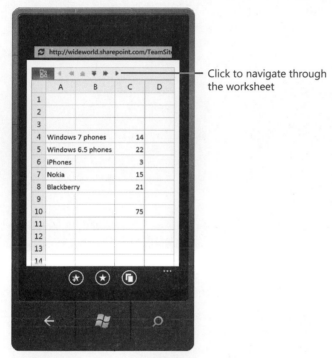

Click to navigate through the worksheet

FIGURE 9-17 The Excel worksheet on Windows Phone 7.

Working with the Worksheet

You can begin to work with the worksheet values and formulas—and display any charts attached to the file—by tapping the Excel icon in the top left corner of your phone display. A menu of tools appears at the bottom of the worksheet. (See Figure 9-18.)

FIGURE 9-18 Display Excel worksheet editing tools by tapping the Excel icon in the top left corner of the display.

The top five tools in the list enable you to display additional portions of the worksheet, either by scrolling (by tapping Next 15 Rows) or by moving to a specific worksheet or cell.

The Find command enables you to search for a specific value—text or number—on your worksheet. If you'd like to review any charts that are included with the current worksheet, tap View Charts in Current Sheet. (These are not displayed by default.)

Making Simple Editing Changes

If you want to edit the worksheet data, tap Download A Copy, and the Excel worksheet opens on your phone. Tap the cell on the worksheet to select where you want to make changes. Then tap the text or values you want to add, and tap the Enter key. Figure 9-19 shows a worksheet on Windows Phone 7 with editing in progress.

You can display a set of editing options by tapping the options button (the three dots in the lower right corner of your display), as shown in Figure 9-20. Additionally, you'll notice that Excel also offers Outline, Comment, and Find tools so that you can easily review and comment on the content in the worksheet.

FIGURE 9-19 Tap to select a cell, and then tap your new content.

FIGURE 9-20 Tap the options button to display the tools you need to sort, filter, and format worksheet data.

Here's a simple introduction to each of the editing techniques you can do on your phone:

- Tap Sort to choose the column and order by which you want to sort worksheet data.

- Tap Apply Filter to filter your data so that you can see the Top 10 values or the Bottom 10 values shown.

- Tap Format to display the Format window so that you can change the look of text and values, change the font color, or select a different fill color. (See Figure 9-21.)

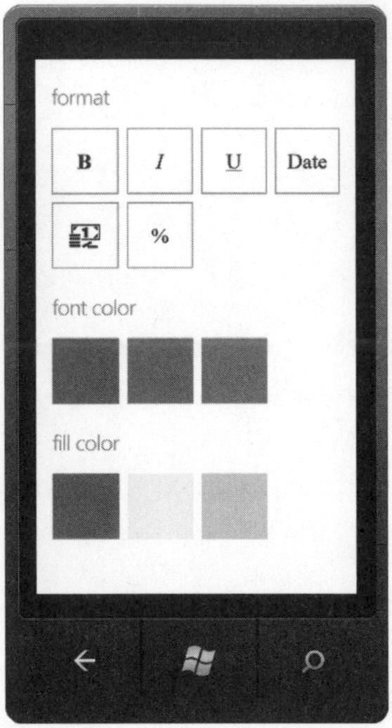

FIGURE 9-21 You can change the format of cells or select a different font color or fill color.

Saving and Sending Worksheet Changes

After you've made changes to the worksheet on your phone, you can tap the options button and then flick down to display Save and Save As. Choose Save if you want to store the file on your phone so that you can work on it more later; tap Save As if you want to save the file under a new name. And finally, tap Send if you want to forward the file along to one of your colleagues, so that she can add her own review comments or finalize the file.

To return to the document library on your phone, tap the Excel icon again and tap Close.

Tweaking a PowerPoint Presentation on Your Phone

Even though your PowerPoint slides might be more design than content, you can review them easily on your mobile device and make simple changes to share with your group. You open your presentation in the same way you open Word and Excel files—by tapping them in the SharePoint document library you've created on your Office 365 site.

When it opens on your phone, the first page of your presentation shows all the slides in the presentation in sequence. You can flick down through the list and tap the one you want. Or—and this is a good idea if you have a long presentation—you can use the Search box to enter a word or phrase on the slide you want to view. (See Figure 9-22.) Tap Find to move to the slides with the search text you entered.

FIGURE 9-22 You can search for a specific slide by entering a word or phrase in the Search box and tapping Find.

Tap the link of any slide you want to view, and the slide appears in your display, along with your PowerPoint options. (See Figure 9-23.) You can use the arrows to move through the various slides or tap + or – to magnify or reduce the size of the displayed content. Tap Download A Copy to edit the presentation on your phone.

Tap to reduce the size of the slide

Tap to magnify the slide

Display the presentation outline

Download the presentation for editing

FIGURE 9-23 You can review the presentation or edit it on your phone.

Mobile Editing for Your Presentation

The process for editing a presentation on your phone is easier than you might think. After you tap Download A Copy in the PowerPoint options list, the current slide opens on your phone. Tap the slide and then tap the Edit tool (to the right of the Comment tool in the tools row along the bottom of your phone). You can select an area by tapping it, as shown in Figure 9-24.

FIGURE 9-24 Tap the area of the slide you want to change.

PowerPoint opens the text area of the slide to enable you to make simple changes in the content. (See Figure 9-25.) Tap to position the cursor, and use the Delete key and the character keys to remove unwanted text and add new content, respectively. When you're finished editing, tap the Done tool. (It resembles a check mark.)

FIGURE 9-25 Make your changes, and then tap Done.

You can then move on to other slides by tapping the Next button, or you can display additional slide options by tapping the three dots by the tools row. As you can see in Figure 9-26, additional options enable you to move the current slide to a new point in the presentation or hide the slide from view.

FIGURE 9-26 You can edit the presentation on your phone and enable ActiveX controls to ensure the animations work properly.

If you decide to move the slide, the process is as simple as tapping and dragging the slide to the new location in the list of slide names. (See Figure 9-27.) The slide is high-lighted so that it's easy for you to see and move (and move *back* if you so choose after you've relocated the slide).

FIGURE 9-27 Reordering slides on your phone is as simple as dragging your finger—literally.

Saving and Sending Your Presentation

Similar to its other Office kin, you can save your PowerPoint presentation by tapping the option dots, flicking down to Save or Save As, and tapping the option you want to use. (See Figure 9-28.) If necessary, enter a name for the file, and then choose to send the presentation wherever you want it to go—to your office email account, to a colleague, to a client.

When you're ready to close the file, tap the Office Button at the top of the display and tap Close. Nice and simple.

Tip ✓ One great feature introduced in PowerPoint 2010 is the ability to broadcast presentations, and now you can view a presentation no matter where you are by simply tapping the link the presenter sends you via email. As the presenter broadcasts the presentation in real time, the slides will appear in the web browser on your mobile device, and you can participate whether you're on the train, in a coffee shop, or sitting at your daughter's soccer game. Nice!

FIGURE 9-28 Save your PowerPoint presentation, and send it on its way.

What's Next

In this chapter, you learned how to use your mobile phone to access and work with files you've saved in SharePoint document libraries in Office 365. Having the option to use your phone to stay in the flow of information for an ongoing project is a great perk, and it helps you get more done, faster and more flexibly. This technology is really just getting started, so you can be sure you'll see many major improvements in mobile connectivity with Office 365 as the software continues to evolve.

The next chapter takes you into the details of managing your email, calendar, contacts, and tasks in Office 365.

Connecting in Real Time

NOW THAT YOU'VE set up an account in Office 365 and gotten your team started in the right direction, this part of the book helps you think through connecting to others through email, instant messaging, and your public website. You also see how all the tools in Office 365 can be used together to help you accomplish specific business goals.

CHAPTER 10

Email and Organize with Office 365

BY NOW, YOU MIGHT be proficient at organizing your contacts, managing your calendar, and staying in touch through email. But being able to coordinate all those things—for yourself and for your team—in Office 365 enables you to keep all the information you need for your group flowing smoothly and easily. Using Outlook Web App, you can easily add contacts, manage your mail, search for colleagues, add appointments to your calendar, and keep an eye on the tasks—individual and collective—your team needs to complete.

This chapter introduces you to the ways you can manage your people and project information in Office 365.

Introducing Outlook Web App

After you log in to Office 365, you can display your Inbox by clicking Outlook at the top of the Office 365 Home page or by clicking Inbox in the Outlook area on the left side of the window. (See Figure 10-1.)

Click either link to display the Inbox.

FIGURE 10-1 Display Outlook Web App by clicking Outlook or Inbox on the Office 365 Home page.

■ Checking and Managing Email

One of the great things about Outlook Web App in Office 365 is that your mail—and contacts—are always right there when you need them, available through any device that gives you access to the web. In Chapter 9, "Going Mobile with Office 365," you learned how to review and send email on your phone; Outlook Web App gives you the online, web-based ability to read new mail, work with received mail, and organize all your communication preferences in just the way you want.

The window is organized in three main areas. (See Figure 10-2.) In the left panel, you see the mail folders as well as the Outlook tools that take you to other views so that you can work with your Calendar or manage contacts or tasks. In the center is the Inbox column, where your new mail appears. The panel on the right is the reading pane, which shows you the contents of the selected message without you needing to open the message in the Web App.

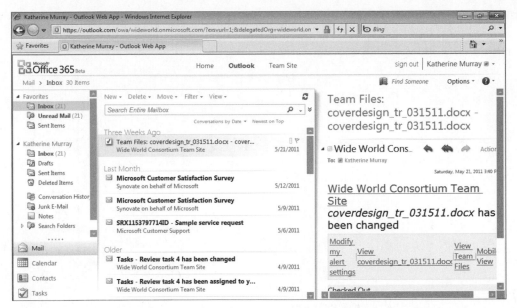

FIGURE 10-2 The Outlook Web App window gives you access to your messages as well as the other Outlook tools.

Checking, Reading, and Responding to Your Mail

Your mail arrives in your Inbox automatically, but you can also have Outlook search for new messages by clicking the Check Messages tool at the top of the Inbox pane in the center of the Outlook Web App window. (See Figure 10-3.)

Check Messages

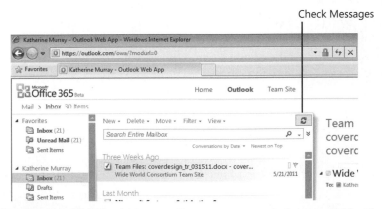

FIGURE 10-3 Click Check Messages if you want to see whether any additional messages are available for downloading.

The messages appear in the Inbox column in the center of the Outlook window. To read a specific message, you can click it in the Inbox column and it appears in the Reading pane on the right side of the Outlook window. (See Figure 10-4.)

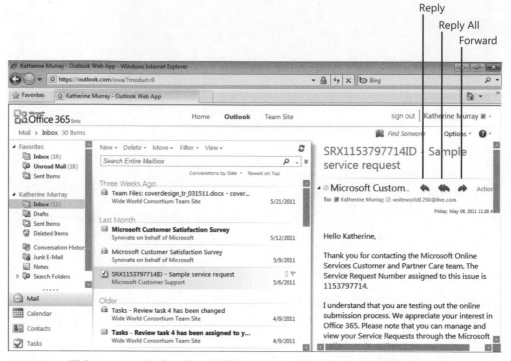

FIGURE 10-4 Click a message in the Inbox to display the message content in the Reading pane.

You can reply to a message by clicking Reply (or Reply All, if the message was sent to more than one recipient) or clicking Forward directly from the Reading Pane. The message opens in a message window so that you can type the content you want to send, add any other recipients you want to receive the message, and click Send.

Creating a New Message

Of course, every message you want to send to others won't necessarily be a response to a message someone else sends you. Sometimes you'll need to create a new message and send it directly to a recipient—or many recipients. Outlook Web App makes this very simple. Here are the steps:

1. In the Office 365 Home page, click Outlook.

2. In the Outlook Web App window, click the arrow to the right of New.

3. Click Message. (See Figure 10-5.)

FIGURE 10-5 Begin a new email message by clicking New and choosing Message.

4. The new message window appears, as you see in Figure 10-6. Type the email address in the To field, the message topic in the Subject line, and the content of the message you want to send.

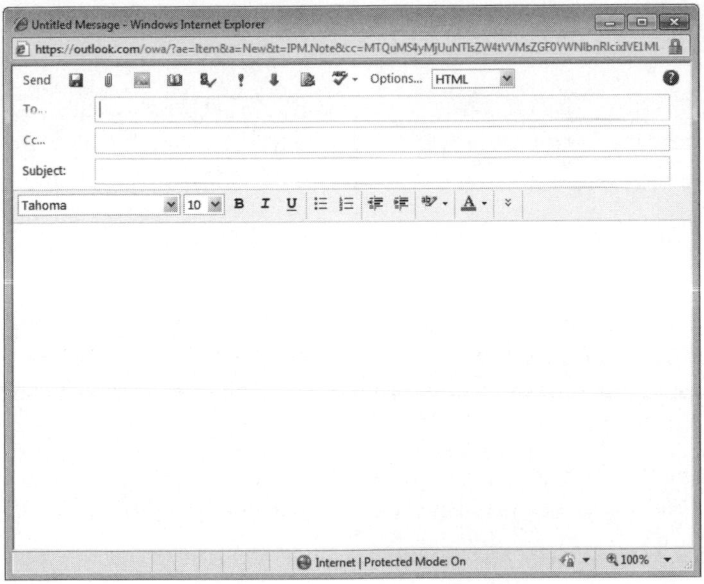

FIGURE 10-6 Enter the email addresses of recipients in the To line, add a subject, and type the body of your message.

5. Alternatively, you can click To and choose the name of the recipient in the Address Book window. (See Figure 10-7.)

6. Click To, and click OK.

7. When your message is complete, click Send to send it to the recipient.

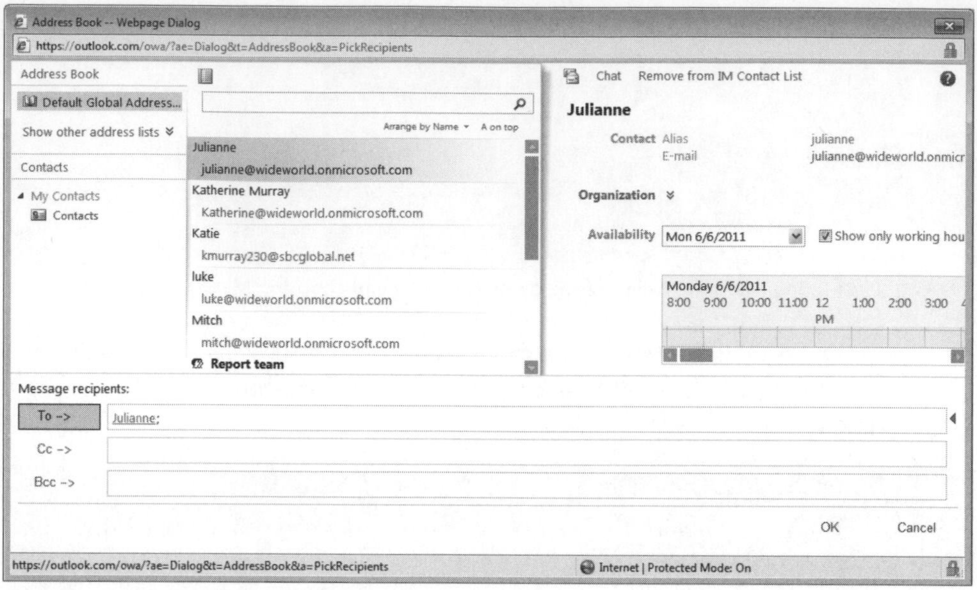

FIGURE 10-7 Click the name of the contact to whom you want to send the message, and click To.

Changing Mail Views

By default, the mail in your Inbox is displayed in Conversation view. This is a new view in Office 2010 that weaves together the various messages involved in a conversation so that you can read it as a complete entity. This helps you keep all discussion about specific topics together so that you can easily follow the thoughts of your group as ideas develop.

You can change the way the messages are organized in the Inbox, or turn off Conversation view, by clicking the Conversations By Date arrow at the top of the Inbox column. (See Figure 10-8.)

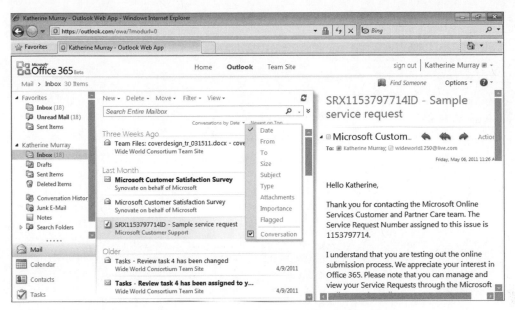

FIGURE 10-8 You can choose to organize messages in the Inbox in a variety of ways.

If you want to turn off Conversation view, click Conversation to clear the check box.

To rearrange the messages in the Inbox, click one of the other categories from the list. If you choose From, for example, the messages are arranged in alphabetical order according to the person who sent the message.

Choosing a New Theme

You can apply a new look to your mail activities by choosing a new theme for the Outlook Web App window. You'll find the controls you need in the Options tool in the upper right corner of the window. Click the Options arrow, and click one of the arrows in the Select A Theme gallery to browse the available themes. (See Figure 10-9.) Click the theme you want, and it is applied to the Outlook Web App window.

FIGURE 10-9 Page through the available themes by clicking the arrows in the Select A Theme gallery.

Note The theme change you make in Outlook Web App affects only the mail utility and doesn't apply to your other Office 365 programs.

Managing Your Mail

The more email you receive, the more important it becomes to have a smart way of organizing it so that you can find it easily later. You might want to organize your projects in different folders, for example, to group items together by the task they represent (such as Design, Writing, Production, and other such categories). You can then move messages into the appropriate folders, delete message you no longer need, search for specific messages, or filter the mail to see only select messages.

Creating New Mail Folders

You can easily create new folders and then move your messages to those folders while you're working in Outlook Web App. Begin by right-clicking the Inbox in the folders view on the left side of the Outlook Web App window. A content menu appears, as Figure 10-10 shows.

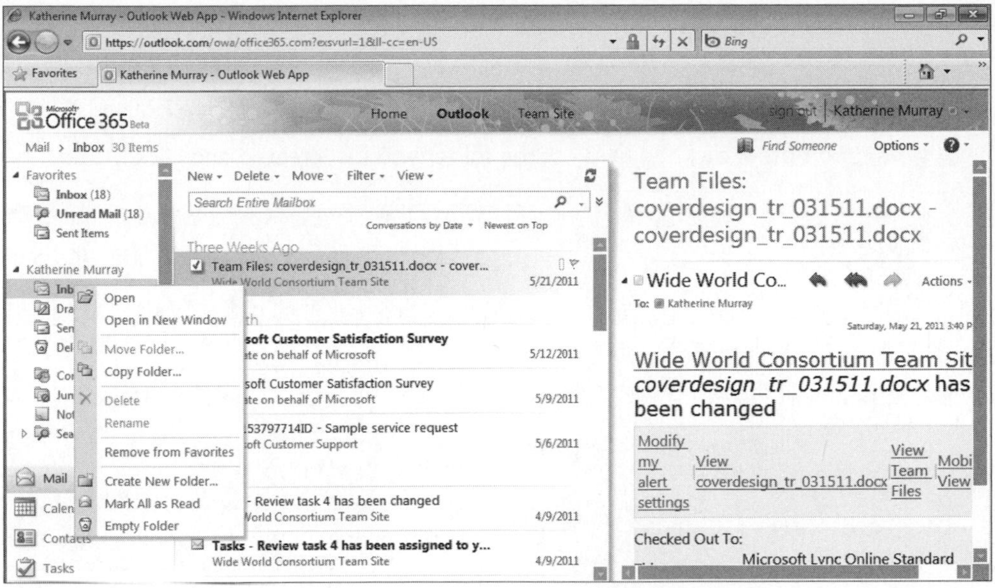

FIGURE 10-10 Right-click the Inbox folder to display a list of folder options.

If you click Create New Folder, Outlook adds a folder in the folder list. Type a name for the new folder. You can create additional folders—and subfolders within folders—to keep your messages organized.

> **Tip** Remember to weed out folders you no longer need periodically to keep the folder list manageable. To remove a folder, right-click it and choose Delete on the context menu.

Moving Messages

The easiest way to move a message to a folder is simply to drag it from your Inbox to the folder where you want it to be stored. When you release the mouse button, the message is filed in the folder. You can also use tools in Outlook Web App to move messages from place to place. This technique comes in handy especially when you need to move multiple messages at once. Here are the steps:

1. Hover the mouse pointer over the small mail icon at the far left of each message you want to select. The icon changes to a check box.

2.   Select the check box to specify which message you want to move.

3.   Repeat steps 1 and 2 to select all messages you want to move to the new folder.

4.   Click the arrow to the right of Move, and click Move To Folder. (See Figure 10-11.)

5.   When prompted, click the name of the folder you just created and click Move.

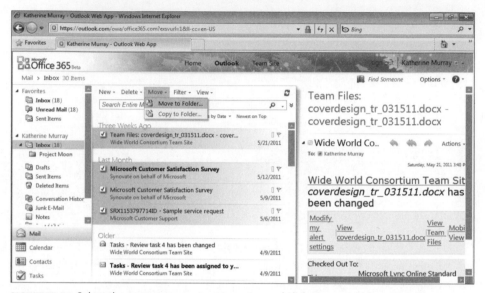

FIGURE 10-11 Select the messages you want to move, and click Move and Move To Folder.

Searching for Messages

When you are looking for a message from a particular person about a certain subject, you can locate the message quickly by searching for it. The search box appears at the top of the Inbox column in the center of the Outlook Web App window.

Simply click in the search box and type the word or phrase you want to find and click the Search tool. By default, Outlook searches the entire mailbox, but you can change where the search is performed by clicking the arrow on the right end of the search box and choosing another option. (See Figure 10-12.)

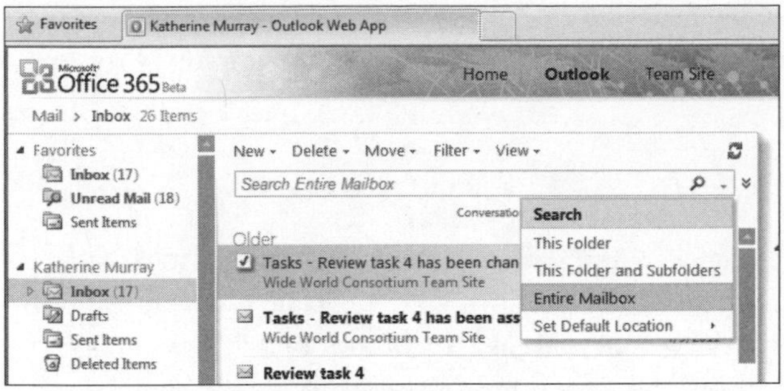

FIGURE 10-12 Choose where you want Outlook to search for the topic you specify.

> **Tip** ✓ Although Outlook searches the entire mailbox by default, you can change the default setting to another folder if you like. First click the folder you'd like to use as the default location, and then click the arrow on the right side of the search box and click Set Default Location. Choose either This Folder or This Folder And Subfolders to change the default.

Outlook displays any messages whose subject line or body text contains the word or phrase you entered. You can then review the messages to find the one you're looking for.

You can further narrow the search by using Outlook's advanced search features. Click the double arrow at the far right end of the search box area to display Advanced Search tools. A set of tools appears as shown in Figure 10-13 that enables you to change where the results are found, who sent or received the message, and how the message is categorized. Select the check box to the left of the item you want to change, and enter the new setting for the item in the fields on the right. Click Search again to initiative the advanced search, and the results appear in the Inbox panel.

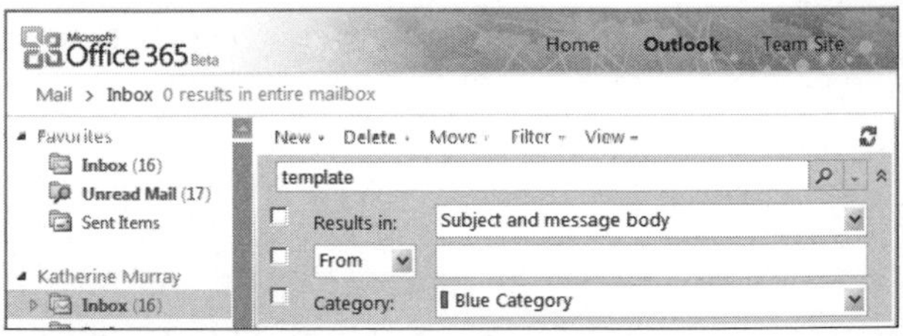

FIGURE 10-13 Enter advanced search settings to narrow your search.

When you're ready to clear the search results and return to the normal Outlook display, simply click the Cancel tool (the red X) to the right of the search box. Your Inbox returns to normal.

Filtering Your Mail

Depending on how much mail you receive—and from whom—you might also want to set up a filter on your email to display only the messages with a certain characteristic. For example, if you're trying to find a message that had an attachment of a PDF you need, but you can't remember who sent it, you can filter your messages to show only those that had attachments.

Here's how to do it. In Outlook Web App, click the Filter arrow in the tools above the Inbox column. A list of possible filters appears. (See Figure 10-14.) Click the one you want to apply to the messages in the current folder.

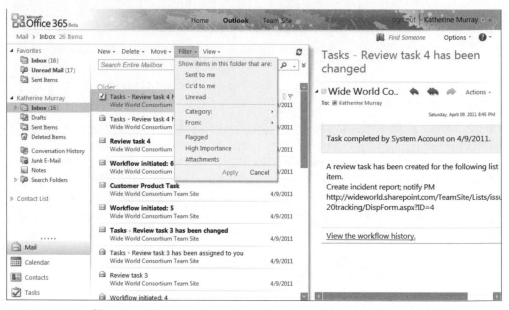

FIGURE 10-14 Use filters to cut down on the number of messages displayed in the current folder.

If you choose the Category filter or the From filter, you have an extra step with each one. When you click Category, a list of category styles appears so that you can choose the category you want to see. When you click From, a text box appears so that you can type the sender's email address and display only the messages that person sent.

The Inbox title shows the name of any title currently in use. Along the right side of the Inbox title row, you see a tool that enables you to add the current filter to your list of Favorites, or to clear the filter and return the display to normal. (See Figure 10-15.) Click Clear Filter to remove the filter and display all messages in the Inbox once again.

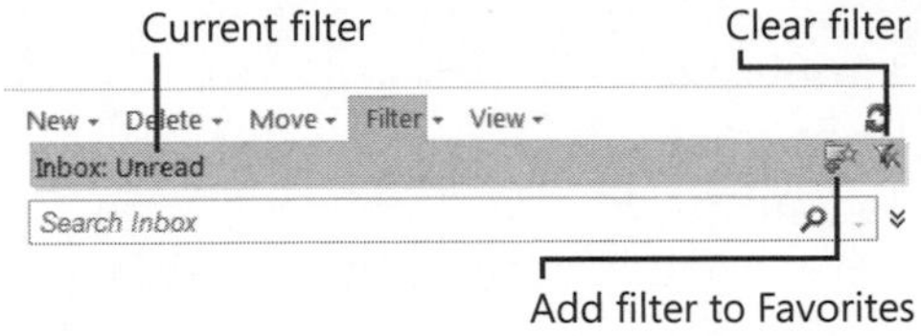

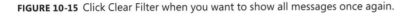

Current filter   Clear filter

Add filter to Favorites

FIGURE 10-15 Click Clear Filter when you want to show all messages once again.

CREATING AN INBOX RULE

Perhaps you'd like to automate your messages so that they're filed automatically into their respective folders. Suppose, for example, that your managers are required to file a manager's report each Friday, but you don't typically look at them until just before your online manager's meeting the following Wednesday. You can create an Inbox rule to move the messages to your Reports folder until you're ready to look at them. This clears up the space in your Inbox for the messages you really need to see.

To create an Inbox Rule, click Options in the upper right corner of the Outlook Web App window and choose Create An Inbox Rule. Click New, choose which messages you want to use and what you want done with them, and click Save. Now the rule will be applied to your incoming messages and the messages will be filed automatically.

Setting Mail Preferences

You can set your preferences for working with Outlook Web App by clicking Options in the upper left corner of the Outlook Web App window and choosing See All Options. In the Mail Options window, click Settings, as shown in Figure 10-16.

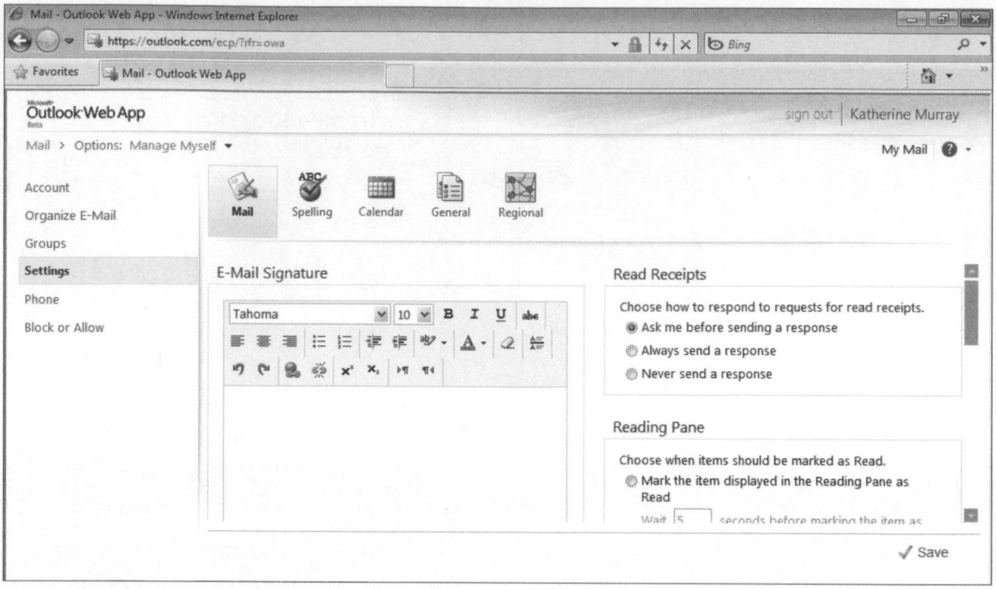

FIGURE 10-16 Click Settings to display and set your mail options.

On the Settings page, you can add an email signature, choose whether you want to receive receipts from the messages you send, whether you want messages you view in the Reading Pane to be marked as read, and how you want Outlook to handle display-ing conversations. You can also scroll down to the Message Options at the bottom of the page to tell Outlook whether you want to hear a sound when new messages arrive, see notifications about new communications, and empty the Deleted Items Folder when you exit Outlook. Click Save to save the new settings you have entered.

Creating a Meeting Request

Chances are good that as you're organizing and leading your group, you're going to send out a fair number of meeting requests. Luckily, the process is super simple:

1. In Outlook Web App, click New.

2. Click Meeting Request.

3. In the Appointment tab of the New Meeting window, enter the email addresses of the recipients you want to invite. (See Figure 10-17.)

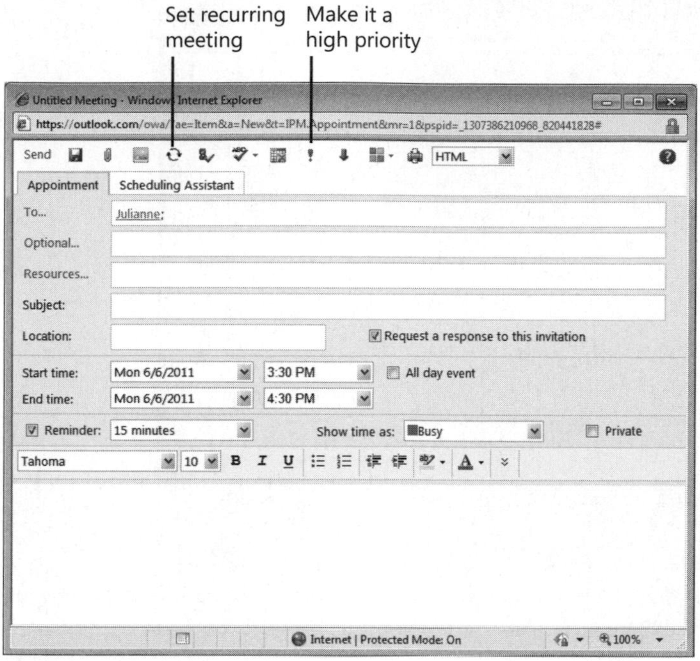

Set recurring   Make it a
meeting   high priority

FIGURE 10-17 Create the invitation to send to recipients.

4. Enter a Subject line and a location

5. Set the Start time and End time, and type the body of the invitation.

6. Click the Scheduling Assistant to schedule your meeting and set resources. (See Figure 10-18.)

7. Click Send to send the invitation.

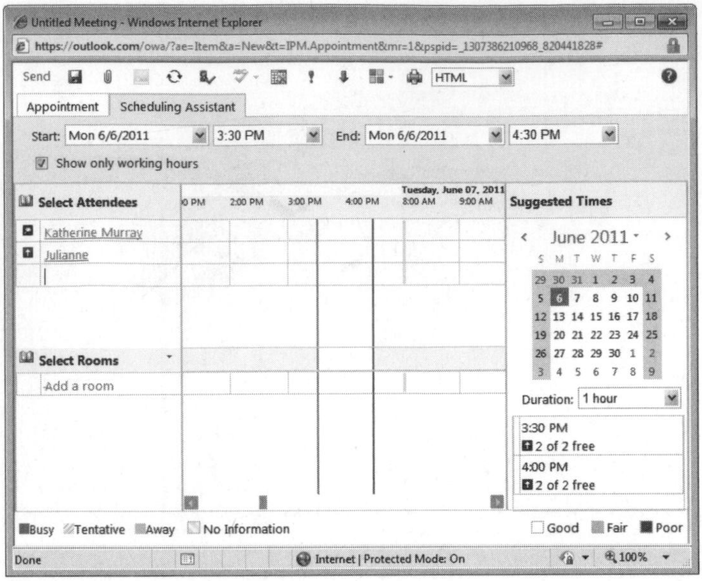

FIGURE 10-18 Use the Scheduling Assistant to check recipients' schedules and arrange for your meeting space if needed.

As you add recipients to the attendee list in the meeting invitation, the Scheduling Assistant will look up the schedule of each participant and let you know if the time is free for each person. If you find a schedule conflict, you can change the time on the invitation and try again.

Working with Your Calendar

One of the great things about Outlook Web App is that all the features are interrelated and you can easily move from your Inbox to your Calendar to your Task list with just a click of the mouse. When you want to view your calendar in Office 365, click Outlook to get to Outlook Web App, and then click Calendar in the bottom left area of the window.

The Calendar window likely looks familiar if you have used any of Microsoft's calendar tools available online or you've used Microsoft Outlook before. (See Figure 10-19.) In the upper left corner, you see a mini-calendar that shows you the current month at a glance. In the center of the window, you see today's schedule by default. On the right side of the window, you see details about the selected appointment.

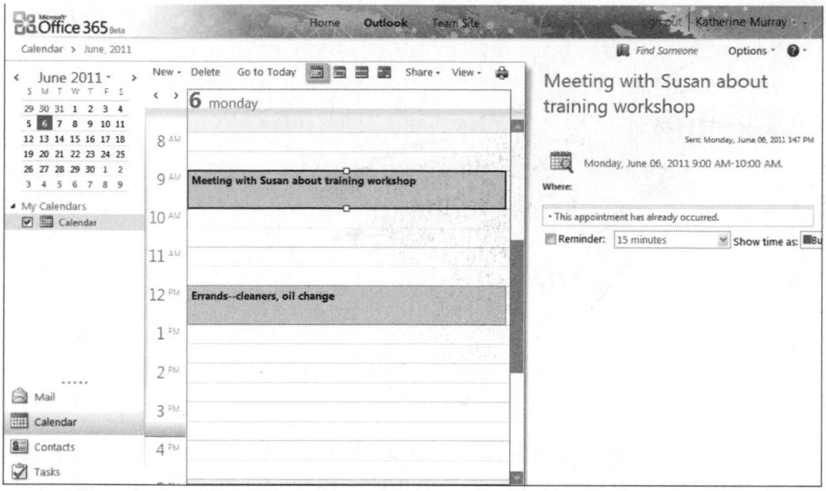

FIGURE 10-19 The Calendar in Outlook Web App enables you to set, share, and modify appointments.

Adding an Appointment

When you want to add a new appointment to your calendar, display the date on which the appointment will occur by clicking the date in the calendar in the upper left corner of the screen.

In the schedule in the center of the window, scroll to the time at which the appointment will begin and double-click the timeslot. The New Appointment window opens as shown in Figure 10-20.

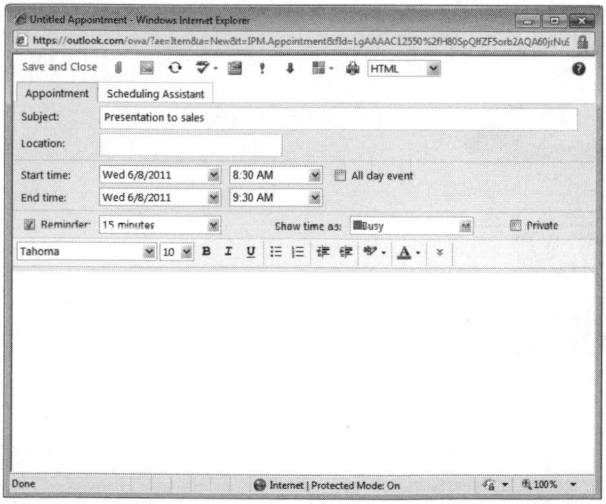

FIGURE 10-20 You can easily create a new appointment by double-clicking the time slot on the calendar.

Enter information about the appointment, including the End time, the location, and any additional notes you want to include about resources you need, people you want to include, or files you want to share. Click the Scheduling Assistant to check the schedules of others in your group and create and send an invitation for others you want to attend.

When you're finished, click Save and Close, and the appointment is added to your calendar.

Changing Your Calendar View

Depending on when you want to schedule your appointment—and how you like to view the events you've arranged for the near future—you might want to change the daily view to Work Week view, Weekly view, or Monthly view.

You'll find the tools you need to change the calendar view in the top of the Schedule panel in the center of the Calendar view. (See Figure 10-21.) To change to a different view, simply click the icon of the view you'd like to see.

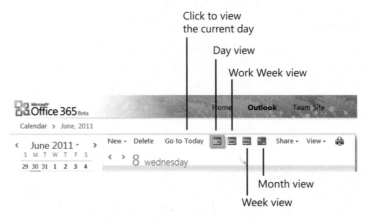

FIGURE 10-21 Click the View icon that reflects the way in which you want to view your calendar.

> **Tip** ✓
>
> You can create a new appointment in any Calendar view. Simply double-click the date on the calendar and a new appointment window will open so that you can enter the details.

Sharing Your Calendar

When you're working in a team and creating new appointments and meeting requests that will include other members of your group, sharing your calendar is a good idea. You can easily share your Calendar in Outlook Web App by clicking Share and choosing Share This Calendar. (See Figure 10-22.)

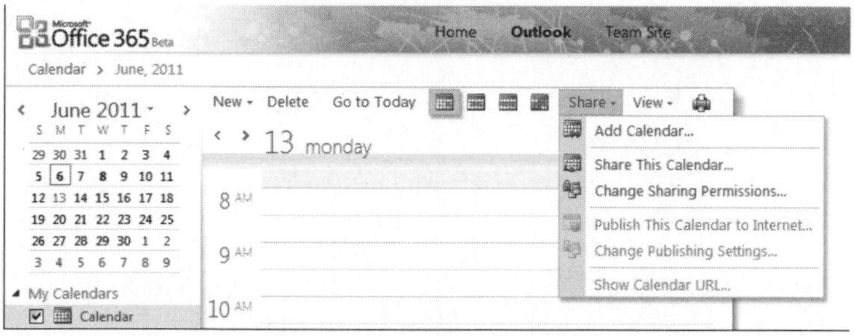

FIGURE 10-22 Click the Share tool and choose Share This Calendar to begin sharing your Outlook calendar with your team.

The Sharing Invitation window appears so that you can send the message to others on your team with whom you want to share your calendar. (See Figure 10-23.) You can type the email addresses of your teammates in the To line, or click To and select your colleagues from the Address Book. In the Share area, click the way in which you'd like to share your information:

- **Free/busy information** enables those you invite to see your calendar in terms of when you are free and when you are busy.

- **Free/busy information including subject and location** gives others more information about your appointments, including where you'll be and what the topic of the meeting is about.

- **All information** enables others to see all details you've entered about the upcoming appointment.

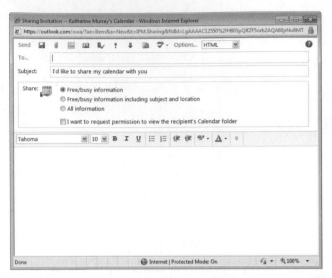

FIGURE 10-23 Send a sharing invitation to others on your team with whom you want to share your calendar.

If you want to ask whether you can have sharing access to your teammates' calendars, select the I Want To Request Permission To View The Recipient's Calendar Folder check box. Type any message you want to include in the body of the invitation, and click Send.

When the recipient receives the invitation, she will be able to add your calendar by clicking Add This Calendar, and if she wants to share her own calendar, she can do so by clicking the Share My Calendar link. (See Figure 10-24.)

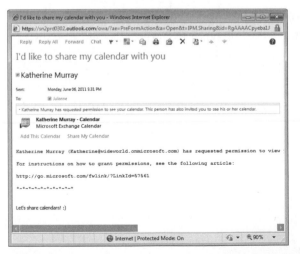

FIGURE 10-24 The recipient of the sharing invitation can click Add This Calendar to share your calendar and Share My Calendar if she wants to return the favor.

After your calendars are shared, you will be able to view the calendars of others alongside your own, which will help the team find times when everyone can meet. To display another person's shared calendar, simply select the check box in the People's Calendars area of Calendar view. (See Figure 10-25.) You can hide the shared calendars again by simply clicking the check box again to remove the check mark.

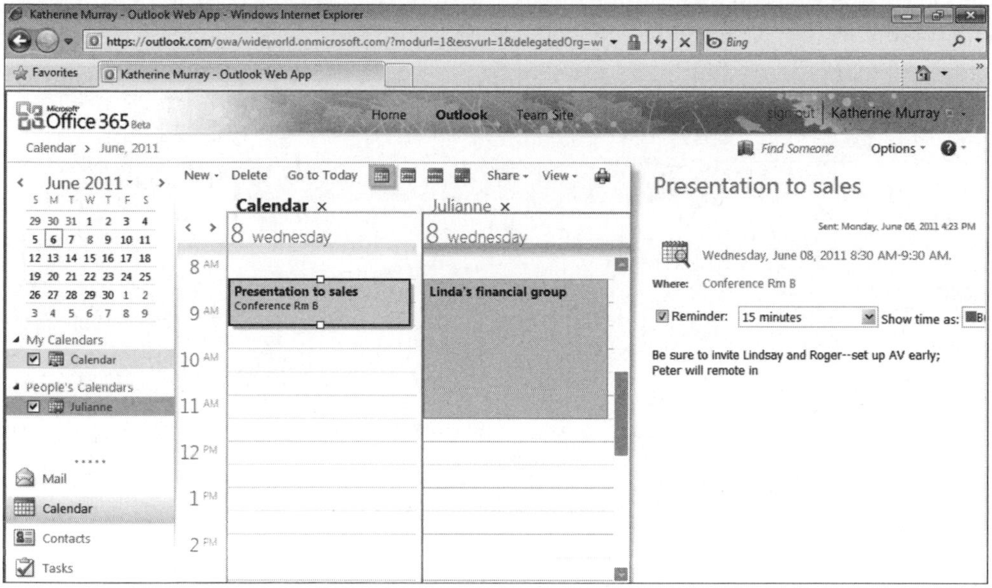

FIGURE 10-25 You can view calendars side by side after calendars are shared.

> **Tip** ✓ You can close shared calendars easily by clicking the Close tool at the top of the calendar column in the center column of the Calendar window.

> **Tip** ✓ If you need space to view a number of shared calendars, you can hide the Reading Pane by clicking View at the top of the Calendar window and choosing Off in the Reading Pane list.

Importing and Managing Your Contacts

You can easily add, manage, organize, and create subgroups of your contacts by working in the Contacts area of Outlook Web App. When you first click Contacts in the lower left corner of the Outlook Web App window, you see a list of all contacts displayed in the center of the screen. (See Figure 10-26.) The right-most panel shows you the details related to the contact selected in the contact list.

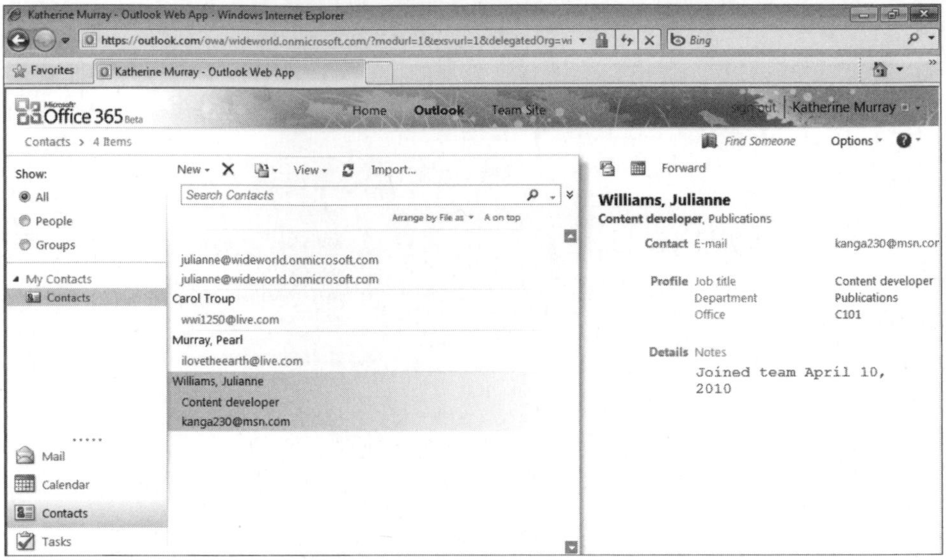

FIGURE 10-26 Click Contacts to display the Outlook Web App contact manager.

Adding New Contacts

The easiest way to add a new contact in Outlook Web App is to click New at the top of the Contacts list and choose Contact. (See Figure 10-27.)

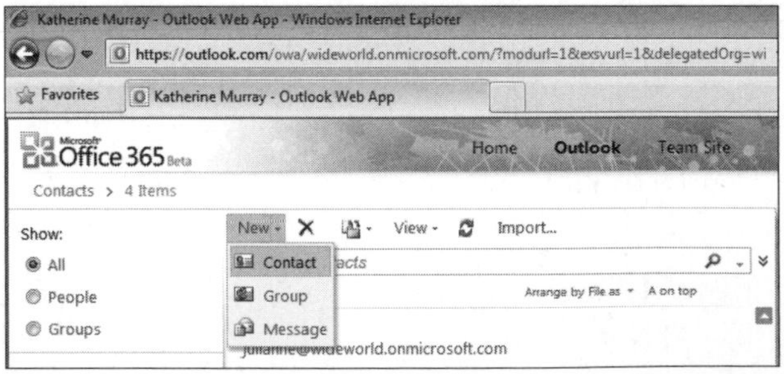

FIGURE 10-27 Add a new contact by clicking New and choosing Contact.

Outlook opens a new contact window so that you can fill in all the information you have for the new contact. Scroll down the page to find additional fields, or click the various category names (Profile, Contact, Addresses, and Details) to move to different areas of the form. (See Figure 10-28.)

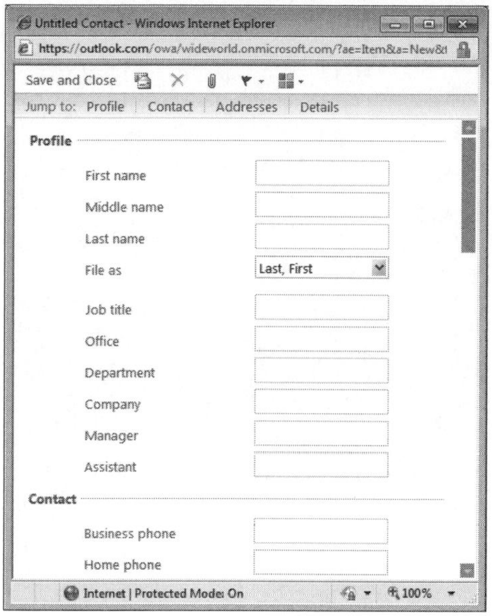

FIGURE 10-28 Enter information about your new contact as completely as you can.

> **Note** You don't need to enter information in all the fields on the new contact form. You can simply enter a name and an email address for starters, if that's all you have. At a later point, you can open the contact window (by double-clicking the contact name in the Contacts window) and add to the information you originally entered or change that information.

Importing Contacts

Outlook Web App includes a tool that makes it simple to add whole contact lists if you like, which makes it convenient to add a company list, a department roster, or a mailing list to your contacts online.

To import contacts into Outlook Web App, follow these steps:

1.   Click Import in Contacts view.

2.   In the Import Contacts window, click Browse. (See Figure 10-29.)

3. Navigate to the folder containing the data file you want to import, and click Open.

4. Click Next.

5. In the Congratulations page, click Finish.

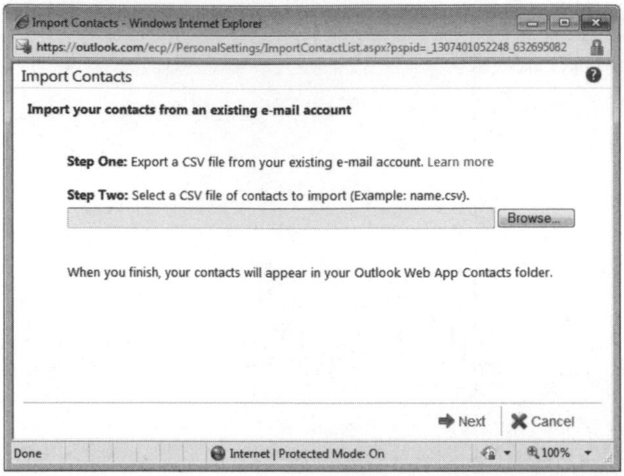

FIGURE 10-29 Click Browse to navigate to the CSV file you want to import.

Searching for a Contact

Now that you have dozens of contacts in your Contacts list, you need an easy way of finding just the person you need at any specific time. To find a contact in Outlook Web App, click in the Search box and type the name of the person you want to find. Click the Search tool, and Outlook begins searching. After a few seconds (depending on the size of your contacts list), any results of the search are shown in the contact list. (See Figure 10-30.) You can clear the contact results list and return to the normal contacts display by clicking the close box at the right end of the search box.

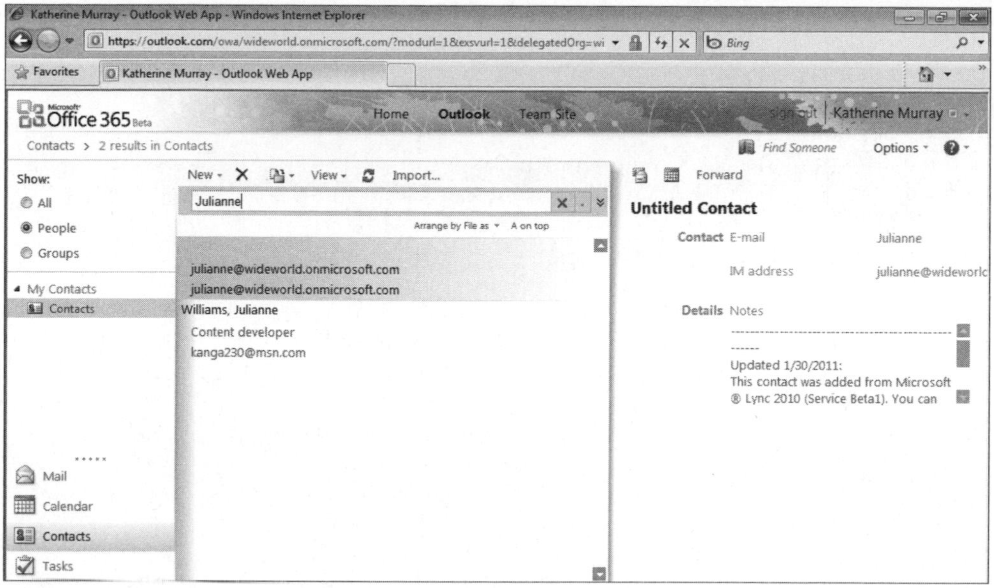

FIGURE 10-30 Outlook makes it easy for you to locate a specific contact no matter how long your list might be.

Adding and Completing Tasks

The final tool in Outlook Web App to explore in this chapter is one you can use to create and manage tasks that relate to your Office 365 projects. Click the Tasks tool in the lower left corner of the Outlook window. (See Figure 10-31.) You can create a new task two different ways:

- Click New, and click Task to display the New Task window.

- Click in the Type A New Task box, and enter the information—text and date—that you want to include.

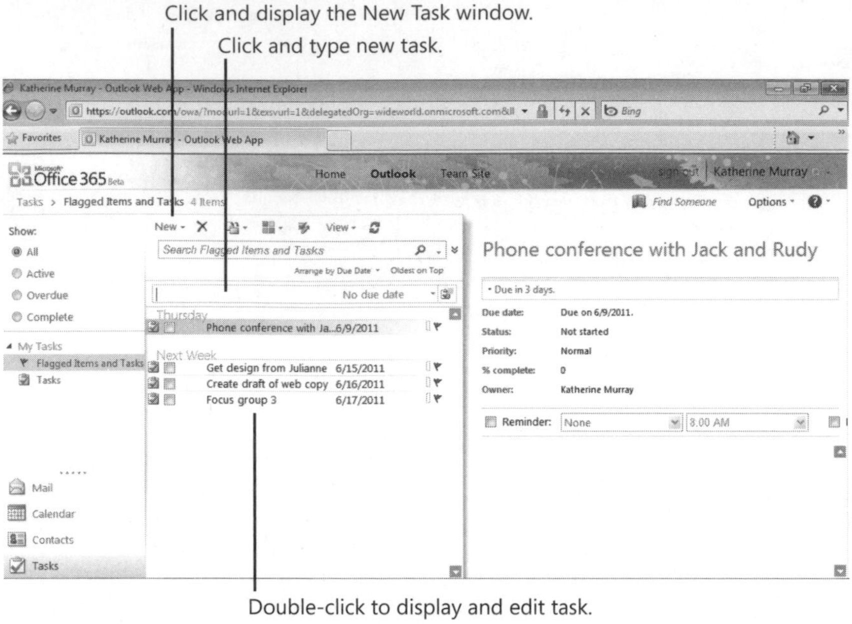

Click and display the New Task window.

Click and type new task.

Double-click to display and edit task.

FIGURE 10-31 Options for adding new tasks or making changes to existing ones.

After you add the task, you can easily sort, categorize, edit, or delete tasks. You can mark a task as complete by selecting the task's check box and then clicking Mark Complete in the tools row just above the search box. Outlook shows the task as completed and adds strikethrough to the text of the task. The icon on the far right of the tasks now shows a checkmark, indicating that the task has been completed.

> **Tip** ✓ In Tasks view, the details shown for the selected task in the Reading Pane are actually editable, which means that you can update some of the data items without opening the task. To make text changes, you'll still need to open the task by double-clicking it.

What's Next

In this chapter, you found out how to use Outlook Web App to work with email, manage your messages, and set email preferences. You also learned how to work with calendars and tasks. In the next chapter, you learn how to use Microsoft Lync to stay in touch with your team in real time.

CHAPTER 11

Talking It Over with Microsoft Lync

IMAGINE WORK with no limits. You can have a great two-day training without flying your team to a central location. You can share the latest reports without sending them through the mail, show images from submitted portfolios, or walk through the sales projections by viewing them on a whiteboard.

What's more, you can show everybody—right now, in real time— what you're working with on your desktop. You can tweak a presentation together. You can talk things through. Good ideas happen that way.

And when your work is done, you can simply close the conversation and go back to what you were doing before the meeting began. No fuss, no bother.

And that's just a part of what Microsoft Lync 2010 can do for you and your team.

This chapter introduces you to Microsoft Lync 2010, the instant messaging and online meeting tool that is part of Office 365. You'll find out how to set up Lync to work the way you want it to, add contacts, have instant messaging conversations and phone calls, add video, share files, and much more.

WHERE DID LYNC COME FROM?

Microsoft Lync was formerly called Microsoft Office Communicator 2007 R2, and it was previously available only for corporate clients as part of the enterprise packaging for Office Professional Plus 2010. With Office 365, Microsoft Lync is available for both Small Business and Enterprise customers. Microsoft Lync enables Office 365 users to

- See the online status of other team members.
- Connect with colleagues through instant messaging.
- Make audio or video calls.
- Host online meetings.
- Share and transfer files.
- Record your audio and video calls.
- Set up dial-in conferencing.
- Share your desktop.
- Use a whiteboard.
- Save notes to your OneNote notebook.

Introducing Microsoft Lync

In Chapter 2, "Getting Started with Office 365," you downloaded and installed Microsoft Lync. To start Microsoft Lync (if it doesn't start automatically when you log on to your computer), click the Windows 7 Start button and click All Programs. Navigate to the Microsoft Lync folder, and click it; then click the Microsoft Lync 2010 program icon.

Signing In to Lync

The Microsoft Lync Sign In window appears so that you can enter your Office 365 user ID and password. The first time you sign in, the Microsoft Lync Sign In window asks you to enter your user name and password. (See Figure 11-1.) You can select the Save My Password check box to have Lync remember your password on your current computer.

FIGURE 11-1 Enter your Office 365 user name and password, and click Sign In.

To the right of the Sign In As selector, you'll see a small green box. This is the *presence indicator*, and it lets others on your team know whether you are available for online contact. You can choose from a number of presence settings by clicking the arrow to the right of the indicator, which causes the following list to appear:

After you make your selection, click Sign In to launch Lync 2010. The program contacts the server and authenticates your account, and then the Microsoft Lync 2010 window appears.

Getting Started with Lync

The Lync 2010 window pops up on your desktop, taking up only a portion of your screen. This design makes it easy for you to have other windows open on-screen while you're communicating with your colleagues in Lync. (See Figure 11-2.) You can do a number of things right away in Lync (and you'll learn more about these tasks in the following sections):

- Add a personal note to tell others what you're doing.

- Change your profile picture.

- Search for contacts you want to add to Lync.

- Launch a phone call, instant messaging (IM) session, video chat, or meeting.

- Set your online status and presence indicator.

- Enter your location.

FIGURE 11-2 The Lync window offers various tools for interacting with your team in real time.

Entering a Personal Note

You can click in the What's Happening Today? area at the top of the Lync window and type a phrase about what you're working on, how your day is going, or just about anything else that strikes your fancy. The personal note in Lync is like a status update in Facebook; it lets your teammates keep up with what's going on in your world.

Simply click in the box and type the phrase you want to share; then press Enter. When your colleagues view your contact info in Lync on their own computers, they will see your note beside your photo. They can also get an update on your added notes by clicking the Activity Feed tool at the top of the contacts list in the Lync window. You can update your personal note as many times as you like throughout the day.

> **Tip** ✓ You can also use your personal note to send quick information to your team. For example, posting "Running late—let's meet at 2:15!" lets others know you need a few more minutes before the staff meeting. Or "Don't forget to send in your expense reports!" reminds others that they need to submit their reports before your meeting begins.

Setting Your Location

Setting your location might not seem like that big a deal if your entire team works in the same state, but when you're sharing files and tasks with people all over the world, knowing the time difference of each person's location helps you coordinate schedules and arrange meetings when it's convenient for everyone.

Click Set Your Location and a text box appears so that you can type your location. You can then click the Location arrow to see additional options, which enable you to turn off the display of your location and remove custom locations. (See Figure 11-3.)

FIGURE 11-3 Click and type your location in the Location field; then click the arrow to change Location options.

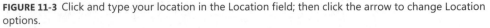

> **Note** If you're an administrator, you can set Location information by editing the settings available for each information user. Click Admin and then choose Users. Click the name of the user whose account you want to change, and then click Settings. Click the arrow in the Set User Location setting, and click the location you want to assign to the user.

Setting Up Sound and Voice

Lync includes a friendly setup wizard that walks you through the process of entering your information and setting up your version of Lync so that you can speak, hear, and see others in your online meetings and conversations. To launch the wizard, click the Options button in the upper right corner of the Lync window, click File, click Help, and follow the prompts on the screen until you get to the Microsoft Lync 2010 welcome page to launch the wizard. (See Figure 11-4.)

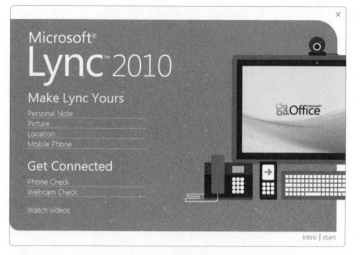

FIGURE 11-4 Clicking Start on this page launches the Welcome To Lync Wizard, which walks you through the process of setting up your computer for online meetings.

Click Start in the lower right corner to begin the wizard. The utility explains the personal note, picture, and location area, and it gives you the chance to enter your mobile phone number so that you can get Lync calls on your phone. Click in the mobile phone box, and type your number; then click outside the box to close it.

If you haven't already done so, plug in your headset or connect your speakers and microphone. Then click Get Connected, and Lync searches for the audio capability on your system. When Lync finds your audio devices, you will see the message, "You can use your computer's mic and speakers for calls."

If you have a webcam connected to your computer, you can make sure it is working properly with Lync by clicking Webcam Check. The wizard checks your webcam to make sure it's working properly; you'll be able to see the live video in the display your screen. Click Next, and then click Exit to close the wizard and return to the Lync window.

CHOOSING ADVANCED AUDIO SETTINGS

There's another way you can fine-tune your audio settings for Lync. Click the Options button in the upper right corner of the Lync window, and click Tools and then Options. In the Lync Options dialog box, click Audio Device.

On this screen, you can choose the device you want to use for calls, and choose the devices and sound levels you prefer for your speakers, microphone, and ringer.

Click your choices, and then click OK to save your settings.

> **Tip** ✓ You can use Lync without audio or video capability, but being able to have real-time conversations—and see others via webcam—can enhance your communications and help your team work productively together.

Working with Contacts in Lync

After you finish entering your information and checking audio and video connections, your next step is to add contacts to Lync. You might have already added user accounts to Office 365, so adding those contacts to Lync is as simple as searching for the contact names you want to add and pinning them to your contacts list. Here are the steps:

1. Sign in to Lync if you're not logged in automatically.

2. In the Microsoft Lync window, click in the Search box.

3. Type the email address of the contact you want to add, and press Enter.

4. Click the Add To Contacts button. (See Figure 11-5.)

5. Click Pin To Frequent Contacts or All Contacts to choose where the contact will be added.

FIGURE 11-5 When you type the email address of the contact, Lync searches for the contact name and adds it to the contact list.

SO HOW DO EXTERNAL COMMUNICATIONS WORK?

By default, Lync is set up to allow external communications, which means that you and your teammates will be able to use Lync to communicate with people outside your Office 365 team.

For using public instant messaging with people outside of your Office 365 approved contacts, however, Windows Live Messenger is the software that is used. You can also set up audio and video calls with external contacts, but again, Windows Live Messenger supports the calls. Audio and video conferences and desktop sharing are not available when you're working with external contacts.

Creating a Contact Group

You can create a group of contacts if you want to organize your team for a specific project or task; or you might group all users who are in a certain location or working with a particular program. After you create a group, you can communicate with all members of that group at once, for example, by sending a group email to the whole team about an upcoming meeting or event. You can create a new contact group when you add a contact to Lync, or you can create a group and then add contacts to it as you go along. To create a group with your existing users, follow these steps:

1. Click in the search box, and enter the email address of the user you want to add.

2. Click the Add To Contacts button, and click Add To New Group.

   Lync creates a new group and selects the group name. The new user is displayed in the group. (See Figure 11-6.)

3. Type the name you want to use for the new group, and press Enter.

FIGURE 11-6 Click Add To New Group to create a new contact group in the Lync window.

To create a new group that you will add contacts to later, right-click Frequent Contacts and select Create New Group. Enter a name for the new group, and press Enter. You can then drag and drop contacts into the new group when you're ready to add members to it.

You can include contacts in more than one group if you like, and you can also rearrange the groups in the Lync window by simply dragging and dropping a selected group to a new position in the list.

Accepting a Contact Request

When you add a new contact to your list, a contact request is sent to the person you're adding. Similarly, when others add you to *their* contact list, you receive a message asking your permission to be added to their list. The Lync message box alerting you to this appears on your desktop if you are online; if you're not using Lync when someone adds you to her list, the message will pop up the next time you log in. (See Figure 11-7.)

FIGURE 11-7 When another person adds you to her Contacts list, you receive a notification you can use to add that person to your list as well.

If you want to add the person to your own Contacts list, click the Add To This Contact Group check box and click the All Contacts arrow on the right side of the message box. Choose the group to which you want to assign the new contact. Additionally, you can choose the privacy relationship you want to apply to this contact by clicking the arrow to the right of Colleagues and choosing the level you want to set for that person. (Read on for more about setting privacy relationships in Lync.)

Setting Privacy Levels for Contact Relationships

No matter how many contacts you add to Lync, you can tailor each contact so that it allows others to see just the amount of information you want them to see. Lync allows you to choose from among five different privacy settings:

- **Friends And Family** This setting gives others the most information about you, enabling them to see all your contact information and viewing any items you include in your profile (such as picture, email address, and more). Friends and family cannot see your meeting details, however.

- **Workgroup** This setting is designed for the team you work with on a regular basis. Contacts you assign this privacy setting to can see all your contact information but won't be able to view your Home and Other phone numbers. This setting also enables others to contact you even if you have your Lync status set to Do Not Disturb.

- **Colleagues** Contacts assigned these privacy settings can see all your contact information but cannot view your Home, Other, and Mobile phone numbers. Additionally, contacts designated as Colleagues will not be able to view your meeting details.

- **External Contacts** This setting shows others only your name, title, email address, company, and picture.

- **Blocks Contacts** Contacts with this setting can see only your presence in Lync—your name and email address—but they will be unable to contact you through Lync. To communicate with you, people you designate as Blocked Contacts will need to send you an email message.

By default, Lync sets up all new contacts with the Colleagues setting. As you saw in the previous section, when someone adds you to his or her Contacts list, you receive a notification, and you can set the privacy level for your relationship when you add that person to your own Contacts list.

You can also change the privacy setting for any of your contacts. In the Lync window, right-click the contact you want to change and point to Change Privacy Relationship. A list of available privacy settings appears, and the current level is highlighted. (See Figure 11-8.) Simply click the new level you want to apply or, if you want to return the contact to the Lync default settings, click Auto-Assign Relationship.

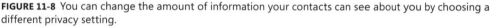

FIGURE 11-8 You can change the amount of information your contacts can see about you by choosing a different privacy setting.

Tagging Contacts

When you're working closely with others—especially if you're working at a distance from them—it can sometimes be helpful to know when people are available online and when they're not. Suppose you're working on finalizing a contract, but you really need the input of a manager who is working overseas. You can tag his contact to let Lync know you want to be alerted when he logs into Lync the next time so that you can ask him questions as you finalize your contract. Here's how to do that:

1. In the Lync window, right-click the contact you want to change.

2. Click Tag For Status Change Alerts. (See Figure 11-9.)

FIGURE 11-9 You can tag individual contacts so that you are notified when their online status changes.

The next time the contact signs in to Lync, an alert will appear on your desktop, letting you know the contact is now available online. (See Figure 11-10.) Similarly, when the contact's status changes—to Away, Busy, or any of the other status settings—an alert will let you know.

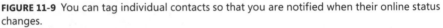

FIGURE 11-10 After you tag a contact so that you receive alerts, Lync lets you know when the contact's status changes.

Tip	If the number of alerts you receive about status changes gets annoying, you can simply cancel the alerts by clicking Untag. If you simply want to close the alert box without contacting the person (it will disappear on its own after a few seconds), you can click Ignore to close the message box.

Changing Contact Views

By default, your contacts in the Lync window appear organized by group, but as you can see from the selections at the top of the list, you can change the view to display your contacts arranged by online status or by relationship. The Display Options on the right side of the views row gives you options for changing the way contact information is organized in the current view. (See Figure 11-11.)

Contacts are organized by the groups they are assigned to.

Contacts are displayed according to their online status.

Contacts are grouped by the privacy levels you have assigned to them.

Click to choose display options

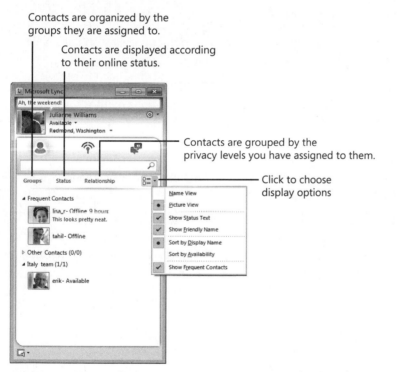

FIGURE 11-11 You can display your contacts in different ways by clicking the view tool you want to use and choosing View Options.

To change the way your contacts appear in the list, click the view you want to use (Groups, Status, or Relationship.) The list is immediately rearranged according to your selection. You can further tailor the information shown for your contacts by clicking the Display Options tool and clicking the items in the list you want to display. To remove any of the existing items, simply click it. The highlight is removed from the item, and that piece of information is hidden from view.

Working with Presence and Contact Cards

Your presence will be visible to all others on your team—and the presence of others will be visible to you. Others will also be able to see your presence indicator in Outlook Web App and when you're working collaboratively on documents in Microsoft Word, PowerPoint, and Excel. You can change your presence at any point in Office 365 where you can see the presence indicator.

So what do the colors mean? Here's a quick list:

 A **green** presence indicator means that the contact is online and available, and all contact methods through Lync are available to you.

 A **yellow** presence indicator means that the person is away from his desk or unavailable at the moment. Limited communications methods will be available through Lync.

 A **red** presence indicator means that the person is online but is currently unavailable, either because she is busy or has set Do Not Disturb as the selected status. Limited communication options will be available to you when you see this presence indicator.

The presence indicator appears to the left of the profile picture in your contacts list, which enables you to see at a glance the online status of your contact. You can click the contact to display the person's contact card. (See Figure 11-12.) This card shows the various communications methods you can use to be in touch with the person.

> **Note** The methods of contacting someone that are available to you depend on the person's status. If a person's status is Offline, you cannot send her an instant message, but you can send an email message if you like.

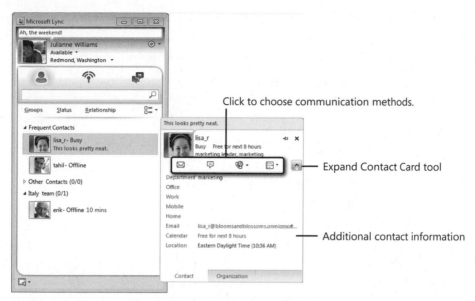

FIGURE 11-12 Click the contact to display the contact card and choose a way to communicate.

Instant Messaging with Your Team

There's a great kind of freedom inherent in instant messaging. You have a question—ask it! Are you wondering how things are going on the new design? Send your team an IM and find out.

Of course, for those of us who *love* to be in touch, instant messaging can be a bit addictive—and annoying to those who don't want to be interrupted 20 times a day. (Hence, the need for the Away or Busy statuses in Lync.)

When you want to instant message one or many people on your team, you begin in the Lync window and follow these steps:

1. Click the contact you want to send an instant message to. The person's contact card appears.

2. Click the instant message icon.

3. In the instant message window, type your message in the lower text box.

4. You can change the format, write the message as ink (if you have a drawing tablet or other pen device), and click Send The Message. (See Figure 11-13.)

5. When your contact responds, the response appears in the text box at the top of the message window. You can reply by repeating steps 3 and 4 as often as needed.

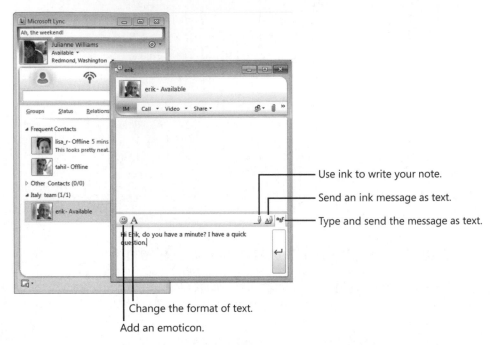

Use ink to write your note.

Send an ink message as text.

Type and send the message as text.

Change the format of text.

Add an emoticon.

FIGURE 11-13 Create and format the instant message in the message window.

Tip

If you want to invite others into your conversation, click People Options in the top right corner of the message window and click Invite By Name Or Phone Number. Choose the other contacts you want to invite from the list that appears, and click OK. An invitation is sent to the participants you selected.

Tip

If you add others to your IM session, you can keep track of who is involved in the conversation by clicking People Options and choosing Show Participant List. This displays all participants at the top of the message window so that you know who is participating.

KEEPING A TRANSCRIPT OF YOUR CONVERSATION—OR NOT

By default, Lync keeps a transcript of your conversations so that the content of your conversations is always available to you for other meetings, projects, or conversations.

Lync stores your instant message conversations in the Conversation History folder that is actually available in Outlook Web App. To view past conversations, display Outlook (by clicking Inbox on the Office 365 Home page) and click the Conversation History folder in the folder list on the left side of the window. All your Lync communications that have been tracked appear in this view, and you can read through conversations to find what you need.

If you want to change the way Lync tracks your conversations—or perhaps turn off the logging of Lync exchanges—display the Lync Options dialog box by clicking Options in the top right of the Lync window, pointing to Tools, and clicking Options. Change the Save Instant Message Conversations In My Email Conversation History Folder option by clearing the check box. Similarly, you can stop keeping track of calls in the same folder by clearing the Save Call Logs In My Email Conversation History Folder check box.

Making a Call with Lync

When you want to call a contact directly through Lync, you can simply click the contact in your Lync window. The Call button appears. Click it, and then click in the Subject box and type the topic of your call. (See Figure 11-14.) When you click Lync Call, Lync dials the contact's listed phone number.

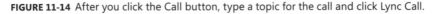

FIGURE 11-14 After you click the Call button, type a topic for the call and click Lync Call.

An alert message appears on the other person's desktop, and the computer "rings" so that the person can hear the incoming call. When the contact clicks the message box, he answers the call. During a call, any participant can make the following adjustments while the conversation is going on, as you see in Figure 11-15:

- **Mute Microphone** Turns off your microphone so that others can't hear you talk

- **Adjust Volume Or Mute Speakers** Changes the volume of the sound you hear

- **Display Dial Pad** Shows a number pad so that you can dial a phone number

- **Network Connectivity** Shows you how strong your connection is

- **Hold** Places the call on hold

- **Hang up** Ends the call

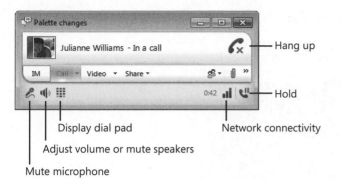

Hang up

Hold

Network connectivity

Display dial pad

Adjust volume or mute speakers

Mute microphone

FIGURE 11-15 You can change settings while you talk if you want to adjust sound levels or look something up.

> **Note**
>
> While you are on a call, your Lync status lets others know that you're busy and some communication methods are blocked. When you hang up, your status changes back to available automatically and other contacts will be able to contact you normally.

Launching a Video Call

If both you and your contact have webcams, you can also have a video call so that you can each see each other while you talk.

When you set up Lync, you went through the process of preparing your webcam, so the camera is ready to go whenever you are. When you want to make a video call, follow these steps:

1. Click the contact you want to talk to on your video call.

2. Open the instant messaging window, and send the contact a note if you'd like; then click Video and click Start Video Call.

3. A call is made to your contact. He clicks the message box and then clicks Accept Video Call.

4. The video appears in the top portion of the message window, and you can continue sending instant messages in the bottom portion of the window if you like. (See Figure 11-16.)

5. When you're finished with the call, click End Call to hang up.

FIGURE 11-16 You can have a video call and send instant messages at the same time in Lync.

Sharing Programs and Files

Another important task you might need regularly if your team works at a distance involves sharing files, folders, and programs. Suppose that someone on your team wants to share the design for the latest product brochure. Instead of emailing it to all team members and then discussing it at some future point, the person presenting the design idea can open the file on her desktop and then share her desktop with everyone in the group.

Similarly, if you want to plan a brainstorming session, you can open a whiteboard and invite everyone you want to attend to put their ideas on the virtual board and see what stands out.

And if you *do* want others to have their own copy of the design to go through in more detail, you can easily transfer files while you're in Lync so that all of you can literally be on the same page at the same time.

Sharing Your Desktop

The process of sharing your desktop is simple. Begin by opening an instant messaging session with one of your contacts. Click Share in the top of the messaging window, and click Desktop. Your desktop appears as an extension of the instant messaging window on your contact's computer. (See Figure 11-17.)

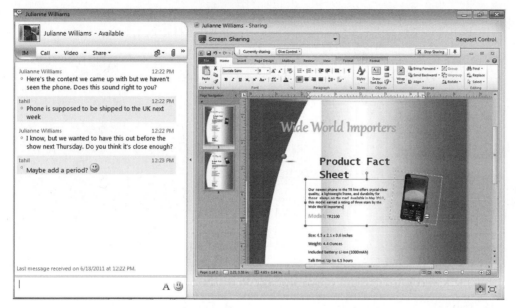

FIGURE 11-17 Your contact sees the instant messaging conversation on the left and your desktop in the stage area on the right.

You can transfer control of the screen display by clicking Give Control at the top of your sharing window and choosing the name of the contact to whom you want to transfer control. (See Figure 11-18.) You can talk or chat about the contents of the display and share what you need to share. When you're finished with the call, click Stop Sharing to end the sharing of your desktop and return to normal view. You can also click Release Control to let go of your control of the other user's computer.

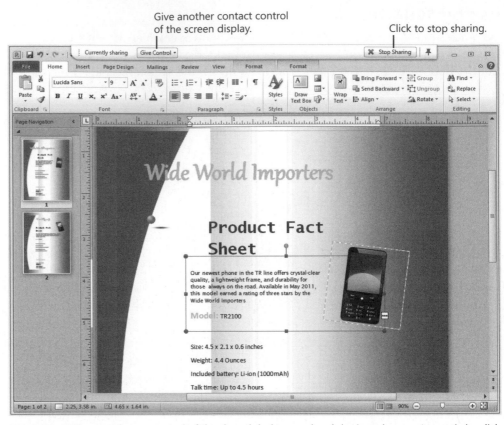

FIGURE 11-18 You can change control of the shared desktop and end sharing when you're ready by clicking the tools at the top of the sharing window.

Sharing Programs

The process of sharing actual programs on your computer is similar to sharing your desktop. Begin by opening the program you want to share, and then, in the instant messaging window, click Share and choose Program. Click the program you want to share with your contacts, and it appears in the stage area of your screen. You can draw, write, construct formulas, or do whatever else you want to demonstrate to your group and, when you're finished, click Stop Sharing to return your desktop control to only your view.

Using a Whiteboard

You can easily create a whiteboard session in which you and your colleagues can brainstorm about new ideas, projects, clients, and programs. When you start a whiteboard, by clicking Share during an instant messaging session and choosing New Whiteboard, Lync creates a Group Conversation that enables all participants to have equal input into what's happening on the screen. You can add images, add text, doodle, add shapes, change fonts, and more in the Whiteboard window. (See Figure 11-19.)

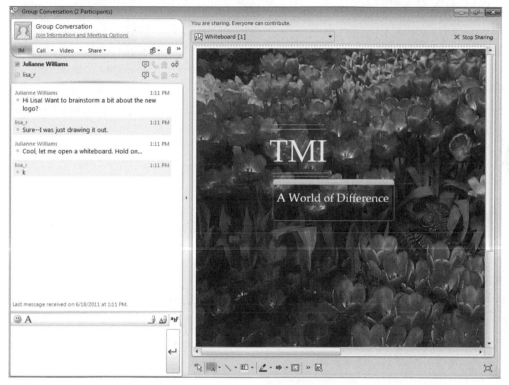

FIGURE 11-19 When you share a whiteboard with your contacts, Lync opens a Group Conversation so all can participate.

You can use the tools at the bottom of the whiteboard to add all kinds of content to the page, as you see in Figure 11-20.

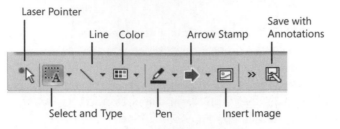

FIGURE 11-20 Use the Whiteboard tools to add content and notes to your developing ideas.

You can save the whiteboard so that you can view it or use the content later by clicking Save With Annotations at the far right of the Whiteboard tools row. The Save As dialog box appears so that you can navigate to the folder in which you want to store the whiteboard. Click Save to save the file.

Of course, you can continue to IM or talk on the phone while you work with the whiteboard, so communication continues in several ways at once. Similar to real-time, around-the-table collaboration, Lync makes it easy to share ideas, work collaboratively, and finish your projects together in real time.

What's Next

This chapter introduced you to Microsoft Lync, the great, instant-contact tool that is part of Office 365. With Lync, you can stay in touch with your team in real time through email, instant messaging, phone and video calls, desktop and program sharing, and whiteboards. This means you can keep the creative vibe going whether you work down the hall from your teammates or on different continents.

The next chapter shows you how to design, create, and manage the public-facing website that is yours as part of Office 365.

CHAPTER 12

Designing Your Public Website

IN ADDITION to all the tools you've already explored in Office 365—which enable you to organize your contacts, create document libraries, design a team site, stay on top of your email, and communicate in real time—Office 365 also includes a free public-facing website you can develop to present your company to the world. You might use your public website to showcase your products, talk about your services, introduce your staff, provide a map to your facility, tell happy customer stories, or much more.

On your public website, you can include text, pictures, video, audio, PDFs, and other content. Perhaps your annual report will be downloadable. Maybe visitors can send in their email address to sign up for your monthly newsletter and get a catalog of your products.

No matter how you use the site, editing it and enhancing it in Office 365 is a breeze. With a full set of web-based editing tools, you can control colors, fonts, alignment, and more. This chapter shows you how.

Tip ✓	Do the web tools look familiar? If you previously used Office Live for Small Business to create, manage, and update a website, the web tools in Office 365 will look familiar to you. Although some big changes have been made here, the tools you'll use are based on the same approach and structure you learned with Office Live.

Getting Started with Your Public Website

Your first step in creating your public website involves clicking the Admin tab and scrolling to the bottom of the Admin Overview page. (Note that you'll see the Admin link on the top right of the Office 365 window only if you have Administrator privileges.) Click the Edit Website link to display your site pages. To begin working on your site, click Home (your website Home page) and click Edit, as shown in Figure 12-1.

FIGURE 12-1 Click a page, and click Edit to begin making changes to your site.

Making Simple Web Changes

The easiest changes to make on your site involve simple text changes. You can click in any of the zones you want to change, highlight the text you want to remove, press Delete, and type the new text. You can use the formatting tools in the Font group of the Home tab to change the look of the text, and you can use the tools in the Paragraph group to change the format and alignment of the text on the page. (See Figure 12-2.)

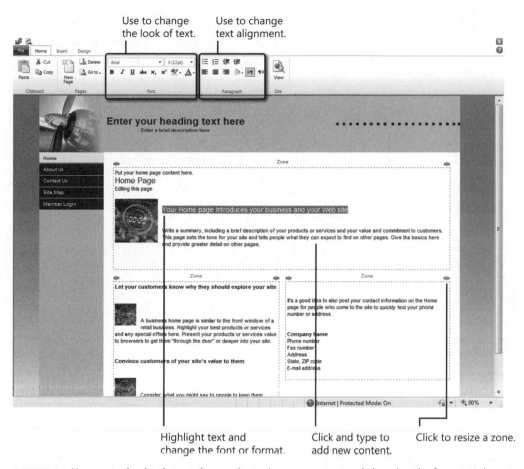

Use to change the look of text.

Use to change text alignment.

Highlight text and change the font or format.

Click and type to add new content.

Click to resize a zone.

FIGURE 12-2 You can make simple text changes by typing new content and changing the format and alignment.

Tip
✓   You can view the way your changes will look on your public site by clicking the View tool in the Site group on the Home tab.

Setting Up Your Site

Some of the choices you'll make early on as you design your site will affect the entire layout of the public pages. Click the Design tab, and click Setup in the Site group to display the Setup dialog box. (See Figure 12-3.) Click the Page Width arrow, and choose the width of the page you want to display; click the Page Alignment arrow, and choose Center, Right, or Left.

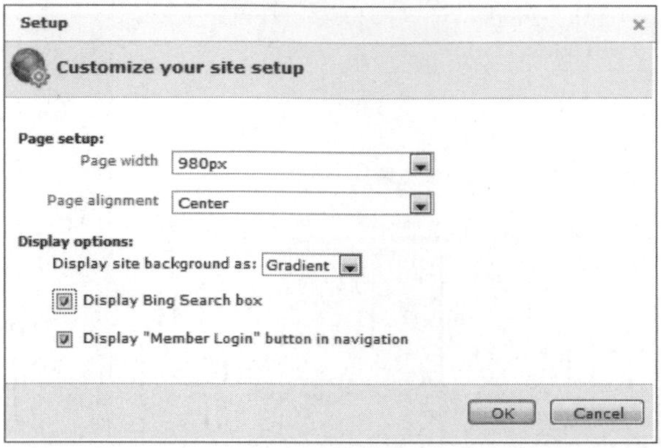

Setup   ×

Customize your site setup

Page setup:

Page width   `980px`

Page alignment   `Center`

Display options:

Display site background as: `Gradient`

☑ Display Bing Search box

☑ Display "Member Login" button in navigation

     OK   Cancel

FIGURE 12-3 Use the Setup options to set the page width and alignment for your entire website.

In the Display Options area, you can choose the way the background will be displayed on the site. Additionally, you can add the Bing search box to the site and enable the Member Login button so that those who are part of your Office 365 team can log in from the public site.

Tip   What's the best page width? When you're designing for the web, you need to think about the whole range of users who will likely be browsing to your site. Although many desktop monitors now have larger screen resolutions (perhaps up to 1440 x 990 or so), netbooks, laptops, iPads, and other devices have smaller screens. For best results, leave the default setting (980 px) or choose the smaller width (780 px) to accommodate your visitors with smaller screens.

Applying a Page Background

One big change you can make to your page right away involves changing the look of the page background. Start by clicking the Background tool in the Page group on the Design tab. In the Page Background dialog box (shown in Figure 12-4), add a background image by following these steps:

1. Select the Use Background Image check box.

2. Click Select, and click Browse For An Image.

3. Navigate to the folder storing the file you want to add, select it, and click Insert Image.

4. Back in the Page Background dialog box, click the Position arrow and choose where on the page you want the picture to appear.

5. Click the Tiling arrow, and choose whether you want the image to be tiled (meaning it will be repeated as needed to fill the page) and, if so, how.

6. Click OK to save your choices.

Tip By default, Office 365 selects the Optimize My Image check box when you upload a picture to your site. Optimizing an image resizes and compresses it so that the picture loads more quickly on your website (which your visitors will appreciate).

Page background   ✕

📄 Use a custom image on your background

Use background image: ☑
          Image file: /siteimages/garfield_08.jpg   Select...
            Position: Top left   ▾
              Tiling: No tiling   ▾

                                          OK   Cancel

FIGURE 12-4 You can add an image to the background of your page by clicking Background in the Page group of the Design tab.

Note The background image you apply to your page will appear only in the center text area; the navigation panel and header areas are controlled by other formatting choices.

Choosing a Theme and Header Style

The way you design your site—with the colors, images, and navigation style—creates a kind of experience for your site visitors that communicates something about your organization and your services. If the colors are dark and the fonts are conservative, people might see your organization as being very serious. If the site is colorful and the fonts are playful, visitors might view your company as creative or whimsical.

You can choose a theme in your Office 365 site to apply a set of colors and a logo design for the site. Office 365 includes a huge range of theme choices that are designed to correspond with the type of business you are running. Even though there are a number of categories, you can choose whatever appeals to you—such as a Scenic & Landscape scene for your computer tech company—as long as you like the look and you feel it fits the overall tone you're trying to convey.

To choose a theme for your site, click the Design tab and click Theme in the Header group. A huge list of choices appears, as you see in Figure 12-5. Point to the various categories to see the galleries of styles you can apply to your site. When you find the one you want, click it and Office 365 applies it to your site.

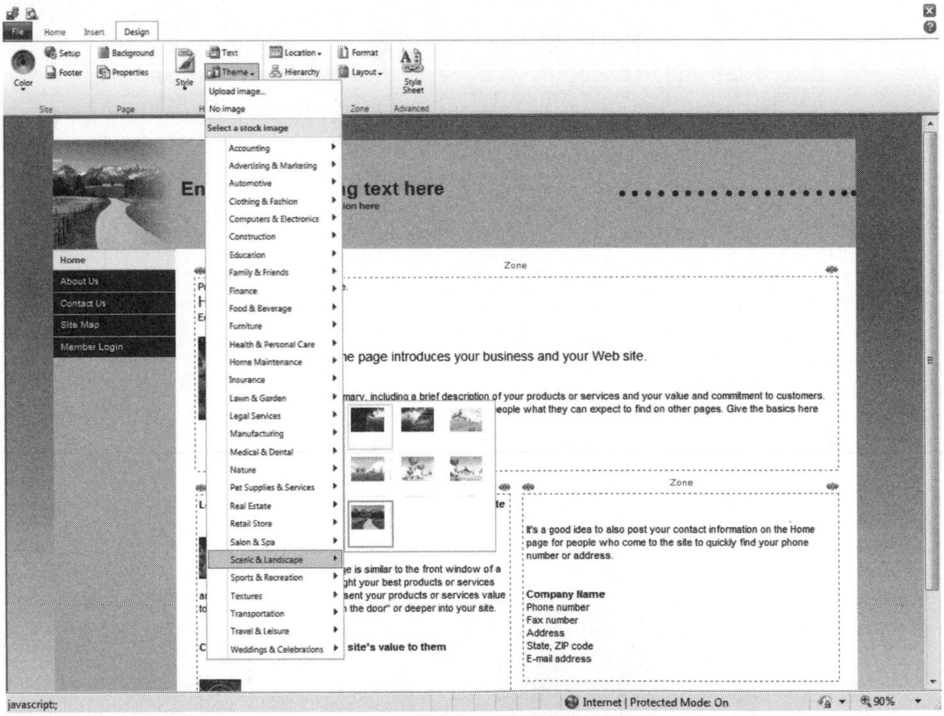

FIGURE 12-5 Click Theme in the Header group to change the theme of your site.

If you don't like the effect, you can change the theme and experiment with many other looks. Just remember to keep your visitors in mind, which means you should consider not only your personal color preferences but also the overall site design and how well (or not) it matches the message you want your visitors to receive.

WHAT'S IN A THEME?

Not all themes are created equal. Each theme you select in Office 365 has been professionally designed to present a specific look and feel. All items in the theme are coordinated so that they look good together and provide a professional, polished look for your site.

Changing the Site Header

The site header is the area at the top of your webpages that gives a consistent look and feel to your site. The header is repeated from page to page so that site visitors recognize the continuity throughout your site.

To change the header, click the Design tab and click Text in the Header group or click the header to display the Header dialog box. In the Header dialog box (shown in Figure 12-6), type the text you want to appear as the header for the site, and use the formatting tools to change the style and font of the text.

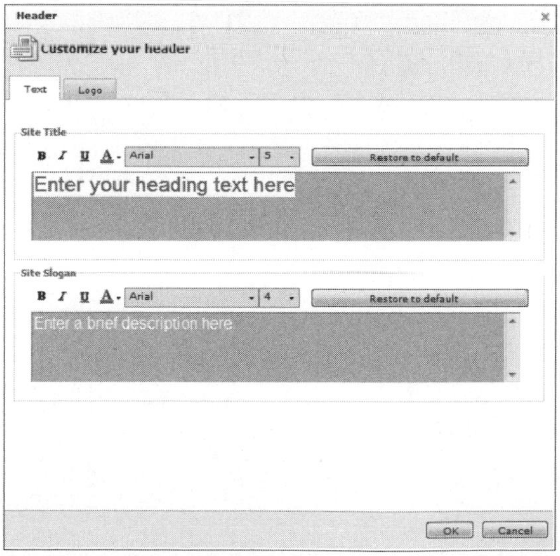

FIGURE 12-6 Enter a heading and a description for your site in the Header dialog box.

You can also add a site slogan, which is a description that will appear below the header, by clicking in the Site Slogan box and typing your description. Again, format it as you'd like, and click OK to return to the site and view your changes.

Add a Logo to Your Site

If you have a customized logo saved as a .jpg or .bmp file, you can easily add it to your site in Office 365. The process is simple—it's similar to adding a photo or piece of clip art to your pages. Here are the steps:

1. Click Text in the Header group of the Design tab.

2. Click the Logo tab.

3. Click Upload Pictures if you need to add your logo image to the dialog box.

4. Click the image you want to use as the logo. (See Figure 12-7.) If you decide you want to forgo the logo altogether, click No Logo.

5. In the Display Options area, select whether you want the logo to appear at the top of each page of the site or beside the page title.

6. In the Size area, choose Small, Medium, or Large for the size of the logo.

7. Click OK to save your changes.

FIGURE 12-7 Add a logo using the Logo tab in the Header dialog box.

WHAT MAKES A GOOD LOGO GOOD?

Are there some characteristics that "good" logos have that other logos don't? Think of the logos you're most likely to recognize. Chances are that you see them everywhere—Coke, IBM, Nike, Dell. What do they all have in common? Colors we remember. A simple, strong design. Bold characters. Think about what makes your logo memorable in the minds of your site visitors, and be sure to use your logo consistently on all printed and web materials.

Choosing a Custom Color Scheme

Similar to the way in which your theme creates an experience for your visitors, the color scheme you select says a lot about your business or organization. Red is a high-energy color; blue is passive; green is relaxing; yellow is stimulating. (Be careful about how much yellow you use because a little goes a long way and used to excess could make your page more difficult for visitors to read.) Visit some of your favorite sites. How do they use color? How does the design make you feel?

You can easily apply a new color scheme by following these steps:

1. Click the Design tab.

2. Click the Color tool in the Site group on the far left end of the Design tab. (See Figure 12-8.) A list of color palettes appears.

3. Click the color palette you like. The colors are immediately applied to the theme you selected, overriding any other colors in use.

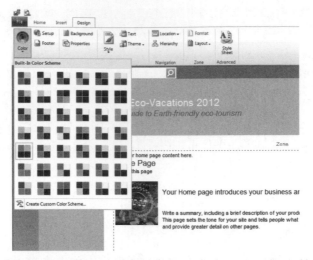

FIGURE 12-8 Choose a color palette, and select a coordinated look for your public website.

Adding and Formatting Text

What do you want to say on your website? Most businesses try for a mix of friendly and factual, welcoming visitors and making sure they are able to find what they're looking for with the fewest number of clicks possible. For example, if you're hoping visitors will download a copy of your product catalog—and you think people will likely be coming to your site to do that—feature the catalog somewhere prominently on your site (either on the Home page or as a link that is plainly visible to visitors) so that they can find what they need and download it quickly. This gives visitors a good feeling about your site, which means they're likely to come back.

There's a delicate balance about how *much* text you want on your site, however. Even though you want visitors to find what they need, you don't want them to wear themselves out by reading too much about it. So keep your content short and sweet. If you must go into great detail about a process or a product, create a new page the user can visit if they decide they want to read more about it.

It's a simple thing to add text on your Office 365 pages, but there's no Undo tool to undo your changes—so it's a good idea to be certain about your edits before you make them. As mentioned earlier in this chapter, the easiest way to add content is to click the zone where you want to change the text, delete what's there, and add your new text. After you've added your new content, you can use the various formatting tools to give it just the look you want.

Formatting Your Headings

Your pages include placeholder text in each of the zones on the pages you work with. You can choose to use the format already there or change it to fit the tone of your site. Here's how to change the look of the zone headings on your page:

1. Display the page you want to change.

2. Highlight the text you want to use as a heading.

3. In the Home tab, click the Font arrow and choose a font from the displayed list.

4. Click Bold, Italic, or Underline as desired.

5. Click the Font Size arrow, and choose a size from the list. (See Figure 12-9.)

6. Click the Font Color arrow, and choose a color from the palette.

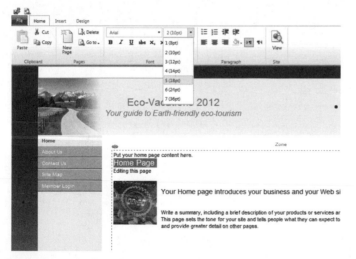

FIGURE 12-9 The font sizes in the Font Size list show both the HTML sizes and the more familiar point sizes for the text.

| Note | Text sizes in HTML are shown in size levels ranging from 1 to 7, with 1 being the smallest and 7 being the largest. In print documents, text size is generally shown in *points*, a typographical term used to indicate the height of a character on a printed line. Because 72 points equals one inch, a 72-point letter will be one-inch tall on the printed page. |

ATTACHING A CSS STYLE SHEET

If you are accustomed to working with web design, you might have a cascading style sheet (CSS) you've used for other web projects in your business that you'd like to apply to your Office 365 site.

You can add the CSS code directly to your site by clicking the Design tab and clicking Style Sheet in the Advanced group. In the Style Sheet dialog box, you can paste the CSS code you want to include on the site. Select the Apply Custom CSS Code To My Web Site check box, and click OK. The new code is added to your site, and you can add CSS styles when you use the HTML module to enter code directly to the site.

Creating Lists

Chances are you know all about bulleted and numbered lists. You use the tools in your word processor, you see them in PowerPoint—you know the drill.

Bulleted and numbered lists are nice to use on websites because they offer information in a succinct, clear format. The reader's eye is drawn to scan a list quickly, and that adds to a feeling of effective communication on the site.

When you want to create a bulleted list on your Office 365 webpage, click in the zone where you want to add the list, click the Bulleted List tool in the Paragraph group of the

Home tab, and type your list. Each time you press Enter, the cursor moves to the next line and a bullet is inserted. Click the tool again to turn the format off. You can also turn existing text into a list by selecting it and then clicking the Bulleted List tool.

A numbered list works similarly. Click the tool and type your list, or select the text and click the tool.

Tip ✓ In HTML, a bulleted list is coded as <UL>, which stands for *unordered list*. The list gets its name from the fact that the items in the list can appear in any order. In contrast, an *ordered list*, or <OL>, is the designation used for a list that must appear in a particular order. In Office 365, an ordered list is called a *numbered list*.

Adding Hyperlinks

Everything you've done so far—add and format text, choose a color scheme, apply a theme, customize the header—is an important part of creating a good experience for your site visitors. But without hyperlinks, the links that take people from one page to another, nothing on the web would work. Links bring visitors to your site and help them find what they need while they are there.

You can add hyperlinks easily to your Office 365 pages. Here's how:

1. On the page, highlight the text to which you want to apply the link.

2. Click the Insert tab, and click Hyperlink.

3. In the Insert A Link dialog box (shown in Figure 12-10), select the type of link you want to create:

   - Click Web Site if you want to enter the address of a site you want to link to.

   - Click Page On My Site if you want to link to one of the other pages in your site.

   - Click My Documents if you want to create a link that enables a user to open or save a document.

   - Click E-mail Address if you want to create a link that opens an email window.

4. For example, if you click Web Site, a Link box will appear. You can click in the Link box, and type the web address of the page, file, or document you want to use as the target of the link.

Note

The Link option changes depending on the type of link you select. If you choose Page On My Site, you'll see a list of pages so that you can select the page in your site you want to use. If you click My Documents, files from your document library appear so that you can choose the document you want to link to.

5. If you want the target of the link (another site, a page in your own site, an email window, or a document) to open in a new window on top of your website window, select the Open Link In A New Window check box.

6. Click OK to save your changes and create the link.

Tip

✓

You should open the target of the link in a new window if the link leads visitors either away from your site or to a page where they are likely to jump to another site. When you select Open Link In A New Window, your website stays open on the user's screen while the new window opens on top of it. When the user is finished viewing the target of the link, your site is still displayed.

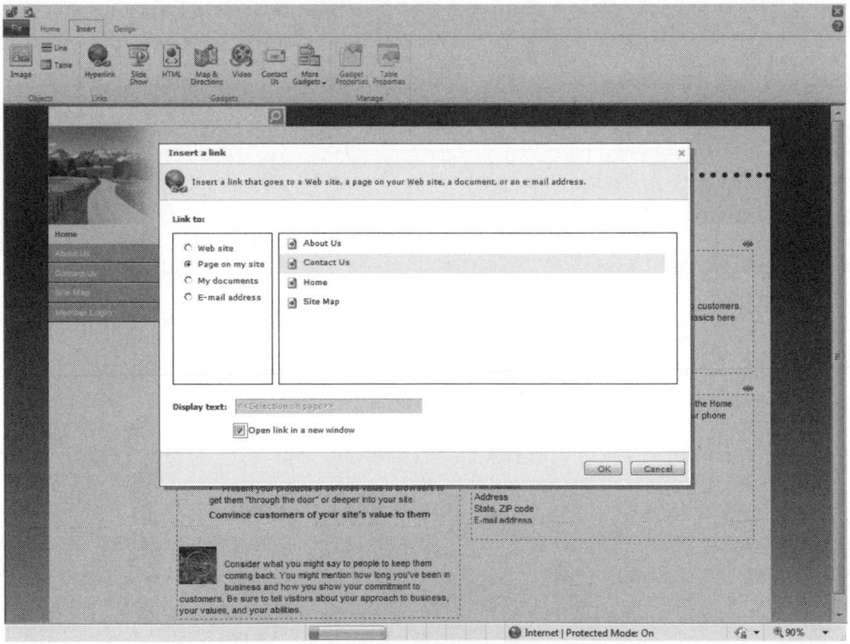

FIGURE 12-10 To add a link to your page, select the text you want to link and click Hyperlink.

Inserting, Formatting, and Aligning Images

As the web has matured, people have come to expect more pictures on web pages. This is part design and part function. Pictures can showcase products, illustrate services, and introduce important personalities. Pictures also give the reader's eye a rest and keep a page from feeling too full of text.

What kinds of images will you show on your web pages? You might want to consider the following:

- Product photos

- Staff photos

- Service-related images

- A photo of your facility

- A map to your office

You begin the process of adding pictures by clicking Images in the Objects group on the Insert tab. The Insert Image dialog box appears, as you see Figure 12-11. Click whether you want to choose images from your computer or from images you've already uploaded to Office 365. Then click Browse For An Image and navigate to the folder containing the image you'd like to add. Click Insert Image, and the image is added to your page.

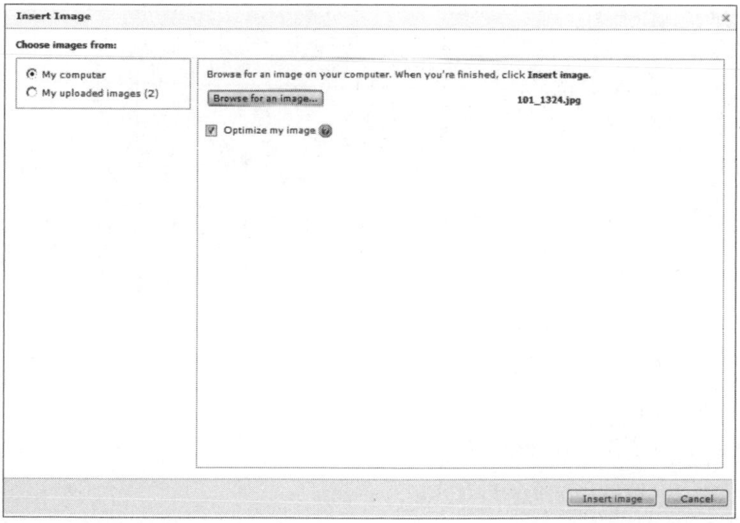

FIGURE 12-11 Click Browse For An Image to add a new picture to your page.

Formatting Your Picture

After you position your picture on the page, you might find that it needs some tweaking. Perhaps it's too big (like the photo in Figure 12-12). Or perhaps it comes too close to the surrounding text. You can fix those problems—and more—by clicking the Image Tools Format tab, which is available when the picture is selected on the page.

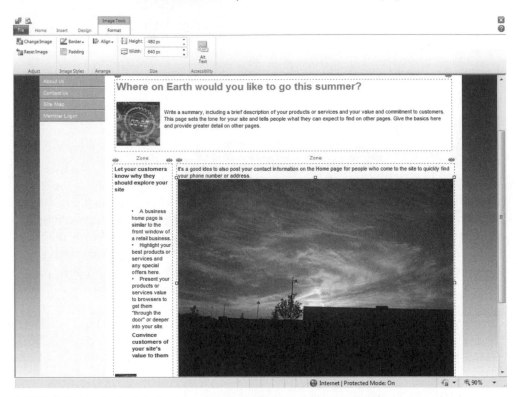

FIGURE 12-12 Use the tools in the Image Tools Format tab to format and align your image.

The Image Tools Format tab provides you with a set of tools you can use to format the image on your page. In addition to working with the alignment (which is discussed in the next section), you can do any of the following:

- Click Change Image to replace the selected picture with a new photo you select from your computer or from your uploaded images.

- Choose Reset Image to remove all formatting changes.

- Click Border to choose the color and thickness for a border you apply to the picture.

- Use Padding to set a margin of space around the selected image.

- Click in the Height and Width boxes, and type new values to resize the photo on the page.

- Click Alt Text, and enter a description of the photo for visitors who can't view the image.

For example, the picture in Figure 12-12 clearly needs to be resized. You can do this one of two ways: You can click one of the handles on the image and drag it in the direction you want to resize the image. Or you can click in the Height and Width boxes in the Image Tools Format tab and type new values for the settings to resize the picture.

Setting the Alignment for Images

Next you need to think about how you want the image to align on the page. The alignment of the image controls how—or whether—text wraps around the picture. To change the way your picture aligns, follow these steps:

1. Click the image on the web page.

2. Click Align in the Image Tools Format tab.

3. Click No Text Wrapping, Float Right, or Float Left.

No Text Wrapping leaves the picture as is on the page and doesn't cause the text to wrap around the picture. If you choose Float Right, text flows around the image on the left. Similarly, if you click Float Left, the text wraps around the image on the right.

Adding and Organizing Pages

When you're first creating your site, four pages might seem like a lot of space to fill. As you begin adding content and photos, you might discover that those pages fill up quickly and you need to add more. You add pages by using the New Page tool on the Home tab. Here's how to do it:

1. Click the Home tab.

2. Click New Page. The Create Web Page dialog box appears. (See Figure 12-13.)

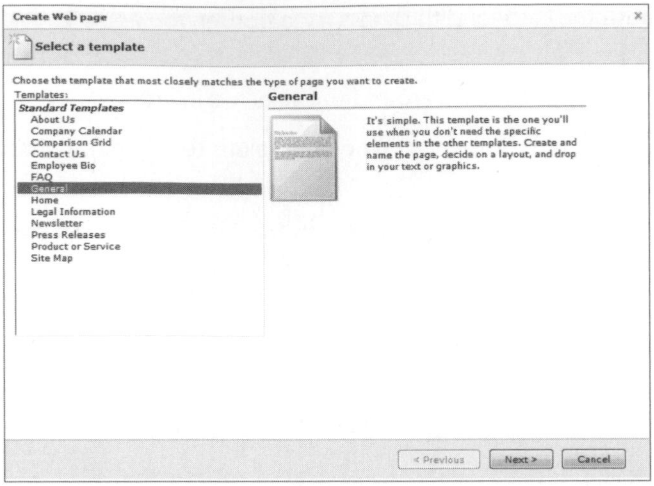

FIGURE 12-13 Choose a template for the new web page you want to create.

3. Click a template for the type of page you want to create, and click Next.

> **Tip** ✓
>
> The various page templates available in the Create Web Page dialog box each creates a specific type of page for a particular kind of information. If you are unsure about which template you need—or don't yet know what you want to put on the site—click General. This template creates a generic page you can customize later when you know what type of content and layout you want to add.

4. On the Choose Page Properties page, type a title for the new page.

5. Click in the Web Address field, and modify the suggested page name if you like.

> **Tip** ✓
>
> If you're creating a new page that will replace an existing one, you can type an existing page name and select the Overwrite Existing Page check box to replace the old page with the new one.

6. In the Navigation area, leave the check box selected if you want the page to appear in the navigation bar.

7. Type the title you want to appear in the navigation bar and, if the page will be a subpage of an existing page, click the Select Parent arrow and choose the page from the displayed list. (See Figure 12-14.)

8. Click Finish to add the page to your site.

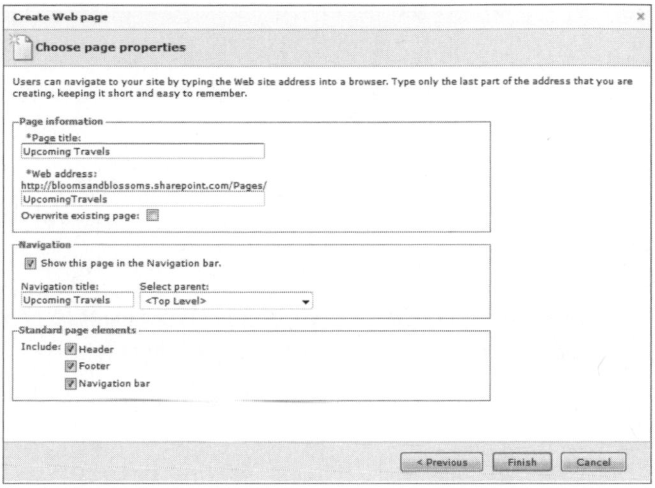

FIGURE 12-14 Enter page properties to assign a title, address, and navigation title for the page.

Selecting a Navigation Layout

By default, Office 365 displays the navigation panel for your site along the left side of the page. But there are a total of three navigation layouts you can use for your site. In addition to the Left navigation which is chosen by default, you can use the Top & Left navigation layout or the Top navigation layout.

To choose a navigation style for your site, follow these steps:

1. Click the Design tab.

2. In the Navigation group, click the Location tool.

3. Click the Navigation style you like: Left, Top & Left, or Top. (See Figure 12-15.)

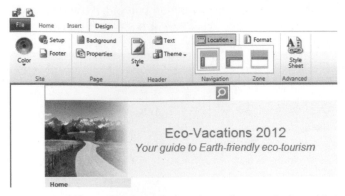

FIGURE 12-15 The navigation style you choose for your site has a big impact on how easily visitors can find what they need on your site.

The navigation changes are applied instantly. (See Figure 12-16.) If you want to change the navigation style, simply repeat the steps and choose a different style.

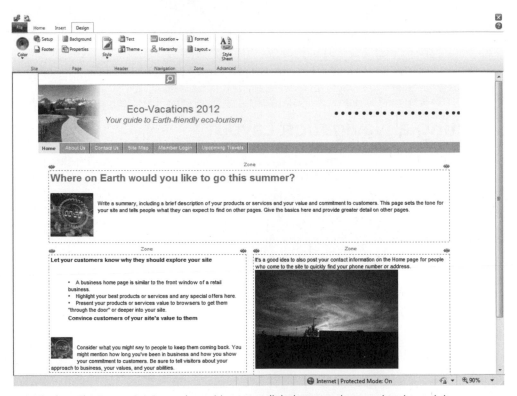

FIGURE 12-16 The Top navigation style positions page links between the page header and the content area.

Adding Gadgets to Your Site

One of the great perks of creating your website in Office 365 is that you can add a number of ready-made gadgets to your website. This means you can add all sorts of interesting extras that visitors to your site will enjoy using.

The gadgets already built into your Office 365 site are available on the Insert tab, as Figure 12-17 shows. Additional gadgets are available in the More Gadgets section. To add a gadget to your page, simply click in the zone where you want to add the gadget and then click the gadget you want to add.

FIGURE 12-17 Insert a gadget by choosing the one you want on the Insert tab.

Figure 12-18 shows the Slide Show dialog box, which appears after you select the Slide Show gadget.

FIGURE 12-18 Adding the Slide Show gadget.

Enter a name for the album and then drag the photos you want to use to the panel on the right side of the window. You can click an Add Caption prompt to add captions for the figures you use. Click the Album Layout Style arrow, and choose whether you want to display a basic slide show or a revolving carousel. Click OK to add the gadget to your site. Figure 12-19 shows the Slide Show gadget on the webpage.

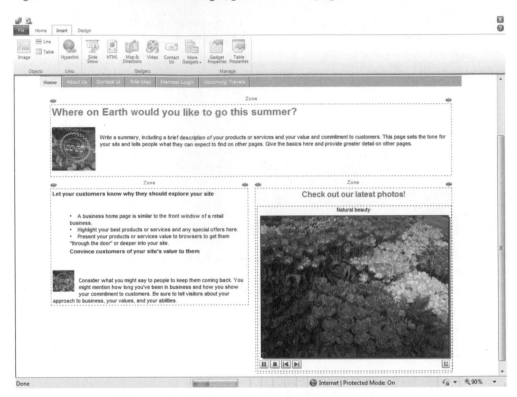

FIGURE 12-19 The Slide Show gadget has been added to the site.

Optimizing Your Site for Web Search Results

One major consideration as you create your site is a single question: How will people find you?

With so many businesses and so many websites online, how will you stand out from your competition? What will bring potential customers to your site?

You can enter keywords and your site description to help your site get noticed by search engines such as Google, Bing, or other major search utilities. When someone enters a word or phrase that describes what they're searching for, if the word or phrase they enter matches the keywords or description you've entered for your site, your site might appear in that person's search results. So the best idea is to choose keywords that reflect what people are searching for. This helps new clients find you online.

You enter keywords and your site description by clicking the Design tab and clicking Properties. In the Choose Page Properties dialog box, click on the Search Engine Optimization tab, as shown in Figure 12-20. Click OK to save your changes.

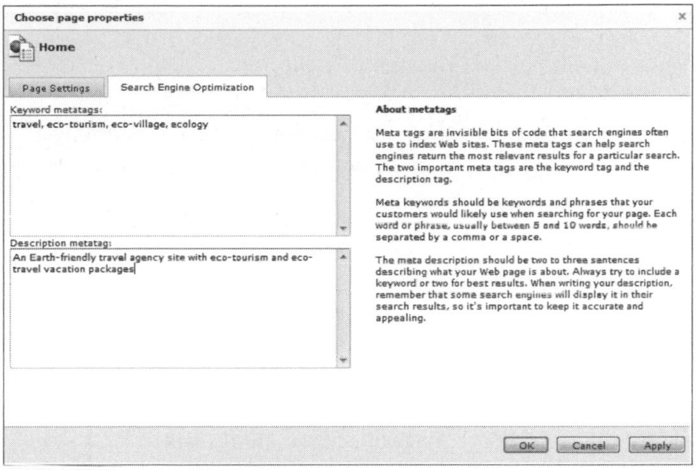

FIGURE 12-20 Enter your keywords and a site description in the Choose Page Properties dialog box.

Previewing and Publishing Your Site

When you've selected your theme and colors, added text and images, and entered keywords, gadgets, and a site description, you might be ready to preview and publish your site. You can take a look at the way the site will look to the public by clicking View in the Site group of the Home tab.

If you're happy with the way things look, you can publish your site by clicking the File tab and clicking Save & Publish. (See Figure 12-21.)

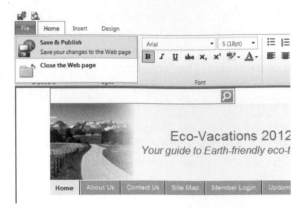

FIGURE 12-21 Click the File tab, and click Save & Publish to publish your site.

When you're ready to close the website and return to your Office 365 site, click the File tab again and choose Close The Web Page. Back in the webpage listing, you can click Home to return to your Office 365 Home page.

■ What's Next

In this chapter, you took a whirlwind tour through all the web features available in Office 365. As you can see, you have many tools for designing your site, adding content, formatting text and pictures, adding gadgets, and optimizing your site for better placement in search engines. The next chapter closes out the book by offering examples of the ways you can use various tools together to manage collaborative projects and reach your team goals with Office 365.

CHAPTER 13

Integrating All Parts of Office 365

THROUGHOUT THIS BOOK, you've looked closely at the various elements of Office 365. After exploring the online interface, you followed specific paths through administering your account, creating a team site, working with document libraries and workflows, using Office Web Apps, and using Microsoft Outlook and Lync to keep your team on the same page and communicating well.

This chapter shines a light on the big, overarching benefit of Office 365—how beautifully it all works together. Here you'll see some examples of how using the various elements of Office 365 together can help you work effectively with your teammates to accomplish tasks that are important for your team.

Using It All Together—Online and Off

One of the great benefits of cloud technology in all its forms is how easy it is to work on your files and stay in touch no matter where you might be working or how you're accessing the web. And even though the idea is to keep the files in the cloud so that you and your teammates can get to them easily, you can also download and work with versions of your projects while you're offline and then sync the files with the site when you log on next time.

Checking a File Out of Your Document Library

When you want to download a file and work on it on your computer—or phone—follow these steps:

1. Log in to Office 365.

2. Display your SharePoint team site.

3. Go to your document library.

4. Click the arrow of the file you want to work on, and click Check Out. (See Figure 13-1.)

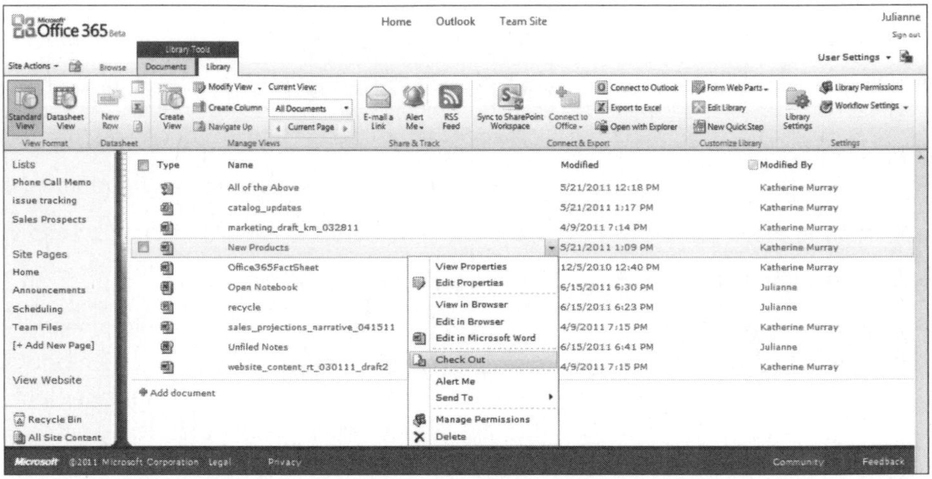

FIGURE 13-1 You can check out a file to open a private copy and keep the file from being edited while you're working on it.

The file is now checked out as a private file for you to edit. Others won't be able to make changes to the file while it is checked out. When you're ready to return the file to the site—and make it available so that others can work on it—you can check it back in.

Checking a File in After You're Done Working on It

You can also check in a file after you've been working on it in the application. When you check in the file, it lets the server know that your changes have been saved and the file is ready to be edited by others. Here's how to check a file in:

1. Click the file you want to work with, and open it in the application used to create it.

2. Click the File tab.

3. In the Info tab, click Check In. (See Figure 13-2.)

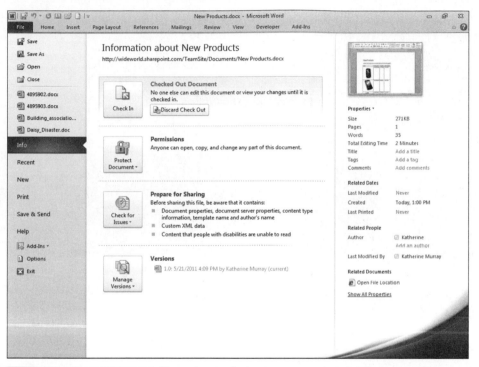

FIGURE 13-2 After working on a file you've checked out, you can return it to free use in the document library by clicking Check In.

After you check in the file, it becomes available in your SharePoint document library again so that others can open and edit the file as normal.

Saving Files to Your Computer

When you want to take a file offline so that you can work on it on your computer or your mobile device, you can simply open the file and then use Save As to save it to your computer or device. Choose a folder where you'll be able to find the file easily when you're ready to add it back to the site—for example, you could store it in your Downloads folder, or in a folder named for the shared project you're working on.

If you have already checked out the file, when you save it, Office 365 will remind you that the file is checked out to you and ask you whether you want to cancel the check-out status or keep the file checked out. If you want to keep others from being able to make changes to the file while you're working on it, choose Keep Checked Out. If you want others to be able to edit the file, click Discard Check Out.

> **Tip** If a dialog box appears giving you the option to Use My Local Drafts Folder, the file is checked out and a copy is downloaded automatically to your SharePoint Drafts folder. This is a subfolder of your Documents library on your computer. The folder will be synched automatically with the SharePoint server when you access your Office 365 account again.

Saving Files to Your Document Library

After you make any necessary changes to the file offline, you can easily save your updated version of the file back to your team's document library. Here are the steps for saving the file back to the site:

1. In the application you are using (Word, Excel, PowerPoint, or OneNote), with the file open on the screen, click the File tab.

2. Click Save & Send.

3. Click Save To SharePoint.

4. Click the folder that represents your SharePoint document library. (See Figure 13-3.)

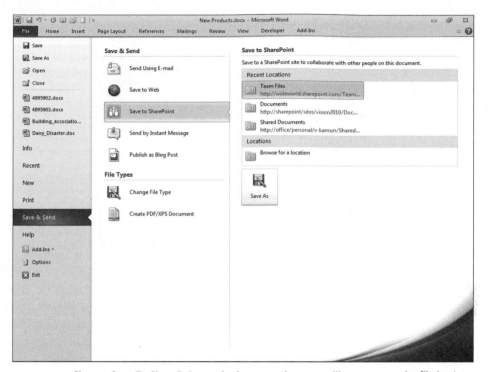

FIGURE 13-3 Choose Save To SharePoint, and select your document library to save the file back to the site.

Tip ✓ If you don't see your document library folder in the list of available folders, you can click Browse for a location and enter the URL of your document library. In the Save As dialog box, select Workspaces at the top of the folders list, and choose the folder you need from the displayed list. Click Save to save the document.

Getting Productive with Office 365

Of course, Office 365 is much more than just a way to manage files that you'll work on in a team. As you've seen throughout this book, you can use the various tools in Office 365 to

- Create a shared team site for your group to gather and share documents and tasks as you collaborate on projects.

- Provide email and calendar tools to help you communicate and schedule meetings and events.

- Access Office Web Apps so that you can work on your files from any point you have web access.

- Offer secure instant messaging and online meetings for your group.

- Design and manage a public-facing website for clients and prospective customers.

Using these different tools together gives you a comprehensive way to manage your team and your tasks in the cloud. The sections that follow offer several examples of the way you can use the various elements of Office 365 to complete specific business-critical projects.

Creating an Annual Report

An annual report is an important tool that communicates to those interested in your business or organization how you have fared during the past year. The general idea is to present things in a positive light, showing examples of tasks you've mastered, obstacles you've overcome, and markets you've grown into.

Thinking Through Your Content

People who read your annual report might be your stockholders, investors, or donors—often they are people who have a vested interest in what you're doing, which means you need to aim for quality. A good annual report might include the following information:

- An introduction from the CEO or president of the board

- An overview of the year

- Specific sections about new products or services

- A section about new capital improvements to your facility

- Biographies or introductions for new staff members

- A financial section that explains sales results and projections

- A brief history of your organization

- Expectations for the coming year

Planning for Production

After you know what types of content you want to be included in the report, think through how you plan to deliver it. Will you produce a PDF to hand out at a company meeting? Do you want the PDF to be available as a download from your Office 365 public website?

Do you want to create a PowerPoint presentation of the report—or at least relevant sales data—to make available online or to show during the meeting?

The ways in which you distribute the information you create will largely be determined by the tools you use to prepare it. You can use Word to create a PDF, PowerPoint to create a presentation, and OneNote to collect your team notes along the way.

How Office 365 Helps Facilitate the Process

The tools in Office 365 will help you in many different ways as you pull together the various pieces for this project. One of the first things you need to do, of course, is choose a deadline that gives you the time you need to complete the project and leaves enough time for you to correct anything that goes wrong before the report needs to go out.

You can also decide who you want to be on the report team and make sure they have the necessary licenses to work with the various programs in Office 365.

After you identify your team and decide on a deadline, you're ready to begin the actual day-to-day work. The following list provides some ideas for ways you can use the tools in Office 365 to complete your annual report:

- **Use OneNote to start your brainstorming** Create a OneNote notebook to store team ideas as you think through things you'd like to include in the report. You can share the notebook online through OneNote Web App and make it available in the SharePoint document library you create. (See Figure 13-4.)

- **Create a SharePoint page for the annual report project** You can create a dedicated page where you can post announcements, questions, files, calendars, and other content related to the annual report project.

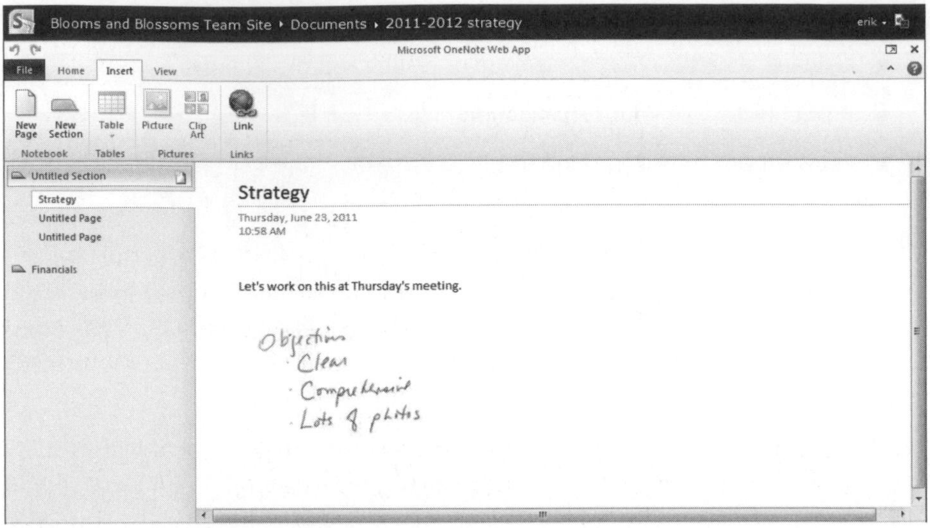

FIGURE 13-4 Create a shared OneNote notebook to gather your thoughts as your team begins to brainstorm about the report project.

■ **Create a document library for the files you'll use in the report** This makes it easy to find just what you need for this project without browsing through a collection of files used for other things. (See Figure 13-5.)

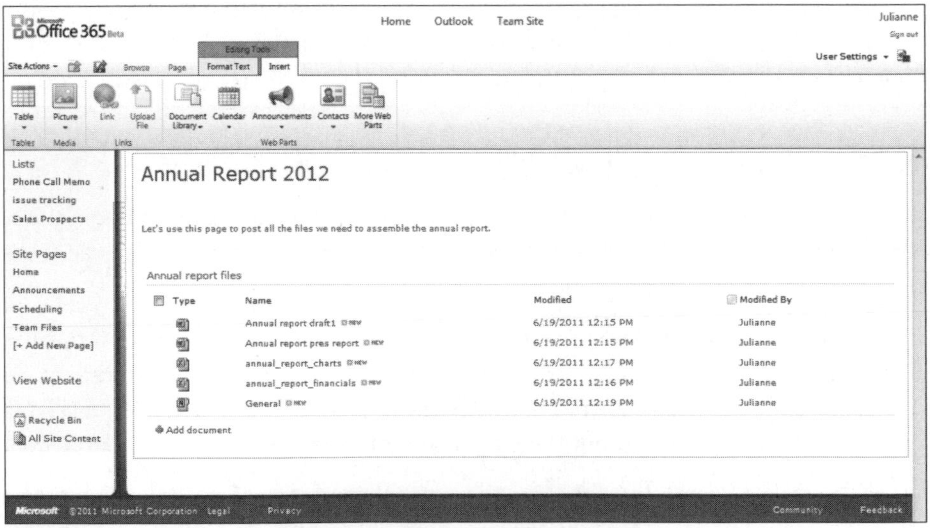

FIGURE 13-5 Add a new page and a document library for this specific project so that you have everything you need on one page.

- **Add a workflow to track report progress** Adding a workflow for the report helps you assign specific tasks and roles for accomplishing the goal, and it helps you to coordinate everyone's efforts.

- **Assign tasks for different aspects of the report** By doing this, you know who is doing what and you can tell where you are in the process by seeing who has completed the tasks assigned to them.

- **Host weekly team meetings in Lync to talk about the report progress** Keeping everybody moving ahead in the process—as a team—is an important part of an overall successful effort. Weekly meetings help the whole team keep track of how things are developing and give you a sense early on of where the trouble spots are.

- **Begin content creation in Microsoft Word** Open your OneNote notebook, and drag notes you need into your Word document draft. Share the file with others so that all team members can add the content they are responsible for adding.

- **Create worksheet data in Excel** You can add worksheet information—including sales figures, new hires, capital expenditures, and foundation donations—in an Excel worksheet. You might also want to create charts that showcase data and place them in the same file, perhaps on a different worksheet. You can link the worksheet data to your Word draft to ensure that the most current data is reflected in the report.

- **Spotlight sales data with PowerPoint slides** You might want to create a short sales presentation in PowerPoint and include those slides as illustrations in the financial pages of the annual report. You can also give the presentation in the annual meeting if you have a speaking spot on the meeting's agenda.

Tracking a Sales Promotion

Often sales promotions are launched and tracked by the folks behind the scenes—or the sales manager or staff—without a lot of company fanfare or communication. But especially if you want your whole group to feel the effects of the promotion (there's a boost of energy, after all) and understand how increases in sales benefit the whole lot of you, it's a good idea to think through your promotion as a way to raise goodwill and enthusiasm companywide.

Thinking Through Your Approach

Your sales promotion might be a small project—just some strategy, a worksheet, and some promotional material for your salespeople—or it might be a bigger event, with updates on your website, blurbs for the company newsletter, and charts and progress reports along the way.

What would you like to accomplish from your promotion? And how will you let people know? Do you want a print component as well as an online piece? Will you be sending out email updates? Walk through your whole strategy from start to finish, and envision the number of people it will involve to prepare the event and pull it off.

Planning for Production

Planning for the way you want to support your sale promotion involves thinking through the process from start to finish. For example, you'll need to work through the following considerations.

What will you use to let everybody know about the promotion? Think "materials" here. For example, you might want to create an internal web page where salespeople can go for more information. Send out a broadcast email to the team introducing the new promotion and linking back to the internal web page.

You might also create some promotion rules that participants can download in PDF format, create some sample sales data in Excel, whip up a few charts to show the kinds of results you're hoping for, and design a brochure that showcases the items salespeople can win as a result of the promotion.

You could also create flyers to post in shared places like around the water cooler or coffeemaker, or if your office is completely virtual, you could post announcements on your team site with links to the website for more information.

How Office 365 Can Help with Your Sales Promotion

There are as many different ways to organize a sales promotion as there are sales promotions, but the tools in Office 365 can help you think through your approach and put pieces in place to track sales information and share successes with your team. You can use Word, Excel, PowerPoint, and OneNote, and create pages on your team site to help everyone get access to the same information. Here are a few examples:

- **Draft your promotion strategy in Word** Working with your team, create and share a Word document that includes your play-by-play strategy for the sales promotion. Be sure to include the contact information for key people on the team, as well as a timeline for the full execution of the promotion.

■ **Crunch the numbers in Excel** What kinds of sales results are you hoping for? What are the ideal numbers you'd like to get in different regions? Do you want to increase a specific type of sales in one area but encourage other sales in different regions? If so, think through how your promotion can help encourage the types of growth you'd like to see in your sales staff. Put some real numbers in the worksheet as your ideals so that you know what you're aiming for. Set your sales goal—even if that number is known only to your top management team—before the promotion begins. (See Figure 13-6.)

■ **Links to other sales worksheets and regions** Another consideration, if you want to make sure your sales data is live and up to date, involves linking the sales reports to the actual sales data as it comes in. You can do this by linking an Excel worksheet to your Word document or by creating a link in your sales promotion worksheet to other sales worksheets used for the various regions you're tracking.

■ **Include your progress in PowerPoint presentations, and make those available on your team site** Keep people in sync with your progress by sharing the good news as it unfolds. Create a PowerPoint presentation, and add it to your team site. That way you can post the slides, with updated sales data, to your team site so that everyone can see the progress that's being made (and perhaps feel inspired to try a little harder next week themselves).

Region	NE	N	E	SE	S	SW	W	NW	C	Asia	UK	Can
2011 Data	Thomas	Jones	Grand	Cartman	Lemans	Brooks	Ross	Woods	Rushman	Toyo	Weatherb	Donald
Quarter 1	1.5	1.3	2.3	1	2.5	1.5	1.3	2.3	1	2.5	2.3	1
Quarter 2	1.8	1.1	2.4	0.75	2.6	1.8	1.1	2.4	0.75	2.6	2.4	0.75
Quarter 3	2	1.6	2.2	0.75	2.2	2	1.6	2.2	0.75	2.2	2.2	0.75
Quarter 4	1.9	1.6	2.3	1.25	2.8	1.9	1.6	2.3	1.25	2.8	2.3	1.25
2012 Projections												
Quarter 1	2.3	1.5	2.5	1.3	2.7	2.3	1.5	2.5	1.3	2.7	2.5	1.5
Quarter 2	2.4	1.8	2.6	1.1	2.8	2.4	1.8	2.6	1.1	2.8	2.6	1.8
Quarter 3	2.2	2	2.2	1.6	2.5	2.2	2	2.2	1.6	2.5	2.2	2
Quarter 4	2.3	1.9	2.8	1.6	2.9	2.3	1.9	2.8	1.6	2.9	2.8	1.9

FIGURE 13-6 Create a worksheet with sales data and projections as you prepare for your sales promotion.

Preparing an Online Training Module

If your team—or perhaps your entire company—works remotely in the cloud, one of the challenges you might face is making sure everyone is trained in a similar way for common business procedures. For example, if you're using a specific kind of issue-tracking software, how do you teach your employees to use it? Or does everyone in your customer service department know how to report fulfillment problems? You can develop online training modules to make sure that your team has access to the knowledge they need to complete their business-critical tasks.

Thinking Through Your Training

Envisioning the type of training you need is an important part of designing a module that hits the mark. There are a number of questions you can ask here, including the following:

- Who will be using the training module?

- Will they have access to the web?

- Will they be able to call in for a conference call while watching a presentation?

- Do you want the training to be self-directed so that participants can work through it on their own?

- Do you want any kind of evaluation method at the end of the training?

- How will you know who has completed the training?

Planning for Production

As in the prior example, way you deliver the training will be largely determined by the type of content you create. If you design your learning module in PowerPoint, for example, you can add audio as a voiceover to give instructions as the participant clicks through the slides. You can also include video to demonstrate key processes.

You cannot, however, use PowerPoint's broadcast feature (new in PowerPoint 2010) to broadcast a presentation complete with sound and video. For now, the broadcast feature supports slides only.

You could create your learning module in a web page on your site and include a mix of documents and presentations. For example, the participant could read an introduction, open a word file to do an exercise, watch a video clip or presentation to learn more, and log their time and email in an Excel worksheet.

How Office 365 Can Help with Your Online Training

One great way to approach training—especially if you think you might do a lot of it—is to create a Training page on your team site. On this page, you could add subpages with a focus on different training modules: Sales, Technology, New Hires, and so forth. After you have an overall idea of your training program in mind, you can get to work using Office 365 to create the pieces. Here are other ideas:

- **Get your team together to brainstorm in Lync** Online training can be a fun, creative project that includes the talents and interests of many people on your team. Create an online meeting in Lync, and invite your team to a whiteboard brainstorming session. You can all talk about what you'd like to see in the training and identify the training goal as well as your primary objectives.

- **Outline the process in a Word document or OneNote notebook** The idea here is to give yourself space to identify all the important steps as you begin to pull together the content for the training.

- **Use Word to draft a document of your training content** Focus first on the outline and the content you want to convey; add illustrations as needed (or create a separate file or folder on your SharePoint site for photos you want to use).

- **Use your OneNote notebook to collect research you will use as the basis for your training** Be sure to include full resource citations and links if appropriate.

- **Build a prototype of your training in PowerPoint** As a first draft, you can include the content and photos (or video clips) your participants will see. (See Figure 13-7.) Share the draft with your team, and use Lync to get together and talk about the draft.

- **Save as a broadcast, and save as video** If the training module you create is not interactive but walks the participant through a process with audio and video, you can save the presentation as a video clip and post it to your team site.

- **Use Word to create an assessment tool** This helps participants see what they learned and let you know what they thought about the training module.

- **Make handouts and tip sheets available on the training page** If you do this, participants can download additional information if they want to review the content that was covered.

FIGURE 13-7 Create a prototype of your training module in PowerPoint.

Happily Ever After...in the Cloud

In this chapter—and throughout this book—you've been invited to think about how Office 365 can help you and your team reach your goals, whether you work in the same office building or you are scattered across the globe. Yesterday's water cooler has become today's Lync chat, and the old processes we used to follow—mailing reports, making long-distance phone calls, flying to meetings—have been replaced (thankfully) with lower-cost, lower-impact options.

Today, using the tools in Office 365, you can build a connected and motivated team that has everything it needs to complete quality projects, anytime and anywhere.

Good luck, and keep finding new ways to be creative and stay in sync with Office 365!

APPENDIX A

Extras for Great Teams

EVERY GROUP is different, just like every cloud is different. So it logically follows that every group in every cloud will be different. One thing that all groups share, however, is that to accomplish the work they come together to complete, they need to have specific, measurable ways to assign tasks, track their progress, get their questions answered, and reach their goals.

This appendix offers ideas to help you organize and manage the overall flow of information in your site. These simple forms aren't meant to replace any of the electronic processes you can use in Office 365, of course. You can use workflows to automate your project review process, for example, or use Microsoft Lync to hold weekly meetings where you check in on various stages of your responsibilities.

But if you're just starting out organizing your team, you might find a few helpful ideas here for gathering your data and keeping it organized and easy to find in the cloud.

Thinking Through Your Group Process

Early in this book, you read about the basic steps of a group process—forming, storming, norming, performing, and adjourning. As you think through the various stages in your project, consider the type of information you want to track:

- What is the scope of your project?
- How long will the project last?
- What will the benchmarks of your project be?
- Will you set internal deadlines for the project? (For example, you might set a date that serves as a deadline for having 50 percent of the project completed.)
- What are the roles your members will perform?
- How will you stay in touch with each other (and with what frequency)?
- Will you use workflows to track your progress?
- How will you notify the team when a problem arises?
- How will plan changes be communicated?
- How will you assess the success of your group?

Team Contact List

You can reach all your team members though your contacts list in Lync and the Admin User page in Office 365, but you might also want to create a contact list with complete names, email addresses, site addresses, responsibilities, and more that you download and make available to the team. (See Figure A-1.)

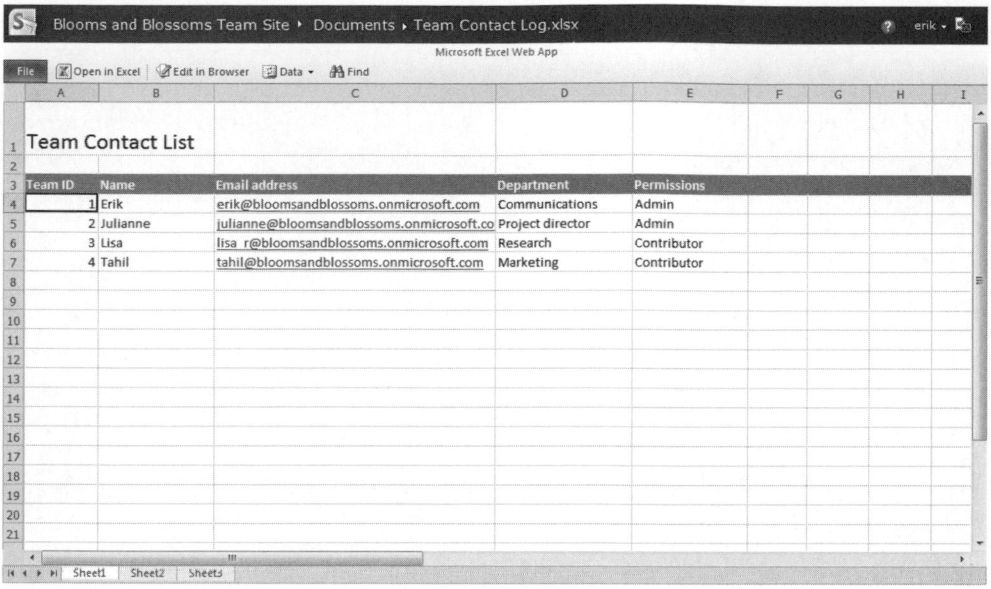

FIGURE A-1 You can create a contact log file so that you can view all user accounts and permissions at a glance.

Excel Worksheet with Licenses and Permissions

Office 365 keeps track of the licenses and permissions you assign to your team members. Depending on the programs you use and the version of Office 365 you've selected, you might have 25 licenses—or more—to assign. If you're working with a large team and want to make sure members have access only to the programs and services they need, you can use an Excel worksheet to manage and track the licenses you've assigned.

Meeting Agenda Template

Will you host team meetings regularly using Microsoft Lync Online? Lync makes it easy to chat and talk in real time, share programs, review progress, and more. You can help organize your team meetings and make sure they are effective by designing and distributing a meeting template members can use to add their own agenda items. Doing this can help you make sure everyone is on the same page. (See Figure A-2.)

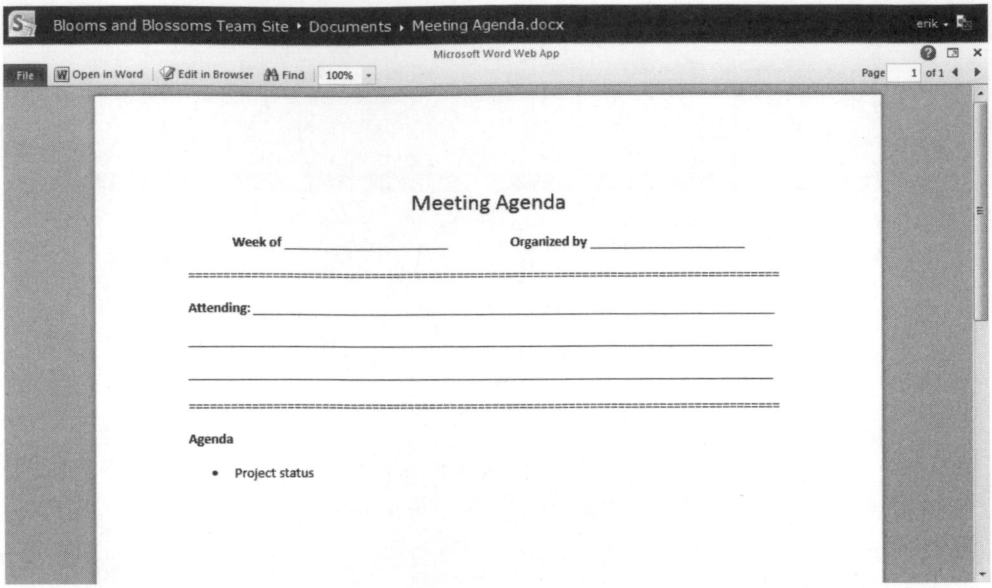

FIGURE A-2 Design a meeting agenda to circulate among team members as you prepare for your weekly meetings.

Tips for Your Team Site

The team site you design in SharePoint is your first resource for all the latest information about your project. Think through your team site so that it accomplishes several information goals and makes things easier on your team. Keep the following suggestions in mind:

- The home page of the team site should list all the most recent update information about your project. Which pieces have been completed? What's next on the schedule? Who is running the meeting next week?

- Secondary pages of your team site should be organized so that their function is clear. One page might be your document library for content; another might be a library for pictures. Another page might include presentation files or video clips, marketing ideas, or event plans.

- Include announcements and notes on your team site to keep your team informed about the latest happenings on your project.

Proposal Checklist

Depending on the type of proposals you prepare—sales proposals, grant proposals, book proposals, or others—the type of information you gather might vary from project to project. As you create a checklist to help you organize the various pieces of the project, consider the following items:

- Who is the proposal for? (Be sure to include all contact information for whomever you put on this list.)

- What type of proposal are you creating?

- When is the proposal due?

- Which departments does it involve?

- How long does the proposal need to be?

- Can you include any elements written previously in other proposals?

- How will the proposal be delivered?

- Who will work on the proposal?

- Have you created an Office 365 workflow to track proposal progress?

Marketing Checklist

A marketing checklist is another tool that can help you think through and plan your efforts. Include on your marketing list the contact info of all team members who work with marketing content, and then plan the ways you want to promote your product, event, or service. Identify the key pieces of information. For example, if you're planning a marketing event, you might want to record information such as the number of people you expect to attend your event, the type of venue you need to rent, the production costs, and so forth. Then devise a form to contain this information that you can make available in a document library on the team site. (See Figure A-3.)

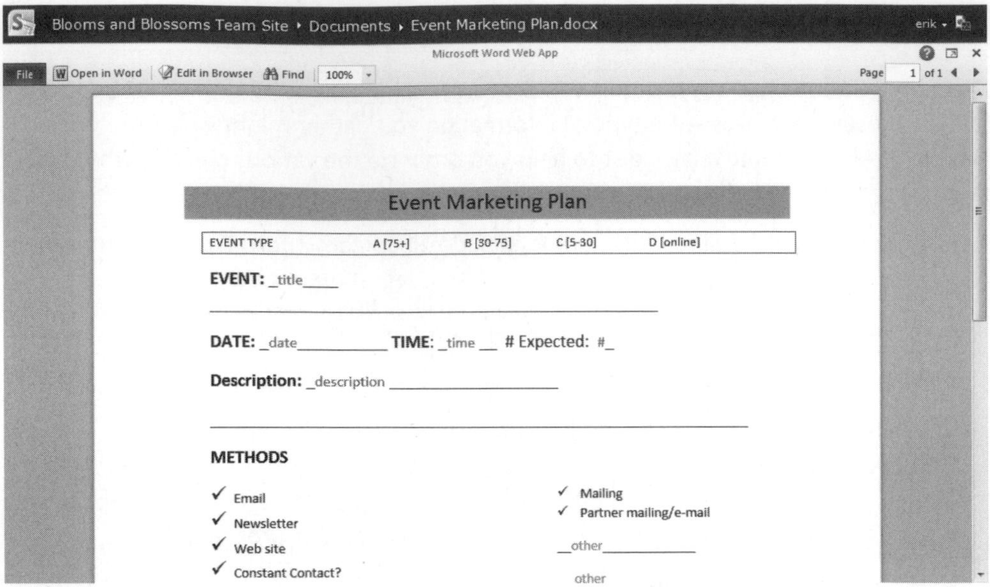

Event Marketing Plan

EVENT TYPE	A [75+]	B [30-75]	C [5-30]	D [online]

EVENT: _title____

DATE: _date__________ **TIME**: _time __ # Expected: #_

Description: _description ___________________

METHODS

- ✓ Email
- ✓ Newsletter
- ✓ Web site
- ✓ Constant Contact?
- ✓ Mailing
- ✓ Partner mailing/e-mail

__other____________

other

FIGURE A-3 Plan the ways you want to spread the word about a product, event, or service, and create a form to capture key details of your plan.

Index

What do you think of this book?

We want to hear from you!
To participate in a brief online survey, please visit:

microsoft.com/learning/booksurvey

Tell us how well this book meets your needs—what works effectively, and what we can do better. Your feedback will help us continually improve our books and learning resources for you.

Thank you in advance for your input!